Beating IT Risks

Beating IT Risks

Ernie Jordan and Luke Silcock

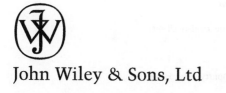

John Wiley & Sons, Ltd

Other Wiley Editorial Offices

John Wiley & Sons Inc., 111 River Street, Hoboken, NJ 07030, USA

Jossey-Bass, 989 Market Street, San Francisco, CA 94103-1741, USA

Wiley-VCH Verlag GmbH, Boschstr. 12, D-69469 Weinheim, Germany

John Wiley & Sons Australia Ltd, 33 Park Road, Milton, Queensland 4064, Australia

John Wiley & Sons (Asia) Pte Ltd, 2 Clementi Loop #02-01, Jin Xing Distripark, Singapore 129809

John Wiley & Sons Canada Ltd, 22 Worcester Road, Etobicoke, Ontario, Canada M9W 1L1

Wiley also publishes its books in a variety of electronic formats. Some content that appears
in print may not be available in electronic books.

Library of Congress Cataloging-in-Publication Data

Jordan, Ernie.
Beating IT risks / Ernie Jordan, Luke Silcock.
    p. cm.
Includes bibliographical references and index.
ISBN 0–470–02190–X (cloth)
1. Information technology—Management.   2. Management information systems.   3. Risk
management.   I. Silcock, Luke.   II. Title.

HD30.2.J67 2005
658'.05—dc22
                                                                                    2004018705

British Library Cataloguing in Publication Data

A catalogue record for this book is available from the British Library

ISBN 0–470–02190–X

Typeset in 10/12pt Garamond by Graphicraft Ltd, Quarry Bay, Hong Kong.

Contents

About the authors

Ernie Jordan is Professor of Management in IT management at Macquarie Graduate School of Management in Sydney, Australia – currently ranked top in Asia and Australia, and number 50 in the world, by *The Economist Intelligence Unit*'s global survey of MBA programs, *Which MBA? 2004.*

Starting from a degree in industrial mathematics in the UK, the path led quickly to COBOL on IBM mainframes in Canada and a period as a lecturer in statistics. Dr Jordan accumulated some ten years' experience in the development of information systems in commerce and industry before re-entering the academic world in Newcastle, NSW and then moving to Hong Kong.

During his eight years in Hong Kong, he made the transition from teaching systems analysis and design to IT strategy, while researching the strategy of a global bank for his PhD at the University of Hong Kong.

Over the last six years, he has carried out research that examines the reluctance of organizations in Australia to develop formal IT disaster recovery plans and his reports have been enthusiastically received by industry and practitioners.

His current research program includes IT governance, IT strategy, operational risk and business continuity. He is a sought-after speaker in the Asia–Pacific region, and can be contacted at Ernie.Jordan@mq.edu.au.

Luke Silcock consults extensively on all aspects of IT management for PA Consulting Group and its numerous major international clients. His twelve years' management consulting experience in Australia, the UK and Asia have focused on:

- Reviewing and assessing IT capability and maturity.
- Designing and leading IT performance improvement initiatives.
- Assuring delivery, reducing risks and avoiding over-spend on IT-enabled business projects.

His assignments for PA Consulting Group – an independent global management, systems and technology consulting firm (www.paconsulting.com) – have assisted dozens of client organizations in different industries including banking, energy and telecommunications.

He has also worked for KPMG Management Consulting in Sydney and London, specializing in IT. Prior to his consulting career he studied Business Information Technology at the University of New South Wales as well as industrial training with three leading companies.

Foreword

In the old days, most of the risks with which each person had to contend were generally local and personal. As technologies pervasively continue to enter our lives, the risks are becoming universal and very far-reaching in terms of those who are affected. Computer-communication systems reach into almost every aspect of our existence, relating to the health and well-being of not only people, organizations and governments, but also of the global environment.

Our increased dependence on computers and networking is unfortunately rapidly tending to increase rather than decrease the associated risks. New applications are being created that are heavily dependent on automated systems whose trustworthiness is wholly inadequate for the given enterprise needs. Systems are becoming ever more complex without constructively being able to cope with the complexity. New vulnerabilities continue to appear faster than old vulnerabilities are being fixed. Threats from evil-doers are increasing. Furthermore, all of our critical national infrastructures are in various ways dependent on information technology – and on each other.

Risks are usually in the eye of the beholder, but are often seriously discounted or even completely ignored. Thus, much greater understanding is needed among everyone who must manage, prevent or remediate risks. Fortunately, *Beating IT Risks* is an extraordinary book that brings many diverse issues clearly before its readers, irrespective of their backgrounds. It is one of the most important, realistic and practical books on this subject ever written – particularly for IT managers.

Some people may tend to consider the wisdom of this book as 'merely common sense'. But common sense is in actuality not very common. In retrospect, considering the historical evidence of flawed systems, wilful misuse, human errors, operational accidents, environmental hazards, many cases of mismanagement and many other causes (e.g. see Neumann 1995), common sense turns out to be extremely rare. Much too often, short-sighted management and system development decisions have ignored the risk implications, with some stupendously bad results – including deaths, injuries, huge financial losses, irreparable personal damages and losses of privacy.

One person's risks are another person's challenges. Indeed, this book presents us all with the opportunity to avoid or enormously reduce many of the characteristic risks that have continued to plague us throughout the computer revolution. I hope you will read it carefully and pay careful heed to its recommendations – which if diligently pursued can save us all a lot of grief. Beware of overly simple solutions, because the problems are complex and the solutions require considerable thought, understanding, foresight and in some cases altruism. Please remember that there are no easy answers to risk avoidance. Risks abound and must be confronted.

Beating IT Risks is quite different in perspective from *beating a drum* – which tends to be monotonal. The book is more like a entire symphony in which all of the voices are in intricate interrelationships. Enabling the reader to learn to understand the big picture as well as the details is perhaps its most significant contribution.

Peter G. Neumann, Palo Alto, California, USA, 21 September 2004

Principal Scientist, SRI International's Computer Science Laboratory,
Moderator of the ACM Risks Forum, Associate Editor of the *Communications of the ACM*
(for the Inside Risks column) and regular contributor to the ACM Software Engineering Notes.
http://www.csl.sri.com /neumann

Acknowledgements

The authors would like to offer great thanks and appreciation to the PA Consulting Group for taking on our proposal with such enthusiasm and commitment. In particular, we'd like to thank the PA Consulting Group team members who helped by contributing case study material, encouragement and insights. A special note of thanks is in order for Clare Argent, John Burn, Jonathan Cooper-Bagnall, Karen Crothers, Frank Decker, Neil Douglas, Dean Evans, Polly Ferguson, Ian Foster, Guy Gybels, Kerry Harris, Greg Jones, Fons Kuijpers, Geoff Larbalestier, John Lunn, Nuala MacDermott, Rob McMillan, Christian Nelissen, Bernie Robertson, Jason Robson, Dawn Whitmore and Nick Woodward.

We would also like to thank Macquarie Graduate School of Management's Bob Hunt and Dave Musson who reviewed the early drafts and gave us valuable feedback.

We have been delighted by the skill and professionalism of the staff at Wiley, with special mentions to Sarah Booth, Lorna Skinner, Rachel Goodyear, Amelia Thompson and Trisha Dale.

Luke would like to give special thanks to his wife Louise and his sons Sam and Rowan for their support and understanding while this book was written.

Ernie would like to thank Amy and Alex whose love and encouragement made all this possible.

1 Thriving on risk

Every time we take a plane we are riding on a pinnacle of risk. The 400 tons of 'impossibility' takes off, gets to our destination and lands – almost always! We take the risk for business opportunities, recreation or just the fun of it. The world is one where we take risks, all the time. It is part of the human condition. It is also part of the business condition. Some of the risks come to the front of our radar; others fade into the background, of others we remain unaware. Logically, we would expect the higher risks to be up on the radar, and the lower risks to be in the background, but that is often not the case.

We need to take risks in every business venture. There is always a possibility that things won't work out as expected. But it is essential that we do take risks. Any active strategy involves clear risks – that may make it unattractive – but a passive, do-nothing strategy also has risks. Typically these are not as clear and so are not as daunting. The important thing is to know what the risks are, to be aware of them and to have options available when the unfortunate eventuates.

This chapter is an executive summary of the book that gives the reader in a hurry access to the ideas, challenges and solutions that we offer. It also serves as a guide to the structure of the book, allowing you to identify your areas of most urgent need and proceed directly there. Of necessity detailed arguments and references are deferred to the later chapters. Chapters 2 and 3 present the IT governance framework and the IT risk portfolio – our two key tools. The subsequent chapters need not be taken sequentially but can be addressed on an as-needed basis. Bon voyage!

One of the challenges of dealing with risk is that there are inconsistent interpretations of the word. We will be using 'risk' to represent both an unwelcome outcome and the possibility of such outcomes occurring.

Risks aren't weighed up and dealt with rationally. The squeaky door gets the oil – and the risk that pesters gets the attention. So we end up with disproportionate responses to different classes of risk and often completely ineffectual responses to some of the most severe.

The legal, social and financial penalties for driving while uninsured are sufficient to ensure that most people carry car insurance. But our driving behaviour may be the higher risk and this is addressed only indirectly. We can imagine that only a very low percentage of risky or dangerous driving manoeuvres are detected.

And so it is with information technology (IT). IT has brought enormous benefits to business over the last 40 years. Directly through electronic products and IT-based services, and indirectly through efficient inventories, supply chains, labour productivity and customer awareness. But against the successes of on-line stockbroking, retail distribution centres, flight reservation systems and the like, there is a pantheon of failures ranging from the London Stock Exchange Taurus project cancellation in 1993 to the strategic flop of the UK's eUniversity in 2004.

These ill-starred initiatives can be ranked alongside some classic infrastructure failures: Auckland's six-week electricity outage – massive alongside the short-lived but extremely serious disruptions in New York and Italy (Hinde, 2003). Information assets also represent a risk – ask CD Universe whose 300 000 customer credit card details were stolen, and extortion attempted. Some of these risks we guard against, but others are disregarded, knowingly or otherwise.

Responses to IT risk are patchy. There is a much higher likelihood that organizations carry out standard back-up procedures to save data, than have IT projects that succeed. Yet the project may cost many millions – and the data that is safeguarded may not be the most valuable or critical. The risk in selection of projects is also high – boards and senior management are seldom well equipped to make these decisions. IT has become an essential part of doing business but organizations seldom are fully prepared for disruptions.

We aim to give you, in this book, ways of weighing up the risks and opportunities in IT and techniques to enable you to find the risks you want to take, and thrive on them.

The challenge

Businesses have got into a situation where IT is significant both to enterprises themselves and to business managers. What's more, there are many risks. IT spans a spectrum from strategic decisions to operational continuity and projects bringing organizational change.

The importance of IT to the modern enterprise screams out through high investment, the pervasiveness of the technology, our reliance on its continuing operation and the pain we suffer when it doesn't work. But above all we see the strategic importance of IT through its critical role in building efficiencies and the ways in which IT enables business to make its strategic moves.

But you can't survive simply by fighting yesterday's battles. IT continues to develop rapidly and to provide opportunities to improve every facet of business. Innovations are not just in terms of computing, but increasingly in dramatic changes to communication and collaboration technology, linking directly and instantaneously to customers and suppliers.

The shine has been removed from the apple many times before, however. A high rate of failure has been experienced in development, deployment and operation of IT – IT has been proven to be high risk:

- Development: Statistics, such as the long-running Standish Group CHAOS reports,[1] show that IT projects generally do not deliver the benefits that were expected of them. It is commonplace that projects come in late and over budget – and many are not even completed. The impacts of IT failures have been significant for the costs of failed development, the loss of anticipated business advantages and for the organizational cost of failure.
- Deployment: Increasingly IT is not 'developed' in-house, rather 'deployed'. Package, off-the-shelf applications are implemented with great challenges in modification, integration and testing. Costs can vary from the trivial to many millions yet management here can be patchy. Only the larger tasks are formally project-managed, and rarely do organizations keep track of the complex configurations of application, middleware and infrastructure.
- Operation: The branch operation of a global corporation may have no direct responsibility for development or deployment of IT – this may all be handled by outsource partners, global fly-in teams or even remotely. Yet local management must ensure that the business keeps running and for this IT may be critical. Your managers need to know the risks that they are facing in trying to manage the service levels being provided to customers.

Strategic failure is often harder to detect – when the wrong initiative is promoted or the wrong vendor selected. In some cases a strategic decision involving IT can be a feint or market-quieting movement, and failure to deliver the IT may well be a strategic success. Loudly trumpeted 'strategic-IT' partnerships during the dot-com boom were often successful in keeping the share price of the 'old-economy' blue chips off the floor. They were quietly folded or downsized after the crash.

To cap it all, business managers should be answerable when IT fails – they'll expect the kudos from success, after all. Their managerial decisions proposed using IT in business operations. The systems, procedures and processes that enable the business to function are their responsibility. Unfortunately, for many the thinking does not extend beyond return on investment or cost-benefit analysis.

Complications and deficiencies

Enterprises and managers don't seem to have a decent way of dealing with IT risks. Firstly the risks are not openly considered, secondly there are few tools to keep the risks in view and thirdly there are inadequate organizational processes to respond to risk.

---

[1] Accessible from www.standishgroup.com

Some organizations regard risk management as 'negative thinking' and paint thoughtful managers as 'over-cautious', timid, or even as lacking leadership. The gung-ho 'crash through or crash' manager may be seen as a charismatic leader – what an indictment! Yet every gambler faces the risk-reward challenge every day, and is completely aware that some risks must be taken in order to get the potential rewards:

- You've got to be in it to win it!
- Nothing ventured, nothing gained.
- No pain, no gain.

Of course IT has risks, as it has potential rewards. The 'dumb-down' thinking that ignores risks or only considers the most superficial ones has no place in a world where IT is, for many organizations, an essential utility that underpins every business activity. Imagine if the same thinking extended to costs, so that only the benefits were considered reasonable for polite conversation, but costs were taboo. Actually this is not so hard to imagine; it was all around us just before the dot-com crash . . .

Risks aren't easily measured, reported and monitored. The use of the word 'risk' to apply to both eventualities and their likelihood is confusing: it leads to statements such as 'this risk is low-risk'. The confusion is increased if the impact or consequence of a risk is also termed a risk: 'Fraud risk runs into many millions of dollars.' But we don't need to create extra confusion; merely dealing with uncertainty, the likelihood of some event, is enough of a challenge.

The best-known measure for uncertainty is 'probability' but this is satisfactory only for activities that are repeated many times – in controlled circumstances – and has little meaning for a one-off activity. Seldom are there good methods for estimating probabilities for single activities. Further, most people have very limited intuition when it comes to very small probabilities and will typically regard them as zero. This is then magnified when we need to combine many probabilities, and classroom lessons on mutually exclusive events and independent events are lost in the fog of time (unhappily, it may well have been a fog when time had not passed). Reporting and monitoring risks is then more difficult as there is no shared language between those estimating the risks and those making decisions on whether to put in more funds or to turn off the tap.

We've painted a picture here of someone – say a project manager – estimating a set of risks for communicating upwards through the organization. But the real situation is that the risk communications should be flowing in many directions:

- Board members may become aware of strategic threats that affect the timing of business initiatives, with or without IT components.
- Business unit managers may be monitoring changing customer attitudes to performance that enhance business continuity risk or the risk of fraud.

- An outsource partner may be failing financially and be unable to deliver in accordance with the contract.

All these risks may be perceived at different points in the organization but need to be brought together for priority setting and action. The processes to enable this collection and rationalization generally do not exist – too often organizations' responses to IT risk are ad hoc and uncoordinated.

The emphasis on IT has historically been one of exploiting the opportunities that are available, with either a nod towards recognition of the costs or, more recently, substantial control of costs. This is an inherently unbalanced approach and risks have to be considered; however, the way IT risks are managed is poor. We see the following seven aspects of inadequate IT risk management:

1. Piecemeal approach: Organizations do not take a holistic approach to IT risk, where risks are determined throughout the organization and then assembled into a corporate score sheet. Most commonly, strategic risks will be assessed at the time that a project is initiated – and then forgotten. Project risks will be assessed only by those responsible for carrying out the project – a guaranteed conflict of interest. Partner risk will be assessed only at contract rollover, if at all. Degrading infrastructure assets are seldom formally valued. And so the story goes on. Each risk component has its own ad hoc treatment, if anything.
2. Communication failure: Technical risks discovered by the network manager or a project manager may well be incomprehensible to the board, where decisions must be made and accountability ultimately resides. The challenge of communicating an issue from technologist to IT manager or business manager and then to a director will be similar to the challenge when the concern is travelling in the other direction. In addition, those responsible for finding risks may not be rewarded for communicating them, giving them a 'whistle-blower' pariah status.
3. Surprises and reactivity: We are continually surprised at how managers are continually surprised when things go wrong. Things do go wrong! Hardware breaks down, software bugs get discovered, staff and customers engage in fraud, telecommunications and electricity stop from time to time – and sometimes for very long times – projects get mired and then go backwards, critical staff leave, and then regulators and lawmakers tighten the screws. All predictable – admittedly very difficult to predict, but predictable nevertheless. So when something goes wrong, the standard approach is one of reacting to the event and finding someone to blame. A one-off – often ill-considered – response to the situation. Seldom are post-mortems held so that real learning can take place – so much for learning organizations.
4. Career damage: In the end blame will be dealt out and an individual manager will be the recipient. At the minimum this is disappointing and embarrassing

but ultimately it is potentially career limiting for individuals who are in management and governance roles. Track records hang around for a long time, and anyone who has presided over a major project failure or corporate IT breakdown will have to carry the burden.

5. Evolving, moving subjects: The nature of IT risks continues to evolve and offer up new challenges. Every day new defects are found in Internet-facing technologies and, almost as often, toolset and middleware developers propose upgrades. Each change means that risks are changed, and until the potential consequences have been worked out, the level of uncertainty is heightened. The impact of a change in one innocuous component can be anywhere between nil and total catastrophe – and ignorance ain't bliss.

6. Creeping goals: Corporate governance and risk management standards are being raised on a regular basis. The Bank of International Settlements' Basel II framework is imposing new operational risk reporting and control requirements on participating banks, which is having serious implications worldwide on banks and some financial services providers. Stock markets are imposing tougher risk reporting requirements for listed organizations, including in some cases explicit requirements for business continuity management. Expectations of other stakeholders are also increasing – such as supply chain partners, customers and stockholders. So not only does IT risk management need to be done, it needs to be continually improved upon.

7. Consistent competitive underperformance: IT failure saps the business's potential to compete, undermining other endeavours; more, it can lead to reputation loss and detrimental effects on the brand of the organization. Outsiders will see any failure as indicative of an underperforming company, perhaps unfairly, but competitors can gain ground merely from the absence of any catastrophes on their part.

Together these seven hazards constitute a theme park of challenges and stumbles that go far beyond the technical concerns of IT. They demonstrate the invasion of IT risks into the daily concerns of the business leader.

The cure for your IT risk headache

Clearly the IT risks themselves will not go away, unless you opt out and go for the sea change and open up a bookshop with great coffee in a sleepy beachside resort. You need to manage IT risk, with initiatives that fit your organization and its situation. But because of the pervasiveness and variability of IT risk, the initiatives are organization-wide and will represent, in time, a significant change in the way in which your organization approaches IT.

There are three key steps in making IT risk work for you, in getting yourself into a position where you can indeed 'thrive on risk':

1. *You need to put in place the right leadership and management through an IT and risk governance framework.*
2. *You need to integrate the way you tackle IT risks by adopting a proactive portfolio management approach.*
3. *You need to manage down complexity by actively managing each type of IT risk.*

1. IT and risk governance

While boards and senior management may not like the sound of it, the issue of IT risk comes back to them. With IT consuming 50% of capital expenditure in leading organizations (US Commerce, 2003), management should work out the detail of the associated risks. Cost-benefit analysis is insufficient for any significant decision; it needs to be complemented by risk-reward analysis. The benefits carry both costs and risks, and as we are now aware of the total cost of ownership, over the product lifecycle, we can also consider the risks over the whole lifecycle. The processes need to be set in place so that risks will be identified, assessed, monitored and reported from project conception to development, implementation, use and eventual run-down.

2. Portfolio approach

IT risks come in seven major classes and the portfolio approach considers all of these, all the time. Whether these risks arising are generic or specific, voluntary or involuntary (Pfleeger, 2000), the portfolio approach enables an overall view of the organization's risk stance, as well as a robust indication of where risks are greatest. Active monitoring of the whole portfolio prepares you better for the shocks and surprises that could take place. While greatest attention can be given to the most critical risks, rising levels of others can be monitored.

3. Manage down complexity

A single project can create risk in several categories, such as infrastructure, information assets and service provider risk. By managing each of the categories, the overall level of risk is reduced and the complexity created by multiple inter-connecting risks is reduced. By consistently working to cut down the highest risk, the overall level of risk can be brought to tolerable levels.

Together, these three tools are active approaches for identifying areas of unacceptable risk and bringing them down. They aim to give the board and senior management the assurance that risk monitoring is taking place and that risk uptake matches the appetite. The remainder of this chapter gives an overview of the governance approach, the IT risk portfolio and then an examination of each class of the portfolio (see Figure 1.1).

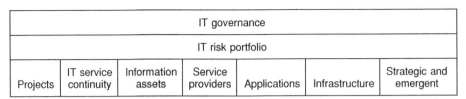

IT governance						
IT risk portfolio						
Projects	IT service continuity	Information assets	Service providers	Applications	Infrastructure	Strategic and emergent

Figure 1.1—Overview of IT risks

IT governance

The most critical step in beating IT risks is to put in place an IT governance framework.

IT risks are large and pervasive. They can be large enough to bring an organization to the point of ruin, yet most organizations do not have systematic or comprehensive approaches to dealing with IT risk. For many organizations, the greatest sources of risk are their products and customers, but IT risk would be a strong candidate for third position. Defective or inappropriate products will doom the organization; customers that go broke, go away or just don't pay are also a significant threat, but after that IT rates high.

For some organizations, IT service delivery is the heart of many business processes; they simply don't function without IT – service delivery is necessary for business continuity. Others have key business assets – such as product specification and customer activity, which are stored digitally and need to be safeguarded. Yet others use IT as the basis for organizational change and development, the key enabler. But the IT-heavy projects – how the change is produced – are themselves fraught with risk, with appalling track records. Projects deliver applications or infrastructure; service provider contracts can cover any area; the board and management can all be thrown off course by strategic or emergent technologies. Any class of IT risk can dominate the thinking, but monitoring all of them is necessary. An IT governance framework is the essential step to understand and take authority over the organization's use of IT.

There's a great pride when managers and board members are able to say, 'Our organization is IT-capable.' It's even better when it's true. IT governance is the link between the rhetoric and the reality. An IT governance framework identifies capability and shortfall, and then works to ensure that these are accurate assessments. It enables assured statements to be made about the organization's IT. While this is the critical step in beating IT risks, it deals with much more than just risks.

So what does it mean when you know that your organization is IT-capable? While there is no consensus on the upward limit of this, there should be consensus at the minimum requirements (Peppard and Ward, 2004). Benefits of IT should outweigh costs – and both should be accurately known. Risks from IT should be tolerated for potential rewards. Then, most importantly, when the business strategy needs some IT functionality, it must be delivered. What more would you want to call your organization IT-capable? It will depend upon the industry you're in and your organization's mission but it should be a matter that the board and senior management can agree upon.

When the IT governance processes are working well, IT risk will be communicated up and down the organization. The level of risk in the IT risk portfolio will be judged as being appropriate for the benefits that you receive and anticipate. This puts risk-reward on an equal footing with the cost-benefit analysis that is widespread. Further, the IT risks that could impact on the organization's strategy or strategic choices will be clearly articulated.

This draws the focus onto one of the key success factors of IT governance: ownership of the IT risk portfolio. Too often risks are dealt with in a piecemeal, ad hoc way. Without the systematic, sustained and consistent approach to the many dimensions of risk that are associated with IT, there is little hope for mastery.

The IT risk portfolio

All IT risks are not the same, but there are enormous benefits from bringing them together and treating them consistently. You need to treat them just like any other business risk, but also in ways that reflect the unique characteristics of IT.

A portfolio approach gathers IT risks together for three reasons: completeness, connectedness and significance:

1. Completeness: Some areas of IT risk may be overlooked in the priority given to the most demanding.
2. Connectedness: A single event, such as an upgrade announcement or a compliance requirement, can have multiple impacts in different classes of risk.
3. Significance: By putting all the IT risks together in a portfolio, the overwhelming consequences posed by the totality of risks will be apparent.

The portfolio approach recognizes that IT risk is ever-present and that continuous monitoring is essential. It is, in effect, a series of alarm bells that together give effective coverage to all IT risk areas. If any of the alarms were missing, the value of the remainder would be seriously downgraded. The universal compass of the set gives enhanced value to each of the components. In addition, any particular event or external stimulus may create alarms in several areas – through their interconnectedness – so there is a heightened chance that the driving force will be detected.

Having gathered together the significant IT risks into our portfolio, we are now better prepared to argue that the returns justify the risks.

Part of the function of the IT risk portfolio is to take away the 'blame' dimension associated with IT. All employees should be comfortable to report 'such-and-such risk has just increased' without being isolated or castigated. So, if risk is no longer 'bad' in itself, how do we measure the risk performance of the

IT function? Fortunately, the portfolio approach enables a global perspective on whether risk is being managed down across the set of categories. It also raises the emphasis on areas that are commonly overlooked, such as business continuity and infrastructure.

When IT goes well, there are business benefits. These opportunities have long been discussed and form the basis for most organizations' approach to IT. We are arguing for a complementary view that identifies, assesses and monitors the corresponding risks.

Projects

Key message: you need to manage IT project risks actively

Projects have a special place in the IT risk portfolio for the obvious reasons that they are unitary, defined activities that can be observed directly, with budgets, start dates and target dates. Projects can fail totally, permanently and irrevocably – and also spectacularly. There are many others that are less than perfectly successful. Newspapers reveal the budget overruns, delays and terminations, usually in bald, budgetary terms. This reporting boosts the reputation damage, but it can seldom reveal the opportunity costs – What if the funds had been applied to some other project? Not only has the capital expenditure been lost, the anticipated benefits have disappeared too.

The failure taints working relationships between IT and business unit heads, as well as any vendors who are involved. It is here that the caustic alternative meaning of CIO originates – 'Career Is Over'! It is easy and quick to build a poor reputation inside the organization and very difficult to rebuild a good one – easier to move to some other company.

If your organization consistently fails to deliver on IT projects, business unit heads will not regard the IT function, and any associated service providers, as valuable partners in the business – quite the opposite. Over time the slippage in IT services, applications and infrastructure will contribute to putting the organization in a vulnerable position – to competition, takeover or failure.

Over the years many approaches to solving the IT project problem have been developed, many books written, much research, experimentation and investigation conducted. Some of it has worked, for some organizations in some situations, but no panacea has been found. In many cases, simple 'bad luck' destroyed all the hard work – the project leader died; some emergency diverted the funds for the project; the programming development environment vendor went broke. You may argue that these were predictable and could have been planned for – yes, this is true, but the likelihood of each would have been so small that it got under the threshold for contingency plans.

The bureaucratic approach to delivery assurance, favoured by government agencies for example, ties a project to a rigid set of outputs and deliverables at each of many stages. The 'Structured Systems Analysis and Design Methodology'

(SSADM) adopted by the British and Hong Kong government, for example, stipulates documents that must be signed off before subsequent stages commence. Developers face the risk of deadlines encroaching while users cautiously hold back signatures. It is also costly to implement and can be inappropriate for some projects. The overhead involved can make such approaches unattractive for internal development.

Some organizations have star teams or star players, who can be left to get on with the job, like the team led by James Gosling at Sun Microsystems that developed the Java toolsets. The excellence of their skills and track record is the way to reduce risk for the project, especially if it is ill-defined or leading-edge.

An alternative approach, less demanding than the bureaucratic one, relies on methods and standards. These can be internally developed or adopted from outside, but their approach to risk is to follow things that have worked in the past. Many organizations will over the years end up with a mish-mash of methods and standards, whose continued adoption may not be warranted.

Project risks can be quite different to other risks. The project may be very large – which is well known as bringing higher risk. This cannot be changed without changing the nature of the project. It may also involve new technology – we simply can't substitute old technology to reduce the risk. Many publications present 'laundry lists' of risk factors, which may unfortunately confuse causes and consequences. We focus on causes and help you to develop a set of indicators that track the movement of the project risk profile, from the day that the project is formally initiated until the day of handover.

IT services

Key message: you need to manage IT service delivery risks actively
IT services underpin many important business processes in many organizations. IT is the way business is done and the failure of IT services brings business to a halt. The losses from outages or service level degradation can often be measured directly in terms of loss of revenue. In some cases it can be loss of life.

Business continuity management is the wider, business risk domain into which IT services fit. This includes non-IT related outages and disruptions, such as those caused by the 2003 SARS outbreak or local incidents such as road closures. The first phase in a business continuity incident may well be termed a 'disaster' and a disaster recovery phase will be concerned with establishing a safe environment and getting the infrastructure operating again. The IT services management role and the business continuity management role may well be adopted by the same individual if the separation of IT services from business process cannot be carried out easily and reliably.

In many business processes, all risks except those relating to IT services are low, so a focus on IT is warranted. It is important, however, that the whole business process is monitored to verify that this is the case.

Many IT functions have not adopted an 'IT services' model and retain their traditional focus on infrastructure, applications and systems. They will know that 'a system is down' but not know the full set of services that it provides. This rates all services equally and does not offer different priorities or service levels. If a telecommunications failure hits a system, which of its services are affected? The mapping of services to systems (and facilities) is seldom complete.

When a comprehensive review of IT services is carried out, service continuity vulnerabilities will be identified. The appropriate actions to deal with these risks will include duplication of resources, increasing the fault-tolerance or resilience of the infrastructure, establishment of secondary facilities, hot sites and the like. It will also be important to work out priorities, so that when resources are scarce, rather than absent, the most critical services are delivered. If, for example, telecommunications bandwidth is reduced, do all applications get a reduction or is the data traffic for accounting more important than the voice traffic for customer service? On the spot decisions are not good enough.

Much of the work involved in IT services risk is in planning. In principle, all threats to essential services will need to be identified, assessed and treated. However, these could be so numerous and have impacts across so many services that an alternative approach may be more effective. A single threat, or a collection of threats, may be dealt with by using a scenario, and then a small collection of alternative scenarios may be invented that together represent all of the important threats.

The planning exercise does two major things – it establishes which facilities need to be enhanced and devises action plans for crises. Enhancements are subject to trade-off and risk appetite hurdles, which should be explicit. Enhancing facilities can be accomplished by replication, hardening or creating alternatives, and the action plans need to be tested and rehearsed. All staff involved in IT service delivery will need to know their roles under particular scenarios. This is achieved only by testing on a regular and systematic basis.

Information assets

Key message: you need to manage your information assets actively
When a family home is destroyed by fire or flood, if there has been no loss of life the greatest anguish will often be loss of the family photo collection. Yet their collection has no value to others. This information asset had a valuable role in the family existence (even confirming its existence!) and would have had an ongoing role. The cost of a duplicate set would have been acceptable, but impractical to establish and maintain. Storing the negatives elsewhere seems an excessive precaution. Much easier (and cheaper) now that we are digitized.

Our business information assets are seldom valued formally and usually protected in a haphazard way. Making back-up copies of data gives a reduction in risk of definite value. On the other hand, should that 'spare copy' end up in the hands of our competitors, the value of the original may be seriously reduced.

Copyright, patent or other legal rights may protect some information assets but that is no guarantee.

While it's hard to put a monetary value on most information assets, the exploitation of those assets leads to monetary value that is easily recognized. Under-exploiting assets is a strategic challenge that may lead to the development of data warehouses, customer relationship management systems and the like.

The organization needs to permit information assets to be exploited in a legitimate manner, for business needs, but to prevent exploitation that is detrimental. So they can't be locked up – but open access is also unsatisfactory. Most organizations have no classification system for their information. Documents are marked 'confidential' but recipients may not know on what basis is the confidentiality and who else is a valid recipient. And then there is the treasured 'need to know basis' – who decides? Many systems permit unfettered access to authorized users and blanket prohibitions to others, with 'appropriate use' seldom defined.

The two goals for information assets are to reduce the risks of accidental loss and the risks of deliberate misuse, abuse and theft. The former can be effectively eliminated, if appropriate, but the latter can be only moderated, to the extent that can be financially justified.

Organizational roles can be very confusing here, with information managers, information security managers, chief information officers, chief knowledge officers, security managers and lawyers all involved. For example, European privacy legislation requires that people's personal data be safeguarded, with unauthorized use, distribution and even destruction not permitted.

Information security management, according to the International Standards Organization (ISO) standard, is concerned with the confidentiality, integrity and availability of information assets. Its ambit ranges from document classification to back-up procedures and password management. For many organizations the implementation of this standard would be sufficient to enable the risks to be monitored.

Service providers and vendors

Key message: you need to manage outsourcing and third party risks actively
The enormous boom in outsourcing in the last 20 years has embedded the role of service providers in many organizations. This ranges from a 'whole of IT' service provision to desktop and network support, helpdesk, and, of course, telecommunications. It is extremely difficult to have no third party involvement in the provision of IT. While services may be less widely used, IT products are commonly supplied and supported by third parties.

The failure of a technology vendor does not have the instant impact of that of a service provider, but the longer-term cost can be much more substantial if that technology is the basis for the organization's infrastructure. A more mundane risk involves upgrades and new versions of core technologies. While these risks can be foreseen, the extent of the consequence may not be apparent until the new version appears, or even later. The costs are not restricted to the licenses for the new versions, but can include rework (and delays) on current projects and unanticipated loads on hardware.

Other risks associated with service providers and vendors include their access to information assets, uneven contractual arrangements, and limited attention. An overriding issue is the danger of thinking that with an outsource arrangement in place you have outsourced the risk. When things go wrong, the problems belong to you. The service provider may well suffer too, but it will be in their cash flow or reputation, rather than their business operation.

The distinctive feature of outsourcing and third party risks is the role of the contract. By their very nature, contracts try to cover all eventualities, especially those where 'things are going wrong'. But relying on the enforceability of provisions is a far cry from the spirit of partnership that is so often espoused when the contract is announced.

Applications

Key message: you need to manage IT application risks actively
You've done it! The project came in on time and on budget, with the users conducting all their tests and finding that all of the specified deliverables are up and running. Time to rest on your laurels? All the challenges are over? While we don't want to sound like merchants of doom, the truth is that, from a business point of view, the project has only just started – the anticipated benefits now need to be experienced and this period is most critical. Business needs to take ownership of the system and make it work for them.

The most obvious risk is that some functionality of the application is missing or incorrect, moreover the specification and the testing had not included it. 'Where's our class list with student photos, email address and employment details – like we had with the old system?' went up the cry when our new student records system was implemented. 'What do you mean "you entered phone numbers in that field that we've just removed"?' While 'key users' are often involved in many projects, it is rare that all users are. Some users of pensioned-off legacy systems will have been able to get that clunky old system to sing like a bird. They will have accumulated a trove of workarounds that have delivered important functionality. Data fields are reused; reports used for quite different purposes than their titles suggest; and informal mechanisms, such as extracts to Excel, have become essential.

The next challenge comes when the application is fully loaded with data, and real workloads accumulate. Here the performance in terms of response time, capacity utilization and batch process operation becomes apparent and it may fall short of the promises. Some applications simply don't scale. They work fine with 1000 records but crash or stall with 100 000. One hundred concurrent users are fine, but 200 demonstrate serious degradation.

Perhaps this problem isn't immediately apparent but comes to light only when the business is much more successful than anticipated. Take-up rates for on-line banking and stockbroking were excellent, maybe more booming than even the optimists expected. And optimists get short shrift in banks!

When the application is fully tried and tested, working satisfactorily, there remains a significant risk. Is it flexible enough to accommodate the totally unanticipated enhancements and modifications that will be required? Browser-based workflow? Integration with a key customer or supplier? Wireless networks, PDAs, customers with mobile phones, SMS or instant messaging? Under this category must also be the ability to cope with inevitable upgrades to operating systems and other infrastructure components.

More dramatically, mergers and acquisitions are seldom decided on the basis of the compatibility of IT – and due diligence may not explore this issue thoroughly. So the two IT heads have to work this out – which may not be realistic if they're fighting for one job. A realistic and detailed compilation of the funds required to merge or replace the IT may take some gloss from the exciting merger announcements.

And then, the final hour approaches, the application is becoming frail, hard to support, hanging on by the skin of its teeth. The risks are increasing and will continue to do so. Time to pull the plug. But the assessment of frailty will be different between key players in the organization. Whose counts?

Infrastructure

Key message: you need to manage IT infrastructure risks actively
In the good old days we had hardware and software, and for many small businesses this distinction is still workable. But over time the usefulness of this separation diminished. Operating systems software clearly belonged with the hardware and gradually more software came to be seen as part of the essential layers that enabled business applications, IT services, to be delivered. The separation of infrastructure and application is now more useful to managers as the two areas have different management needs, different risk issues and produce benefits in different ways.

Infrastructure investments are by their nature long term. It is anticipated that new applications will be added from time to time – and others phased out, while the infrastructure changes slowly. In fact, changes to the infrastructure will be additions of capacity, addition of new infrastructure elements, and repair and maintenance. These should be taking place in the framework of an architecture, an overarching design that aims at long-term evolutionary growth.

Infrastructure investments tend to be large and the direct business benefit may be missing. Infrastructure may simply be 'enabling' – a necessity for being in business, but no return on investment may be calculable. In such a context, the risks can be high, if not extreme. Many of the major project failures that attract the headlines are infrastructural in nature.

The failure of public infrastructure such as roads, rails systems and ports is usually obvious, and the causes are few. The same causes apply to IT infrastructure: inappropriate design for the applications and services that build upon it; inadequate capacity to deal with the workloads; insufficient maintenance to keep it in proper repair. But IT infrastructure has additional risks and opportunities for failure, such as selection of standards, interoperability of components – especially during upgrades – and the capacity to support unanticipated applications in the future.

When infrastructure fails, all the applications and IT services that are built upon it are also threatened. The cost of rebuilding infrastructure that has gone beyond its useful life can be enough to challenge many organizations.

There is a paradox that faces the infrastructure designer: legacy systems are risky and so are new systems. You're damned if you do and damned if you don't (hang on to legacy systems). Legacy systems become progressively more difficult to support, more expensive to maintain and more 'frail'. They are, however, 'the devil you know'. Their wholesale replacement by new systems can be equally risky. Phasing out maintenance of an old, fragile system when expecting the timely introduction of new, can be 'very brave'.

Strategic and emergent risks

Key message: you need to manage IT strategic risks actively
Every CIO worth his or her salt says that they align their IT with the business – that the IT strategy matches the business strategy. The reality can be far away – some CIOs are not even sufficiently close to those determining the strategy to be advised. Further, business strategies may change very quickly; how does the IT react? Usually, with difficulty or not at all. On the other hand, in some organizations business strategy is driven by IT; what the IT can do determines the range of possibilities for business strategy. In such cases the board approaches IT decisions with great care.

If the IT fails to support the execution of business strategy, the impact can be a failed business strategy. Why should such an eventuality come to pass? It is completely avoidable. Those responsible for articulating business strategy need to know – absolutely – the IT implications. Leaving an organizational hiatus between the CIO and the strategy team is, of itself, a high risk.

In strategic terms we are faced with a dilemma – this much-abused word indicates two unsatisfactory alternatives – between diversity and standardization. Diversity brings greater alternatives, at high cost, and standardization lowers costs, while reducing possibilities. Standard operating environments for PCs may prevent the implementation of wireless networks, digital certificates or other innovations. Allowing one division, department or business unit to develop a non-standard network may be very expensive and magnify network security issues. Thus the risks generated fall into different categories.

We can face a similar problem at the level of the application, where the standard and custom models affect strategic outcomes. Customized or in-house applications can be so highly tuned to precisely what the organization needed when they were developed that they don't have the flexibility to adapt to new environments or new strategies.

In strategic terms, IT is always risky. It is a matter of trading off one class of risks against another. Having a flexible IT architecture will enable innovators to create business change that drives shareholder value and may aid speed to market, agility and responsiveness, but a highly standardized one will cut costs today, reflected in today's profit margin. But as today's standardization becomes tomorrow's obsolescence, the strategist will take a circumspect look at the virtues of standardized approaches.

Emergent technologies have many predictable characteristics, but their success is not one of them. Being on the leading edge of adoption of new technologies may give a strategic advantage, but it is very high risk. The technology may be quickly superseded; followers may be able to emulate your success at a small fraction of the costs; and the technology may simply not live up to its promise.

Most organizations avoid the leading edge, so they face the challenge of having to integrate or adopt whatever technologies become 'normal parts of business'. Today most organizations have websites, customer call centres, email and Internet connections, as competitive necessities – to keep the playing field level – rather than some specific benefits. The challenge of adopting new technologies as they emerge depends upon the IT architecture, which may well not have been designed in their anticipation.

IT and other enterprise risk classes

Key message: you need to consider IT in relation to other enterprise risk classes
Clearly you can't put a fence around IT risk and separate it from the remainder of your organizational activity. Many of the risks that we have discussed are specific to IT or are those where IT has a significant contribution. There are others where the contribution of IT is smaller or where IT may assist in the mitigation of the other risks. Let's examine this latter point first.

IT can contribute to the active management of other classes of enterprise risks directly or indirectly. A risk management information system (RMIS) can be a very effective tool in monitoring all risks that impact the organization. The danger is that many important classes of risk may be omitted from consideration by the system – many organizations use a RMIS only to monitor physical assets and it is a tool principally for the benefit of the insurance function.

IT can also assist other risk classes by the specific design characteristics of the IT systems. An accounting system that is easy to validate – a trial balance that can be performed in minutes, for example – assists the auditor to ensure that trans-actions have not been 'lost'. Standardized audit trails, recovery routines and data logs will all make the detection of fraud, integrity and validity much easier. Similarly the operation of business risk controls – such as market risk or credit risk for bankers – can be facilitated by their incorporation in IT systems. The 'information asset' category of IT risk will be complementary here, and the differing views of the auditor and the IT security manager will be valuable.

IT can heighten or expose the enterprise to other risks, such as brand and reputation. Banks that send inappropriate letters to deceased (former) customers look like fools. As do utilities that send out bills for zero, especially if it comes with a threat. Multiple invoices for the same goods, multiple receipts for a single payment, the list goes on. Lack of a single view of the customer is especially common. This can undo much good brand building.

The integration of IT-related risks with other risks needs to be through teams, where all stakeholders are represented. Auditors and IT staff are commonly involved in risk issues, but how often is marketing? Yet their ability to represent both the customer and the brand can be vital. We will be recommending small active teams for distinctive components of the IT risk portfolio, and for the components of other risk portfolios. The multiple perspectives within the teams and the multiple perspectives across teams are the critical initiative in aiming for completeness of risk assessment coverage and in hoping to overcome the boundary or territory issue: it's not our (silo's) responsibility.

2 IT governance framework

The first step, and we argue the most critical step, in dealing with the IT risks that the organization faces is to establish a coherent framework for leadership and management of IT – an IT governance framework. This ensures that the board, senior management and all managers who have responsibilities for making IT decisions have a common understanding of how the organization deals with IT risk. But the governance framework is not concerned simply with risk – the benefits, opportunities and effectiveness of IT investments are of equal status.

IT is frequently about new and emerging technologies, that boards can never be expected to be on top of. So how can they approve projects involving these new technologies? How can they be sure that senior staff are up to the job?

Board members should not be in effect delegating governance issues to line management.

The most spectacular examples of IT governance failure in recent years have been the 'investments' that many organizations made into e-business. Whenever a claim is made of a 'significant investment' then the board is implicated. The failure of the project is simply an investment that failed. Every major project failure – the literature abounds – has an element (at least) of IT governance failure.

This chapter sets out why you need to have an IT governance framework and how to design and implement an effective framework for your organization.

Governance over IT, as with all other facets of an organization, is the responsibility of the board of directors. It is unfortunate, however, that IT is routinely relegated to the bottom of the director's priority list, even in many information-intensive industries (Jordan and Musson, 2003).

IT shouldn't be relegated, but it may be delegated, with appropriate monitoring and review roles established to ensure the executive management team adequately address and manage the affairs of the organization.

For effective governance of IT to cascade down an organization, IT management responsibilities must flow through a formalized structure and be embodied in individuals' roles. Policies and guiding principles, endorsed by the directors, set the scene for the development and alignment of processes, standards, procedures and at the lowest level, work instructions.

Table 2.1—Qualitative and quantitative benefits of
an effective IT governance framework

Qualitative benefits	• Tighter alignment of IT activities with desired business outcomes; • Better integration of IT communities across the organization; and • Better working relationships between the IT delivery units and the business units who benefit from IT when it works and feel the pain when it fails.
Quantitative benefits	• Better return on investments in IT; and • Rational allocation of IT spend according to a balance of rewards sought and risks incurred.

The mechanics of governance requires the formation of committees and working groups. These enable decision-making processes and ensure sufficient communication, particularly when cross-company business impacts and outcomes must be balanced and optimized.

Often the question of how a company should organize its IT is dominated by structural questions: What should be centralized? What decisions can be made by business unit managers?

This chapter provides a comprehensive, integrated set of tools and perspectives from which to design, develop and implement an IT governance framework that matches the prevailing culture and aligns with the characteristics of your business.

An effective IT governance framework provides clarity of direction and ensures managed progress towards agreed goals and can deliver a range of benefits, as shown in Table 2.1.

IT governance goals and objectives

Skipping over, for the moment, the issue of what an 'IT governance framework' is, what can we expect having implemented one? By specifying how we expect it to perform, some of the key components will become clear. While an IT governance framework is not solely concerned with risk, we concentrate now on the outcomes that deal with IT risk.

The board needs to know how much IT risk the organization is taking.

Why the emphasis on the board? An underlying principle of corporate governance today is that the board has responsibility for the risks that the organization is undertaking. In some jurisdictions, this responsibility extends to a personal warranty. This does not mean that the organization does not take risks, but that all the risks are identified, monitored and reported (to the Stock Exchange, in the case of listed organizations). Thus the need to be able to report on the current risk undertaking of the organization demands that the board itself be informed. An important corollary is that the board should be confident that the reporting it is receiving is reasonably accurate and complete. Clearly there is an audit requirement to demonstrate that for each identified risk an action or countermeasure has been instigated to establish control.

> **The board needs to be able to respond to an IT risk assessment with requirements for the risk to be moderated.**

Should the board throw its metaphorical arms in the air at the unacceptable level of IT risk, it needs to be able to give directions to management as to changes that are required. This refers both to the board's own capacity to make such judgements and to the organization's capacity to respond. These pronouncements need to have meaning and relevance to those at the IT risk coalface; they should also have some certainty of reaching them. Thus the IT governance framework needs to deliver two-way communication.

> **The board needs to be confident that the organization is able to make the requested changes, without bringing other risks into existence.**

This third requirement suggests that the IT governance framework should itself not be an additional source of risk. That IT risk governance, as a process, is one that is well-behaved, auditable and capable of delivering consistent and reliable results. It also suggests that, when certain risks need to be traded off against other risks, management have thought about this in advance. This requirement strongly supports the need for the portfolio approach – so that the reduction in one risk is not made at the cost of increasing risk elsewhere, to the point that the total risk is increased rather than decreased.

> **A shared language is developed between technologists, business unit heads and senior management for dealing with IT risk.**

This is where a great benefit of an IT governance framework is delivered. With a common language for expressing IT-related risk throughout the organization, the opportunity for enhanced communication is created. This then permits ready identification of risks and appropriate remedial action to be more easily accomplished.

Extending this thinking to go beyond IT risk, we can see that IT governance needs similar capabilities in dealing with opportunities, benefits and costs. These can be summarized:

> **The board must be assured that the organization is able to identify needs and opportunities to exploit IT, and is then able to satisfy them.**

This overall statement of capability – that the organization is IT-capable – is at the heart of IT governance. It boils down to being able to work out what you want and then getting it. It does not mean that you must identify and develop these applications inside the organization – buying in the appropriate skill potentially demonstrates just as much capability. The board itself does not have to know how to do this, or what the applications are; merely be assured that the organization does. This is not a timid assignment of all activity to the management of the organization; to 'be assured' is in itself an active, demanding position. It is not blind trust, but informed thoughtful trust – if warranted.

Different approaches to governance

IT governance is not new; a range of organizations has adopted it in various forms (Schwarz and Hirschheim, 2003). In some cases there are no significant differences from the IT strategy or IT policy or IT management practices that went before. Organizations that have already adopted IT governance are approaching it from different perspectives that have their own strengths and weaknesses. We outline a model that builds on the strengths of the different perspectives.

Legalistic and regulatory approaches to governance tend to dominate the debate, but there are alternative viewpoints that enhance the understanding. These enable an organization to find the approach or blend of approaches that are most suitable. We find that seven perspectives on governance are dominant, as shown in Table 2.2.

To some extent the field of IT governance theory is emerging. It is clear, however, that structures and roles, processes and outcomes are key elements. These will be assembled by examining the seven perspectives and selecting the most effective, which collectively form a cohesive framework.

Table 2.2—Governance perspectives, views and proponents

perspective	view	proponent
Corporate governance	Accountability	Director
Investment	Funding	Investor
Compliance	Rules	Compliance manager
Enterprise-wide risk	Risk	Risk manager
Audit and control	Control processes	Auditor
Engineering and systems	Effective systems	Systems analyst
Life sciences, biology and ecology	Holistic	User

The corporate governance perspective

The current corporate governance movement is top-down in its orientation with an accountability focus (OECD, 1999). Regulators responsible for the transparent operation of stock markets or the prudent guardianship of public assets (and assets of the public) have created amendments to listing rules, reporting requirements and political pressure for increased accountability of boards (Tricker, 2000). As the body responsible for protecting shareholders' interests, the board needs to ensure that, for all risks the business takes, there are rewards available that are worth achieving.[2]

While matching rewards to risks is a worthy endeavour, it is doomed to failure if the organization does not participate actively and provide the information that the board must rely upon to make its decisions. But traditionally the flow of information between the organization's IT function and the board has been limited, and the board seldom feels sufficiently confident about the IT function for it to direct. Wider issues of IT risk are too dispersed for the board to develop an overview for itself.

The director's perspective on IT governance starts with an understanding that the enterprise is established to meet external stakeholder's objectives. These stakeholders include shareholders or investors, customers, employees, regulators and the wider community.

The directors are appointed by the shareholders to steer the company. They have a set of obligations to strive to meet, in addition to demonstrating transparently the fulfilment of the expectations of the diverse range of stakeholders (Tricker, 2000). A critical role, in IT terms, is confirming that the company has sound systems of internal control (for example: ICA, 1999). Many directors have

---

[2] The Australian Stock Exchange requires listed companies to establish a sound system of risk oversight and management and internal control (ASX, 2003) as part of a sweeping set of changes to corporate governance requirements. Similar rules exist or are appearing around the world.

become personally more comfortable with using IT in recent years but most will have little direct experience of managing IT.

When it comes to IT risks, this has the unfortunate consequence of creating a 'gulf of understanding' between those supposed to be steering and those rowing (Peppard and Ward, 1999; Schwarz and Hirschheim, 2003). In turbulent currents – as the world of IT often generates – this can be dangerous.

Unfortunately past failures of IT in many companies have created a level of mistrust. Today's promises of IT managers and delivery teams are overlaid with heavy director scepticism and in some cases fear. IT practitioner language can further diminish transparency.

The way out from this situation requires IT-adept managers to adapt and sharpen their language and presentation skills to ensure the full business implications of IT are communicated. Directors in turn need to equip themselves with additional knowledge and skills enabling them to ask intelligent questions and also avail themselves of the skills of independent trusted advisors to sort the truth from the IT fiction.[3]

The next and perhaps most important step requires directors to appropriately elevate the priority of IT governance to its rightful place in the context of the board and its subcommittees and to spend the time that is necessary to get it right.

The investor perspective

Investors the world over are advised to select a mix of investments and manage their total portfolio of wealth with the aim of producing acceptable returns over time without exposing their funds to an undesirable risk of loss. What if IT could be managed on similar lines?

The investor perspective seeks a consistent management approach to an organization's total IT wealth – tied up in hardware, software, networks, people and information. The aim of managing the IT investment portfolio is not to eliminate risk but to match the exposure to risk to the appetite for risk.

> *Businesses should think of their IT initiatives as investments that are intended to pay off over their entire lifecycles. While it is true that the nature of IT-related risk changes as an IT investment progresses through its lifecycle, an integrated approach to IT-related risk management allows for intelligent tradeoffs between development costs and risks on the one hand and operational costs and risks on the other.* (Markus, 2000)

---

[3] The IT Governance Institute offers further guidance to board members in its Board Briefing on IT Governance (www.itgi.org) and associated Control Objectives for Information and related Technology (COBIT) resources (ISACA, 2001).

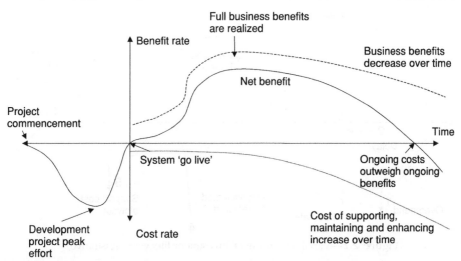

Figure 2.1—IT investment lifecycle, showing cost and benefit components (illustrative)

Planned and in-progress IT projects are commonly evaluated from both a risk and return perspective – some projects are found to have a greater *certainty* of delivery to defined time, cost and quality parameters – these are the ones that more easily jump the funding hurdles. If this common project appraisal method is extended to a view of the operational IT assets through their useful life, it becomes evident that IT investments with a greater certainty of payback through being deployed effectively and used productively should be similarly favoured.

Most IT assets commence with a period of negative returns associated with the investment required to acquire and implement, as illustrated in Figure 2.1. Only after implementation is business value released. Over time the objective is to bring cumulative returns into positive territory – the initial investment plus the ongoing cost of running and maintaining the IT asset outweighed by the cumulative benefits.

The investor seeks to understand the *predictability* in returns from IT investments, as determined both by the business application of the IT investment and as an inherent characteristic of the technology and its supply. As far back as 1979, Abe *et al.* (1979) used the term 'bankruptcy' to describe software project failures. Current research topics include the application of real options theory to IT infrastructure investment evaluation (Thorogood and Yetton, 2004) and have even extended to return-on-investment calculation of intrusion detection systems (Iheagwara *et al.*, 2004).

Revisiting the IT investment returns curve there are a number of points at which this variability or uncertainty can be felt, including:

1. Project overspend increases the initial outlay.
2. Project runs late and achievement of business benefits is deferred.
3. Business take-up and usage is less than planned, diminishing business benefits.

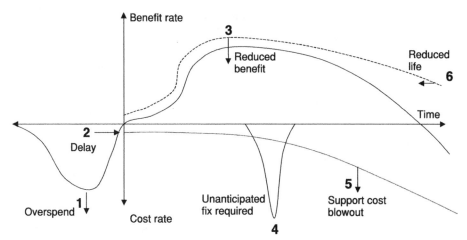

Figure 2.2—Variability in the IT investment lifecycle (illustrative)

4. A merger or acquisition requires significant redevelopment effort to accommodate the unforeseen needs.
5. System is more costly to support, maintain and enhance than planned, increasing ongoing costs and lowering net benefits.
6. Business requirements change or system requires replacement sooner than planned, reducing the asset's useful life.

These six investment traps are shown in Figure 2.2, where the idealized lifecycle becomes distorted by the negative impacts. Time, costs and benefits can all take hits.

At any point, the investor will demand information on the performance of their IT investments: the portfolio should be returning value to the business greater than the ongoing cost to service and maintain it. When profiled over the lifetime of each investment asset, the net returns should exceed the cost of capital plus an allowance for risk appropriate for the investment. This operates similarly to the demand in the marketplace for investment returns to be commensurate with the level of uncertainty.

The investor will however seek to apply the risk management concept of diversification – not putting all the IT 'eggs' in one basket. Within the portfolio of IT assets there will be both performing and non-performing assets. The investor seeks to maintain a majority of assets as performers in the 'payback' phase – accruing ongoing benefits greater than ongoing costs.

The investor perspective does run into some important limitations, such as:

- Ultimately the IT assets of a firm realize value only *in situ* and through the business utilizing the assets, and cannot be traded – as can other investments such as shares in listed companies;

- Market pricing mechanisms exist mainly for IT 'inputs' and not for composite and complex IT assets – information about asset values are only internally derived;
- Information to support whole-lifecycle, total cost of ownership analysis of IT systems is rarely captured, tracked and analysed with rigour; and
- Significant intangible benefits are derived from IT that are not easily translated into quantified or monetary terms.

Milis and Mercken (2004) consider the application of traditional capital investment appraisal techniques to IT investments and determine that the use of a balanced scorecard technique for the appraisal of major IT investment projects is appropriate.

Further limitations are explored in detail by Verhoef in ground-breaking research focusing on the application of quantitative methods to IT portfolio management in low-maturity environments. He comprehensively argues that 'the nature of software does not resemble the nature of a security' (Verhoef, 2002, p. 8) and sets out an IT-specific set of objective and quantitative management tools and techniques.

We conclude that this is a valuable perspective that needs to be incorporated into any IT governance framework.

The compliance perspective

The compliance manager seeks to demonstrate the organization is doing the right thing. Not blindly following the rules, but intelligently applying them to yield the best results.

Compliance is firstly about understanding externally imposed legislative and regulatory obligations and determining how best to meet them. Once the rules are clear, the focus for those in compliance roles is:

- to assist others understand and interpret policies;
- to implement procedures and systems able to capture sufficient evidence to assure compliance; and
- to report this in a meaningful way.

Issues of non-compliance must also be dealt with effectively.

In many organizations, the compliance management remit extends beyond the externally imposed 'thou shalt'. Often compliance managers will seek out and encourage adoption of 'best' or 'leading' practice, leveraging external reference models or standards or otherwise proactively developing internal policies and rules by which to 'self-regulate'.

Typical compliance manager objectives might include:

- Promoting adherence to the rules and procedures – although recognizing that pursuit of 'zero non-compliance' outcome is not desirable or optimal for the business as it comes with too high a cost;
- Demonstrating that compliance risks and acts of non-compliance are being identified and managed;
- Giving mandate and clear guidance for those who are required to act in the occasion of a non-compliance;
- Strongly discouraging ongoing non-compliance;
- Dealing flexibly with current and future compliance risks, some of which are not known or foreseeable;
- Demonstrating consistency with other business practices adopted, including alignment and integration with risk management practices.

In IT management, issues of compliance, standards and certification overlap. For many years it has been a requirement that commercial IT service providers are able to demonstrate their capability, partly through achieving and maintaining compliance to a variety of standards, some fads and some enduring. For example, Indian IT software developers during the 1990s focused on achieving certification to advanced levels of the SEI Capability Maturity Model.[4]

Over the years there has been a significant increase in the compliance and certification activities carried out around IT, including in-house operations. In some cases, as in other fields where compliance is required, particularly where the main benefit apparently sought is *being seen to be* compliant, this activity has been imposed as an adjunct to business-as-usual and in a fragmented and uncoordinated fashion. The results can be odd. For example: systems developed by third parties certified compliant with demanding software development process standards may be tested by in-house teams who operate largely without a documented methodology.

The achievement of benefit or the reduction of risk does not directly result from compliance or standard certification efforts. However, in many cases within IT, the prescriptions offered for doing the right thing will align with broader business requirements and objectives.

The enterprise-wide risk management perspective

Risk management has been around a long time with its focus on specific assets. In particular, physical assets have been the prime major concern, with vulnerabilities identified and, frequently, insurance measures taken. Other forms of assets, such as process knowledge, information assets and brand quality, have not been as amenable to the risk management approach. However the comprehensive identification of assets and the determination of their vulnerabilities is a valuable activity.

[4] Software Engineering Institute at Carnegie Mellon University.

Its bottom-up approach also means that important messages may not find their way to the board or senior management. The risk manager has limited influence on the organization's strategy or opportunity to make a positive contribution to the organization's achievements – tending to deal with the assets that are in place. In addition, the risk manager seldom ventures into the IT domain, except when working on business continuity matters. Organizations with a strategic view of risk – such as those with 'chief risk officers' – are the pleasing exceptions.

The risk manager's perspective on IT governance starts with an understanding that risk is inherent in all aspects of the company's operations. At the highest level the predictability with which the company is seen to meet objectives, such as profitability, will directly influence the risk margin required to satisfy investors.

Furthermore, operational risks are increasingly being measured within the company, particularly in the banking sector; capital is being rationed so that returns demanded from a line of business, product, service and customer group are aligned with the risk incurred. This quantification of risk is an important part of the decision-making process required for IT investments. Many companies are increasingly attempting to use risk-adjusted return criteria when appraising IT investments.

The risk manager also understands the relationship between risk and reward. The more risk a company can take on and manage well, the higher the returns to shareholders. This is spectacularly evident in some industries such as insurance, investment and banking but is to some extent true for all companies in all industries.

For other classes of risk, the risk manager will consider the use of insurance as a means of transferring risk. Generally IT risks are not insured with policies.[5] However, there are some methods for transferring IT risk that bear similarities to the purchase of an insurance policy. Outsourcing IT to a third party – potentially with a premium for improved service and contractual penalties for underperformance – is an example of such a transaction.

Broader concepts of enterprise-wide risk management inform the IT risk management picture. Corporate risk policies and procedures will provide an obvious baseline from which to extend or apply to IT risk categories. Generic risk management processes, such as those embodied in risk management standards, will be applicable to the field of IT with little variation – e.g. identification of risk, assessment of potential impact and likelihood, etc.

---

[5] Recent research from Gordon *et al.* (2003) discusses recently developed cyber-risk insurance policies and identifies three major issues: pricing of the insurance policy when extensive histories do not exist; adverse selection – wherein the organizations at risk are more likely to take out the policy; and moral hazard – that once insured the organization becomes less inclined to take actions that reduce the probability of loss.

The concept of a portfolio view of IT risks, an accepted part of traditional risk management practice, is central to the approach outlined in this book.

Some refinement of the risk management perspective is necessary to cater for effective IT risk management adequately. The most important impacts from IT failures are generally business impacts. Many aspects of IT are measured in a relatively unsophisticated way that moderates rigorous quantitative analysis. Relationships between causes and consequences are often complex and difficult to analyse and understand. IT risks are difficult to unpick from the fabric of the business, difficult to price and difficult to transfer. IT risks continue to evolve at a rapid pace.

The main implications are that a balance of qualitative and quantitative techniques are needed. IT risk management is best integrated into the business – rather than left as an IT functional responsibility – and specific techniques are required for the diverse and rapidly evolving set of IT risks.

The audit and control perspective

Auditors have contributed enormously in risk management through their thorough approach to organizational processes, especially those that deliver documents or records that form the basis for the organization's financial reporting. Processes that deal with physical goods or financial resources will be examined for their reliability, integrity and efficiency. This very nature has a tendency to make the audit process itself reactive, dealing only with the existing processes and procedures. Omissions *within* processes are more reliably detected than omissions *between* processes.

Auditors also suffer somewhat like risk managers in the organizational environment. While having much more power than risk managers, auditors are enormously circumscribed in the areas that they can examine.[6] They must focus on the 'how' and to a great extent ignore the 'why' of business processes. Traditionally auditors have an accounting background and the accounting world view has dominated in the extension of audit to information systems.

An auditor's perspective of IT is significantly influenced by management control concepts. Inherent risks will exist in a system or initiative. These are reduced or mitigated through the correct design and application of management controls. The relative strength or weakness of these management controls can be tested – through the application of various audit and review techniques (Pacini *et al.*, 2001).

The resultant residual risk is considered against materiality filters to determine whether it exceeds a predetermined threshold (Moulton and Coles, 2003a define an 'enterprise pain threshold'). In general this is expressed in financial or monetary terms as a proportion of targeted net profit.

---

[6] Although auditor interest in fields such as business continuity management is increasing (Roessing, 2002).

Those items exceeding the threshold will be highlighted for a further tightening of management controls to reduce their likelihood or severity. The auditor will recommend corrective actions to prompt management to embark on the implementation of these controls. Unfortunately many of these recommendations will be interpreted as compliance measures and may be implemented in a minimal and passive style without a full understanding of the business value to be released from better managing risks.

The audit and control perspective has some weaknesses, specifically in its tendency to be backward-looking, highly filtered and summarized and often crude in the conversion of residual risks for comparison on a monetary / materiality basis.

The system thinking of the engineer – the next perspective – will typically cause complete disconnects in communicating with audit.

Other issues appear when IT-related standards are applied in a checklist manner by auditors. IT practitioners and complex IT issues are rarely able to be properly analysed with a process-oriented cookbook distillation – reviewers with limited content knowledge produce widely disparate review findings from the same set of facts.

Typically audit findings that are not clearly of a material nature are abstracted into a laundry list of 'finding – implication – recommendation – action' rather than a prioritized and balanced view of what is important. The result can be resistance or mandated and unrewarding compliance.

It is finally the unremitting thoroughness of the auditor that reveals the detailed blow-by-blow of the many IT failures in public corporations and government agencies. The authors are indebted to the work of government auditors around the world who have broken open the disasters and shortfalls of IT developers and service providers.[7]

The engineering and systems perspective

Where the activity of the organization is the operation of a system, such as railways or ports, the engineering or systems perspective has been very effective in identifying areas of risk and vulnerability. The total operation of the system can be expressed in terms of components and subsystems that need to inter-operate so that the objectives of the whole system are achieved. This identifies 'single points of failure', coordination problems, interface issues, and the like. Grounding in the firm theoretical base of systems theory means that essential mechanisms such as feedback, error correction and adaptive behaviour can be built in.

As the 'systems' perspective is conceptually more difficult and the 'engineering' one is more readily understood, there is a tendency for this approach to

---

[7] In particular the US General Accounting Office (GAO), the United Kingdom National Audit Office (NAO), Australian National Audit Office (ANAO) and the Australian state-based New South Wales and Victorian Auditors-General.

become mechanistic – how about airline cabin staff's safety announcements! Furthermore, this approach de-emphasizes the business issues in its focus on the performance of the 'system'. Also for many business organizations the system metaphor is not apparent – 'project' or 'process' seems to fit better. The assessment of IT risks relating to a single, well-defined IT application can be useful, if that application – system – has a central role in the operation of the business.

Engineers approach the topic of IT risk with a primary concern for the delivery of predictable systems that operate according to their specification. It is unfortunate that this quest for stability, reliability and precision is notoriously associated with the 'gold-plating' of IT solutions that meet their specification but don't actually meet the business need. The engineer will be unhappy with approximations and be more interested than others in indications that the system is not working. This can be harnessed to provide valuable forward-looking, predictive and proactive risk data.

Engineers will also typically underplay the surrounding aspects of IT – managerial, cultural, psychological, political – that create ambiguity and threaten some of the assumptions embodied in the system-level view.

Even engineers disagree: the process engineering perspective[8] focuses on the activities undertaken within an organization and their interrelationships while the product engineering perspective focuses on the configuration items within an IT environment. Engineers are skilled in decomposing the layers of interaction within an IT environment – and in understanding the interconnected nature and interactions between multiple components to achieve an 'end-to-end' view of performance.

The complexity of this can become apparent to the business manager who may need to sign off the design of a system and will need to navigate through a myriad of diagrams, models and views of the underlying system that are essential to the engineer but uninformative and confusing to the outsider.

Customer and service orientation can be lacking and often system boundaries that are conceptually useful at one stage of analysis can constrain thinking and activities (i.e. give a tunnel view) beyond this stage. Even a task as simple as the naming of a system – with the requisite and oftentimes arbitrary designation of what is 'in scope' and 'out of scope' can have significant consequences.

There is a constant dynamic between the business and user community articulation of requirements and demand, and the translation by system engineers into a specification for what the set of IT systems is required to do. For example, the requirements for a 'fast' system are not strictly compatible with the requirement for a 'secure' system.

Given the fast-changing pace of IT and the great variety in technologies deployed, there is a significant tendency for system engineers to be specialized in one or few technology 'towers'. The holistic view may be lacking.

---

[8] The process engineering approach uses established techniques such as hazard and operability analysis and failure modes and effects analysis (Trammell *et al.*, 2004).

In the end, whenever there exists stability, reliability and precision in the operation of an IT application or, more significantly IT infrastructure, the engineering perspective has delivered. These goals are built into the IT governance framework, so that the technical challenges are rigorously exposed, evaluated and dealt with.

The life scientist, biology and ecology perspective

Biologists and ecologists have long understood systems, as naturally occurring and significant. Natural systems exhibit organic growth, evolving as environmental circumstances change and deal with inter-connectedness between components in multiple ways. Single points of failure are rare in natural systems as are simple interfaces between systems or components.

Knowledge management systems exhibit more of the characteristics of natural systems than other well-defined systems and represent one challenge in IT governance. Other systems for which the biological perspective is helpful are those that are ill-structured in their use, such as email, telephone and instant messaging.

The natural systems perspective is to be self-sustaining, which means that growth is the objective. In business terms, uncontrolled growth is particularly challenging.

The life scientist approach to the topic of IT challenges the more traditional and common views identified above. Extremely rich and useful analogies can be drawn from this field. This perspective considers the 'health' of the organization operating within a wider context or environment.

IT is like the nervous system within a human, comprising of the brain's processing and memory capacity and the network of nerves that coordinate and control the activities of muscles, organs, etc. throughout the body. Clearly IT cannot be separated from the rest of the organization in the same way that the nervous system cannot be separated from the human body.

Health policy increasingly recognizes the benefits of prevention over cure (WHO, 2002). It is the proactive and defensive actions that an organization can take that are proven to be vastly more cost-effective than recovery and restoration. Consequently there are many health metaphors that can be used in the IT domain (see Table 2.3).

We use the concept of health checks throughout this book to highlight this perspective. Put simply, there are many IT risks with irreversible consequences – causing organization fatalities.

An integrated perspective for your organization

Each perspective in the IT governance process brings a unique contribution. Effective management requires the integration of these various contributions and minimizing their limitations. We argue that an IT governance framework is incomplete if it falls down from any of these perspectives (see Table 2.4).

Table 2.3—Example health metaphors used in IT

term	usage
Virus	Infection of IT systems. Protections and treatments from 'infections' can be likened to disease control in a population. The inter-networked nature of IT increasingly suggests exposure will occur. It is the resilience of the organism that will ensure it fights disease.
Transplant	Putting in a new system can be likened to a transplant. The system must be tested for compatibility with the existing systems.
Evolution	An organization's ability to evolve can be significantly constrained by its IT. The dodo could not fly. A set of systems cannot be changed overnight but must 'evolve' to meet a new or emerging set of requirements.
Renewal	In the remaking of the organization, the body must continue to function. A limited amount of an organization's energy can be devoted to renewal. In an IT context many organizations find an increasing percentage of spend being allocated to support, maintenance and operations, with little left over for discretionary projects.

Table 2.4—The seven governance perspectives

perspective	contribution
Corporate governance	Ensure that shareholders' and legal needs are met
Investor	Ensure an optimum balance of risk and return from IT investments
Compliance	Ensure the right rules are defined and applied
Enterprise-wide risk	Ensure that impacts from IT on any part of the organization are surfaced
Audit and control	Ensure that controls are in place to cover likely faults
Engineering and systems	Ensure that the systems and processes are functioning effectively
Life sciences, biology and ecology	Ensure that the organization is adaptive, agile and responsive to its environment

There will be significant benefit in individuals developing an explicit understanding of their own point of view – and seeking to develop the skills of identifying with other participants. To aid this process, management teams can role-play the 'seven hats of IT governance'.

While each perspective is legitimate at all times, in different situations it will be more useful deliberately to weight the influence of a particular perspective over the others. No one perspective is 'right' in the sense of being a complete and accurate representation of reality, so it is the usefulness or utility of the perspectives as models to aid management decision-making and actions that should be the guiding criteria. The successful organization will be able to vary and adapt its approaches to achieve better outcomes over time.

Building a framework for your organization

There is not a single, one-size-fits-all IT governance model (Schwarz and Hirschheim, 2003; Williams, 2001). The framework we propose is such that organizations are able to choose approaches that accommodate their unique needs and issues. Nevertheless there is a need for a framework, to ensure that the approach taken is robust and complete. We first consider processes and outcomes and then examine structures and roles.[9]

Governance processes and outcomes

The overarching outcome of IT governance can be the statement of organizational IT-capability that was given at the beginning of the chapter:

> **The board must be assured that the organization is able to identify needs and opportunities to exploit IT, and is then able to satisfy them.**

This was then expanded to express IT risk-related outcomes:

> **The board needs to know how much IT risk the organization is taking.**
> **The board needs to be able to respond to the IT risk assessment with requirements for the risk to be moderated.**
> **The board needs to be confident that the organization is able to make the requested changes, without bringing other risks into existence.**
> **A shared language is developed between technologists, business unit heads and senior management for dealing with IT risk.**

But risk is the flipside of reward and we've led with the problems. Opportunities from IT abound. IT governance is equally concerned with getting the goods.

[9] You may find our definition of strategy and policy as a risk management concern misplaced in Chapter 3. Whether governance or management, it is a key element.

So the second group of outcomes from IT governance focus on delivery and concern the rewards, benefits or achievements that IT brings to the organization. These complement the risk-related outcomes:

> **The board needs to know how much benefit the organization is receiving from IT.**
> **The board needs to be able to respond to an IT audit or review with improvements to be investigated.**
> **The board needs to be confident that the organization is able to implement proposed initiatives predictably, delivering promised benefits, with emergent risks being surfaced.**

More than delivering on requirements and ensuring that benefits are obtained, IT governance needs to ensure that the strategic view ahead is clear. The final group of outcomes relate to the ability of the organization to devise requirements that meet its strategic goals or positioning. The relationship between strategy and IT, often referred to as strategic alignment, is typically patchy. Organizations do indeed develop some applications that are valuable to their strategy, but it is rare that a comprehensive set of applications exist that map fully onto the business strategy. This mismatch is sufficient to warrant special attention in an IT governance framework, especially as the board has ultimate responsibility for the organization's strategy.

> **The board needs to know what the organization's IT strategic stance is.**
> **The board needs to be able to respond to an IT strategic review with critical assessments.**
> **The board needs to be confident that the organization is able to respond to this criticism and implement its chosen strategy, with emergent risks being surfaced.**

The IT Governance Institute brings together these themes in their all-embracing definition of IT Governance: 'A structure of relationships and processes to direct and control the enterprise in order to achieve the enterprise's goals by adding value while balancing risk versus return over IT and its processes' (ISACA, 2000, p. 3).

Both the succinct COBIT definition and our expanded set of goals underscore communication between the board and those responsible for IT. Key reporting processes that enable these outcomes to be achieved concern the articulation, criticism and amendment of three fundamental reporting processes:

- IT risk reporting;
- IT benefit reporting; and
- IT strategy reporting.

These processes are interconnected and the reports should be consistent – after all, strategy is delivered through a trade-off of risk and reward. How any documents are produced will vary with the organization, as will their form. In larger organizations these will be formal but smaller organizations may be able to simplify.

Clearly this reporting and communication layer sits on top of the established IT management and delivery processes. The risk management processes are taken up in Chapter 3 and the description of the individual risk classes set out in Chapters 4 through 10 provide the links to the core IT delivery processes.

Governance structures and roles

Structures need to be in place that will ensure communication of IT risks, opportunities, needs and issues throughout the organization. As they get closer to senior management and board level, there will be a greater need for formal structures, but informal arrangements, such as chat rooms and issue forums, can be adequate for dispersed information collection. Everyone in the organization will have some role, at least in being aware of risks that they are creating, and what they have to do when crises take place that demand their involvement. This is an extension of the idea that creating a safe, hazard-free work environment is as much a responsibility of the employee as the employer.

Formal structures will depend very much on the size, maturity and environment of the organization, but the most critical are those reporting to (and receiving demands from) the board, and the overall steering role, where business unit heads meet IT service heads on a regular basis. The communication channel with the board is best formalized, which develops an expectation that changes in the risk portfolio will be regularly reported, so that even when no projects are in progress, there is still some situation update.

The steering role will for many organizations be formalized as a steering committee or strategy committee. In small organizations, the CEO or another executive may well form a committee of one. This is the critical forum where business needs for IT are expounded, infrastructure developments are put forward and the methods of meeting these needs are debated. This steering role determines the IT capability of the organization (Peppard and Ward, 1999). How well this steering role is performed is a central issue of IT governance. This role also has responsibility for the IT risk portfolio. It needs to make sure that the risks are determined reliably and brought before it. The steering role makes the decision concerning the monitoring of each of the IT risk components. Do they need to be formalized? Are they to be coordinated?

Ad hoc structures can be created for single issues or projects as long as they fit within the framework. This can be accommodated in various ways, from formal reporting to representation on larger, established forums. The ad hoc team's usefulness is enhanced if the membership is comprised of those with a direct interest and those accountable. The danger with ad hoc structures is that their performance is less certain. Risks are reduced through predictability. Strong guidelines from the steering role on the structure, performance reporting and accountability of ad hoc groups are to be expected.

The final critical governance role is the review and assessment of the performance of the other roles and structures that have been put in place, in other words some audit is necessary. It is this independent feedback channel that gives assurance to the board that the other elements of risk governance are working. This audit may fit in within other audit roles, but it is qualitative rather than quantitative, so the word 'audit' does not necessarily mean that the 'auditor' gets the job.

Design and implementation issues

The consistent message to now has been that there are many approaches to IT governance and that a single best approach does not exist. So a framework needs to be designed that is appropriate to the organization, its industry and the environment. An IT-mature organization may well have the skills to design its own framework and to guide its implementation.

Leadership of an IT governance initiative, with its strong emphasis on risk, ideally falls into the chief risk officer (CRO) role. Few organizations have adopted this title but the role is pivotal. In some organizations this role will be filled by the chief executive officer (CEO), in others the chief financial officer (CFO) and occasionally the chief operating officer (COO). It can also be argued that the need to balance strategy with risks and benefits places the leadership role with the CEO. Whoever has the leadership role, it is imperative that their communication channel with the board is excellent, preferably as an executive director.

A word is warranted about our deliberate omission of the CIO from the contenders for the IT governance lead role. As the CIO charter is to manage and deliver IT services to the enterprise there is a clear potential conflict of interest. After all, the CFO doesn't head the audit committee.

Within the board the oversight role needs to be clear. The chairman may choose to retain that as a personal responsibility, keep it for the board as a whole, include it in the domain of the audit committee or adopt some other approach. The choice will be dictated by the expertise available and how critical IT is to the well-being and strategic performance of the organization.

IT governance models and approaches

Traditional approaches to IT management have included centralized, decentralized, federal and distributed structures, which also serve as useful labels for IT governance models (Peppard and Ward, 1999; Schwarz and Hirschheim, 2003).

The centralized IT governance model relies on a strong, positive, capable IT steering committee that is able to interact with the board directly, or through a one-step intermediary. All infrastructure proposals emanate from this group and all IT proposals need to gain its backing. It will have substantial delegated authority. It may be chaired by the CEO, another executive director, or a senior business manager. IT risk is one of its key areas of responsibility (along with benefits and strategy) but, as an holistic approach is necessary, this will not mean that a subcommittee is formed. In each of its formal meetings, risk reports will be produced for the board. Urgent risk matters will be dealt with on a pre-arranged basis (chairman and two others, for example), and those risks beyond a specified level will require participation of the full committee. Each segment of the risk portfolio will be the responsibility of an individual, who reports to this committee. In smaller organizations one individual may take responsibility for several of the segments. This committee should have a formal meeting with the board on a regular basis, at least annually.

The fully distributed IT governance model has, in effect, a full IT steering committee for each division. Each of these steering committees behaves in a similar fashion to the above, except that there will need to be an intermediary role to deal with the board – unless each division has its own board. The intermediary role may be an individual or a small team, which is able to interact with each of the divisional steering committees. It will also need to have excellent channels of communication with the board.

In the federated model, there is some balance between the central authority and the subordinate divisions. Each division will need to accommodate the IT steering committee role, which it can do through an individual, a small team or a formal committee. The central authority will have an IT governance group that includes representation from the divisions as well as those functions that are centrally managed. This IT governance group is the direct channel to the board.

Centrally managed risk management functions may include IT service continuity, information assets – especially if there is a strong legal basis to those assets – security and partner relationships. There is then the potential for each of the federal units to take charge of its IT strategy and benefits for itself, along with risks that are wholly within its territory.

The rate of change of use of IT in the organization may have an overriding influence if, for example, a new technology is creating a fundamental change in the way the organization approaches its customers or suppliers. In such cases there will be a tendency to adopt a more centralized approach. Correspondingly, if IT use has completely stabilized in the organization, the IT governance role can become more rudimentary. There is the proviso that, although development and implementation may have effectively ceased, the organization's dependence on IT through IT service continuity and information assets may be very high.

Similarly if the use of IT in the industry is changing, there is a need for heightened activity in the IT governance function. Other environmental issues, such as reawakening regulators or impending legislation, should also cause changes to the IT governance model, rather than be dealt with through ad hoc fixes.

In designing the IT governance model for the organization, it is particularly important that two-way channels be established for all employees who may be the initial warning of risk issues, participants in mitigation or recovery activities, or the originator of an initiative.

Matching the IT governance model to your organization

In many organizations there will be a 'natural' approach to IT governance that mirrors the financial reporting and control structures, but in others this could be a disaster. It is important that customer and supplier perspectives be included in the model. If the business units are responsible for service delivery but have little authority over financial matters, an IT governance structure that followed financial reporting would not reflect the range of business activity.

In order to find the best match, the three dimensions of benefits, risks and strategy need to be covered. If these are the responsibility of different management processes, IT governance will have a major challenge in unification. Benefit delivery through IT cannot be undertaken independently of risk assessment or strategic goals. And whether the benefits are for internal or external customers, they are all vulnerable to risks.

Another key question in matching the IT governance model to the organization concerns the board's skills and capabilities. If the audit committee has a long track record of dealing with IT-related matters, it is likely that its role can be extended, and the existing channels take on the new approach. Similarly if the role of CRO is strongly established as an executive director, it is natural to take advantage of this.

Implementing the IT governance framework

IT governance should not be an entirely foreign practice, even in organizations that have no formal framework in place. As has been suggested above, it is possible to build on existing strengths in audit, risk management, strategic planning, for example. If there has been an established practice of IT management, with formalized mechanisms, a comprehensive review may be sufficient to identify gaps between existing practices and a full IT governance framework.

Standard approaches for the implementation of IT governance in an organization will vary and the following illustrate the range:

- When the board has little IT competence and there is no formal IT steering role, a significant education program would be necessary, using external expertise, to chart an evolutionary path. It is critical that all three dimensions of the IT governance outcomes are addressed, so that balance is created in the beginning and preserved during development. Where IT has been characterized by ad hoc practices, there is some groundwork that must be done before even the basic components of the IT governance framework are implemented. The slogan could be 'crawl, walk, run', with education being the critical first step – education for board members and for all managers 'owning' IT-enabled business benefits or strategy.[10]

- In the middle ground, where the board has some capability and there is some IT leadership in the organization, the critical first step is for the board and management to come together to establish the need for IT governance. The existing capability may be effective to self-assess and determine what enhancements to the board and management are needed so that a planned development can take place. In this situation plans are the key.

  A staged and prioritized development is generally feasible, with structures and roles being developed over time. It is likely that the initial focus will need to be on building competencies across the IT risk portfolio, as many organizations will already have established practices to develop IT strategy and to identify opportunities for IT-enabled benefits. Existing strengths in handling particular classes of IT risks can be leveraged. As the understanding of the risk portfolio grows, new structures and mechanisms can be introduced so that the IT governance model becomes more robust. The other critical development will be the establishment of communication channels between the board and the managers charged with components of the IT risk portfolio. When these channels are functioning well, additional participants can be included.

- For those starting out from a high position, when the board is IT-competent and there is a capable IT steering group, a short formal review of the completeness of existing processes will enable a gap analysis and then a series of implementation stages, dealing with the most critical first. In this situation audit and performance review is the key.

Over time as the IT governance framework and underpinning risk management competencies become established, review becomes the byword. Critical review, including reflection on and performance evaluation of the IT governance model that is in place, enables the organic development of the framework itself. Appropriate review of all 'failures' and 'unwelcome events' becomes the norm.

Other chapters are concluded with a health check but this is omitted here. Should you want to review your organization's IT governance, an assessment of the extent of achievement of the objectives set out in this chapter will be informative.

[10] A useful external reference model to build from is the IT Governance Institute Control Objectives for IT framework (www.itgi.org).

Case study: Aventis

Developing a comprehensive Enterprise Risk Management and Business Continuity / Disaster Recovery planning program

Aventis, headquartered in Strasbourg, France, is one of the top ten pharmaceutical manufacturers in the world. Its Aventis Pasteur division is one of the top three producers of vaccines in the world. The company employs more than seventy thousand employees in more than 130 countries with annual sales exceeding 17B euros. Aventis was created in 1999 with the merger of the French company Rhone-Poulenc and the German company Hoechst.

As part of the project to merge the companies and to assure that the best programs and systems were implemented, Aventis senior management looked to its Risk Management department to map out an enterprise risk management implementation process, and tie together corporate risk tolerance identification and financing, corporate governance and risk reporting first, and then to develop and implement a business continuity (BC) and disaster recovery (DR) plan.

Critical steps taken to prepare the company for implementation included:

1. Interviews with top management to understand risk tolerance and appetite, and map out risk categories;
2. Identifying and engaging representatives of each major business function;
3. Getting senior management to give a clear message of support for the project, making involvement mandatory; and
4. Making business continuity and disaster recovery a business priority. The Chief Information Officer insisted that the program must be the responsibility of the business, and its management be outside of IT. IT would be enablers along with other specific functions by business unit.

Key milestones:

1. Risk financing objectives were mapped out and capabilities developed prior to the 2001–2002 insurance market implosion and supported by risk reporting;
2. The Enterprise Risk Council chairman position was elevated to Strategic Risk Officer, reporting to the CEO;
3. Establishment of a Business Continuity Council, representing the business, to guide implementation within each function; and
4. Alignment of IT DR investment to business exposure (underpinned by business impact analyses).

The Enterprise Risk Council, and the BC/DR program, use materiality of risk as the driver for reporting and action. For enterprise risk, exposure and probability are reported quarterly to the Council, and summarized to management. For BC, all systems and processes within each business function are assessed to determine their level of exposure and recovery time objective (RTO). All systems with high exposure will have documented recovery plans. Any IT system that falls below the high exposure threshold will meet minimal standards which are themselves compliant with basic governance (Sarbanes Oxley for example) and provide basic recovery ability. Service levels for DR ensure consistency and cost-effectiveness of DR infrastructure and plans.

'By engaging the business in the development of the solutions, and always thinking in terms of appropriate shareholder protection, we found that we always knew which was the correct decision to take, to get the process to fit our company.' Andrew Tait, P.E. Director of Risk Management, Property Insurance and Business Continuity, Aventis.

Printed with permission of PA Consulting Group and Aventis

3   IT risk portfolio

Having established that you can't do without IT, that IT risks are significant and need to be managed properly, the question then turns to how IT risks should be managed. Certainly this is one of the first questions you should expect from your key IT governance participants!

The IT risk portfolio approach that is described in this chapter enables proactive management of IT risks by providing a structure for business managers to apply when considering the different classes of IT risk, making management decisions and taking action.

When implemented into your organization, systematic and repeatable processes will ensure that important IT risks are identified, confronted, addressed and managed.

Introducing the IT risk portfolio

As IT risks are all, ultimately, also business risks, it is necessary for the management of IT risks to integrate into your wider business risk management context.[11]

There is a need for IT experts, specialized in a particular class of IT risk, to provide advice to management and carry out necessary specialist activities, such as advising on external network connectivity and recommending security measures. However, it should not be necessary for each of these specialists separately to build the 'bridge of understanding' across the void that invariably exists between business managers and IT experts over these specialist topics.

More useful is a single integrated IT risk management approach that both business managers and IT specialists can adopt and use as their 'bridge of understanding'. This is the IT risk portfolio management approach.

---

[11] Models such as COSO (COSO, 2003) developed in 1992 by the Committee of Sponsoring Organisations of the Treadway Commission describes a widely accepted business risk management framework (www.coso.org).

The need for the IT risk portfolio came from a respected researcher:

> *The business world is beginning to see the value of an integrated approach*
> *to identifying and managing business risk; the time is right for the IS field*
> *to begin developing an integrated approach to identifying and managing*
> *IT-related risk. Not only will such an approach be useful to businesses in*
> *their attempts to obtain maximum value from their IT investments, it will*
> *also help bring together a large part of the IS literature under a common*
> *conceptual umbrella. By viewing system development and maintenance*
> *along with package acquisition and outsourcing as part of the business's*
> *IT investment process, risk management becomes the centre of attention.*
> *By viewing system development failure, security breaches and competitive*
> *threats as different types of the unitary phenomenon of IT-related risk, it*
> *becomes possible to make intelligent end-to-end tradeoff decisions through-*
> *out the lifecycles of systems in organizations.* (Markus, 2000, p. 176)

Why do it now? A strident call has come from no lesser than the President of
the United States:

> *There is critical infrastructure so vital that its incapacitation, exploitation,*
> *or destruction, through terrorist attack, could have a debilitating effect*
> *on security and economic well-being . . . The Secretary shall coordinate*
> *protection activities for each of the following critical infrastructure sectors:*
> *information technology; telecommunications . . .*
>
>   (US Homeland Security, 2003)

. . . and the OECD:

> *As a result of increasing interconnectivity, information systems and*
> *networks are now exposed to a growing number and a wider variety of*
> *threats and vulnerabilities. This raises new issues for security.*
>
>   (OECD, 2002)

First seek to manage IT risks like other business risks

A portfolio approach to managing IT risks spans the collection of all of the different
classes of IT risk. You would first want to apply accepted business risk management practices consistently across these different classes of IT risk. At the risk of
oversimplifying,[12] we summarize below the key points of the Australian / New
Zealand Risk Management Standard (AS/NZS 4360) currently being considered

---

[12] We agree with Charette (1996) that the mechanics of managing IT risk are far from
merely mechanical.

by the International Standards Organization (ISO) for international adoption (AS/NZS, 1999).

The initial step is for risks to be identified and classified, with an assessment of the likelihood or probability of occurrence and a consideration of the potential for impact on the business.

Having identified the risks, you then have to work out what should be done. Various actions are possible: to act to avoid or prevent the risk from occurring; to act to lower the likelihood of it occurring; or to act to prepare to minimize the potential impact should defined risk events occur. In some cases there is a possibility of transferring the risk, although in general it is not possible to obtain insurance coverage for most classes of IT risks so this will typically be attempted through contracting with third parties such as IT outsourcing providers.

Usually the IT risk management actions will involve a number of people and will need to be coordinated, with some form of management plan required to guide this activity

There may be a focus on planning business actions as well as IT actions. For example, you may eschew a traditional disaster recovery plan with a standby second data centre site. In its place you may invest in achieving readiness for IT service outage events, building the capability to stem the losses and to enable a rapid recovery to an alternative mode of operation.

Alternatively, you may determine that a passive approach is preferable and that the level of risk in a particular case is tolerable. In this case only the monitoring and review actions need to be assigned so that if a change occurs in the nature of the risk, its probability or potential impact, it will be identified and reported to you.

Ultimately all risk management plans should perhaps trend towards this passive or maintenance approach, where no further risk management actions are warranted. Keeping doing what we are doing today reduces risk over time. Eventually the residual risk – net remaining risk after considering the effect of management controls – arrives at a tolerable level. At this stage of maturity, you will be focused on exceptions, emerging risks and changes to the portfolio.

Information about your portfolio of IT risks needs to be maintained over time and be designed to yield clear answers to questions such as: 'What are the top IT risks, how are these risks being managed and who is managing them?'

It should also be possible to determine the cost and effort associated with the risk management actions that are planned and to ensure adequate funding provisions exist. Most importantly it should be possible to determine that your most significant risks are receiving the most effort and attention.

It is worth stressing that only with an integrated, business-oriented IT risk management approach is it possible to undertake sensible trade-offs, across the IT risk portfolio and across other business risk areas.

The residual risks being carried by your organization should be stated and understood. While unplanned and unexpected loss events can occur, as this is the very essence of risk, the key is to ensure these possible loss events are acceptable and aligned with the organization's risk appetite.

A portfolio of IT risks

At this point we need to clarify precisely what we regard as an IT risk:

> **An IT risk is something that can go wrong with IT and cause a negative impact on the business.**

This definition is in keeping with others (Markus, 2000; Pfleeger, 2000; Keil *et al.*, 2000) in that it emphasizes the role of IT as a cause agent of unwelcome outcomes. The negative outcomes are not restricted to IT but can be anywhere in the business.

It is widely acknowledged that risk is the flipside of opportunity. A simple rephrasing of the IT risk definition will serve to highlight this: *an IT opportunity is something that can go right with IT and cause a positive impact on the business.* The IT risks described in this book are stated in the negative, such as a project failing to deliver. In practice an organization that is managing its risks is also managing its opportunities.[13]

A portfolio management approach for IT risks is an integrated approach to gathering together all the significant IT risks and managing them using common and systematic methods.[14] It is also about recognizing the unique characteristics of different classes of risk and undertaking appropriate analysis and treatment for individual risks. We cannot average one extreme risk with five low risks and come out as 'below average'.

The focus is to establish a capability that promotes action by managers, directing this action toward the things that can go wrong with IT so as to reduce negative impacts on the business. Furthermore, the focus is on proactive

---

[13] The accounting fraternity advocate considering risk and opportunity in parallel and perceive risk management as a driver of shareholder wealth (IFAC, 1999) framing IT risk with a portfolio of e-business IT risk consisting of three categories: IT infrastructure, IT application and IT business process risks (IFAC, 2002).

[14] There have been various approaches, for example Dhillon and Backhouse (1996) consider the risks arising from the IT system's place in the organizational environment, focusing on an objective of integrity and wholeness of systems, social as well as technical. A further complementary approach is set out by Bandyopadhyay *et al.* (1999) who define three levels of IT risk management: the application level, the organizational level and the inter-organizational level and four sequential steps that act at each level: risk identification, risk analysis, risk-reducing measures and risk monitoring. Moulton and Coles (2003a, 2003b) develop an all-encompassing IT risk management model as an outgrowth from information security management.

management action as the adage 'prevention is better than cure' is highly applicable to the field of IT.[15]

The different classes of IT risk described in this book are not mutually exclusive or collectively exhaustive. In short, they overlap and may omit an unusual or organization-specific risk. Why have seven specific IT risk classes been chosen and how do these risk classes relate to one another?

The seven specific IT risk classes are chosen to focus management attention and action. They are based on how IT professionals, business managers and end-users interact when working together and are selected to be comprehensive, understandable and practical. Definitions of each of the classes of IT risk within the portfolio and the interrelationships between these risks follow.

Classes of IT risk

We define seven classes of IT risk, where, in each case, IT can go wrong, but the consequences are negative to the business:

1. Projects – failing to deliver;
2. IT service continuity – when business operations go off the air;
3. Information assets – failing to protect and preserve;
4. Service providers and vendors – breaks in the IT value chain;
5. Applications – flaky systems;
6. Infrastructure – shaky foundations; and
7. Strategic and emergent – disabled by IT.

Projects – failing to deliver

This class of risk is concerned with IT projects failing, considering both designated IT projects and business projects with a significant and critical component of IT. For many organizations this is the most obvious IT risk. We exclude the cases of IT vendors developing IT or software products – for these this is their core business activity.

Projects are undertaken to implement new systems, upgrade or enhance existing IT systems or improve the way systems are used. When a project is an outright failure the planned upgrade or enhancement of IT systems does not occur. The business fails to realize the improvements from a new or improved way of working that would be enabled by IT.

A project can fail in a range of other ways and to a greater or lesser extent. The three key performance failures are in timing, quality and scope. The list of examples is ugly: completing late, consuming more resources and funds than

[15] Others have written about different forms of risk consequences and how to manage them; for example, Rayner (2003) focuses on reputational risk. In the field of IT an orientation of risk management action around potential consequences is not feasible.

planned, delivering less functionality to the users than planned, delivering a sub-standard product, disrupting the business during implementation, and so on.

Actively managing this class of risk requires capability in project management and all aspects of software engineering, IT acquisition and implementation. Even partial failure can be critical.

IT service continuity – when business operations go off the air

This class of risk relates to IT service outages and unreliability causing disruption to the business. It deals with operational or production systems and their ability to keep running reliably to support the needs of users.

Researchers have highlighted a change in the role of the IT function:

The traditional role of the IT organisation as the developer and maintainer of IT systems has been usurped by a variety of factors and its function now includes a significant service component. Peppard and Ward, 1999, p. 35

The traditional focus of people involved in IT has been: 'System, system, system' and it is, for some, a great shock to now think: 'Service, service, service.'

Business processes that are reliant on IT can grind to a halt when the systems are 'down'. When the service is up but suffering a period of poor performance – such as response time degradation – a serious impact on productivity of users and customers can also result.

Actively managing this class of risk requires capability in incident and problem management, customer support and IT service management, business continuity management and disaster recovery.

Information assets – failing to protect and preserve

This class of IT risk relates specifically to damage, loss or exploitation of information assets held within and carried by IT systems. For many organizations this starts with not recognizing the information assets held.

The impact of information asset risk can vary significantly. For example, critical information may find its way to a competitor, customer credit-card details may be stolen and used for fraudulent purposes, or simply publicized – damaging customer relationships and company reputation. Core business processes reliant on critical information may be severely degraded, as when an account enquiry function without accurate account balances becomes ineffective.

Actively managing this class of risk requires capability in security management and information management.

Service providers and vendors – breaks in the IT value chain

Today service providers and vendors play significant roles in the delivery of IT projects and day-to-day running. When an IT service provider fails to deliver there is thus the potential for immediate and significant impact on IT systems and services. Other impacts can be felt in the long term; such as a weakness in the IT service delivery partner's technology leadership, which quietly erodes overall IT effectiveness.

Vendors are relied upon for many of the applications that drive businesses today, yet their products have faults, their remediation may be patchy and they may choose to phase out your key application.

Actively managing this class of risk requires capability in vendor management, outsourcing and contract management.

Applications – flaky systems

This risk class deals with failures in the IT applications. Applications are typically systems that users interact with and in most organizations will be a combination of package software and customized software that will to some extent be integrated together.

Applications are hosted and run on infrastructure – some infrastructure is shared with other applications and some infrastructure is dedicated to running a single application. We deal with infrastructure risk as our next class, understanding that for many IT people a system consists of an application and some infrastructure.

The impact of an application failing to perform as expected and required can range from a minor irritation – a known bug for which workarounds are available and understood – to a major catastrophe. The impact primarily depends on the field of endeavour in which the application is deployed and used. A single application failure can have knock-on effects across a chain of systems – and where multiple company systems are interconnected, across a whole chain of companies.

Other than the operating or functional characteristics of applications, there are many non-functional characteristics where 'failure' is not so recognizable and the impact is felt in the long term. For example, systems that are not easily maintained and enhanced over time may form a constraint to introducing further change; applications that are poorly documented or not well-structured may be difficult to fix with confidence – new and significant defects can be introduced by a software developer when only minor changes are made.

Actively managing this class of risk requires software engineering capabilities particularly for maintenance, enhancement, integration, testing and release management, configuration management, system administration, monitoring and problem management.

Infrastructure – shaky foundations

This risk class deals with failures in the IT infrastructure. Infrastructure is the generic name for the various centralized and distributed computer and network resources upon which applications are hosted and run. Also included within the definition of infrastructure is platform software such as operating systems and database management systems.

Most IT infrastructure components are sourced from vendors and are replaceable, with some obsolete equipment the exception. For any given item of infrastructure, the replacement value is only one of the issues to consider when a loss occurs. Far more important is the impact on IT services in the meantime and the difficulties in confident and rapid restoration under various loss scenarios.

An IT infrastructure failure can be permanent – when a component 'blows up', is burnt, stolen or otherwise breaks beyond repair – or temporary – when the energy supply is shut off or network connectivity is lost. The impact of failure can depend on the level of resilience and redundancy in the systems – whether failure at a single point causes the whole to cease to function – and the availability and readiness of standby facilities.

Longer-term issues arise with the infrastructure choices. Systems that aren't compatible with newer models may need to be completely replaced – most decommissioned computer systems are still functioning as they were when implemented! Infrastructure replacement can lead to an application overhaul – all of which might have been unnecessary with a 'better' infrastructure choice.

Confounding infrastructure choices is the pace of change and movement in the vendor community and technology standards. This is perhaps the least controllable of the risks in your portfolio.

Actively managing this class of risk requires operational capabilities particularly in configuration management, system administration, system monitoring and capacity management as well as long-range planning and architecture skills.

Strategic and emergent – disabled by IT

This risk class deals with the IT capability letting down execution of the business strategy. Impacts are not immediate but will be significant in the business-planning horizon and beyond.

At risk is the ability of the firm to continue to move ahead towards a strategic vision. To remain competitive it is necessary for advances in IT to be understood and matched against potential opportunities for exploitation by your business. Once alignment of IT with business strategy is clear, opportunity can then be exploited through timely and effective adoption and integration. Obtaining strategic benefits from IT begins with a great IT strategy.

Gaps in IT strategy result in tactical and ad hoc approaches to IT. Occasional shocks can occur, as a major IT system is found to be a dead end or an island. More usual is a gradual increase in the difficulty and cost of introducing step-change and a greater allocation of limited development effort on existing systems rather than new.

Actively managing this class of risk requires capabilities in strategy, architecture and planning.

Understanding relationships between IT risk classes

The classes of IT risks are interdependent. Risks in each different class can impact on other classes.

Understanding these relationships will help you capitalize on virtuous-cycles – avoiding upstream risks to eliminate downstream risks, tackling potential problems at source and focusing on prevention rather than cure.

The following series of figures and supporting notes describe these key relationships between IT risks that fall within each class.

Strategic and emergent risk relationships

Poor management of strategic and emergent risks can drive project risks (see Figure 3.1). Key amongst these are the risks in project selection and direction: that the wrong projects are pursued and/or the right projects are not. Also, during the course of IT projects strategic direction corrections or re-alignment may be required. If the corrections do not occur, the project no matter how well conceived at initiation may ultimately be a failure.

Poor management of strategic and emergent risks can drive application and infrastructure risks. Applications and infrastructure components have to be selected but in the absence of a clear strategy and target system architecture these decisions will be made on a tactical or ad hoc basis. Many risks can result from an unmanaged increase in technology diversity, impacting development, maintenance and enhancement activity – difficulties in changing and integrating different systems – and operational support – difficulties in identifying, diagnosing and fixing problems.

Poor management of strategic and emergent risks can drive service provider risks. IT outsourcing decisions are often also IT strategic decisions as their impact will last for many years. A poor sourcing strategy and selection process can drive significant risks into the service transition period and beyond as ongoing service

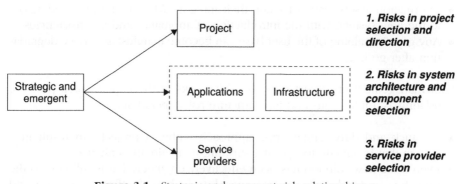

Figure 3.1—Strategic and emergent risk relationships

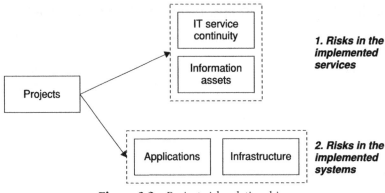

Figure 3.2—Project risk relationships

delivery by individual providers fails to meet your needs. When multiple suppliers are required to work together, a strategy that guides this 'multi-source' arrangement is essential – otherwise gaps, overlaps and disconnects occur and assuring the delivery of end-to-end services becomes extremely difficult.

Project risk relationships

Poor management of project risks can drive risks in the implemented service (see Figure 3.2). This translates as IT service continuity and information asset risks, including:

- A late or undelivered project results in a continued reliance on the existing, unimproved IT services.
- Delivery of new and different vulnerabilities, flaws and weaknesses along with the new system. New and changed systems go through a post-implementation period that requires heightened alertness and responsiveness in the user base and IT support team. Defects that must be fixed may require unwelcome outages.
- Information assets may not retain their integrity when being migrated across to the new system, with the introduction of anomalies and inconsistencies.
- Any gaps in training of the user base can become manifest as service degradation after go-live.

Poor management of project risks can drive risks in the implemented product, translating as applications and infrastructure risks, including:

- A 'quick and dirty' engineering approach within a project can result in a system that is difficult to operate, support, maintain and enhance.
- Even if the new solution has been effectively engineered, it is still new to the operators and a learning curve must be climbed. Ineffective training and

handover from the project team to the operations and support team can create a lasting legacy of risk in the production system.

• Poor product choices are made in projects – without regard for an overarching strategy and without adequate consultation and involvement of those who will be responsible for the system downstream. Future applications and infrastructure teams can be hamstrung and those reliant on them sorely disappointed when a 'not invented here' and a 'no guarantees' response is encountered when problems arise.

Service provider and vendor risk relationships

Poor management of service provider risks can drive project risks (see Figure 3.3). A major milestone in any project is the successful contracting of the solution delivery partners. This milestone will require a watertight contract for each service provider relationship. This should be a complete and sufficient statement of work and a sufficient level of shared understanding between both parties as to how the service provider's work will be managed and delivered. Unfortunately in some projects this milestone is not reached until the end; in some projects, never. When 'delivery to contract' is unclear, it is no surprise that poorly managed service provider risks may manifest themselves in product and service delivery risks within the context of the project.

The possible risks are as extensive as the set of project tasks and deliverables that may be reliant on service providers, which can extend to responsibility for the entire project. Particularly acute are the interrelationships between project tasks and service provider engagement – for example, the difficulties in defining a full scope of work without having completed analysis, additional details

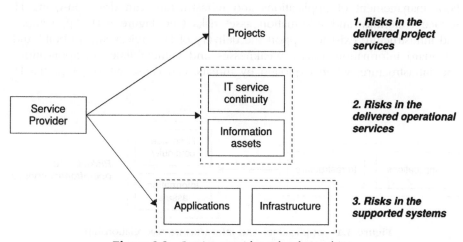

Figure 3.3—Service provider risk relationships

discovered in technical design that require a change in system and project scope, etc. Management of multiple suppliers, potentially in prime and sub-contractor formation adds another level of complexity and difficulty to project risk management.

Poor management of service provider risks can drive ongoing application and infrastructure risks. When IT services are outsourced and the systems are in the hands of service providers these risks intertwine. Outsourcing is effectively a decision to contract for services, transferring responsibility for applications and infrastructure asset management to providers. They are then held responsible for the delivered service, to a defined standard of performance, for an agreed cost. Even in an outsourcing context, application and infrastructure risks will still exist in their own right (i.e. applications can be flaky, infrastructure foundations shaky), however there will be a reliance on the outsourced service provider to manage these risks on your behalf. While some view outsourcing as transfer of risk, we view it as a transfer of risk management responsibilities. The Australian National Audit Office report that a major outsourcing project did not transfer the risk as intended, but retained most of it (ANAO, 2001).

When a more straightforward vendor relationship exists – i.e. IT products are purchased from a vendor and licensed for use – it is simpler to separate the risks into either a product failure or a vendor failure. If a product fails then the vendor is relied upon to fix it – any vendor service failings in the 'break–fix' cycle can have serious consequences. If the vendor fails, then no matter how solid the product, because of various risks associated with the lack of support, lack of an upgrade path and so on, it will be necessary to migrate to a new product, generally much more quickly than planned.

Applications and infrastructure risk relationships

Poor management of applications and infrastructure can drive on-going IT service continuity and information asset risks (see Figure 3.4). Applications and infrastructure exist to support the delivery of IT services and to build and safeguard information assets. Weaknesses and vulnerabilities in applications and infrastructure, when exploited by threats, can cause whole or partial IT

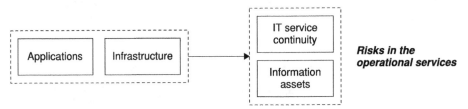

Figure 3.4—Applications and infrastructure risk relationships

service failures. In many businesses, temporary loss of primary computer systems can cause significant pain through temporary disruption of business processes, while permanent damage to critical application and data servers can truly represent a 'worst case' scenario that can cripple business operations. Some organizations are equipped with disaster recovery plans and facilities to allow a re-establishment of applications on a standby infrastructure. In such an instance data back-up and recovery procedures are vital if information assets are to be recovered.

Other relationships exist between the classes of IT risk that are not illustrated on the series of IT risk relationship diagrams, primarily for simplicity. These include:

- When loss or corruption of data residing in operational systems occurs there may be related IT service continuity impacts. Integrity of information processing in many cases is reliant on integrity of information.
- The qualities of the applications and infrastructure selected and utilized on a project can be a significant contributor to project risk. Using new and untried or inappropriate technologies on projects can result in difficulty in estimating project effort and a 'trial and error' approach to design.

Impacts of IT risks

Many different corporate objectives can be directly or indirectly impacted by IT risks. At one extreme a major IT risk event may prove a fatal blow to a company; at the other extreme an IT risk event may be a minor irritation.

A range of example business impacts that can result from different IT risks is shown in Table 3.1. These generic categories and diverse categories only hint at the range of potential consequences. Which of your corporate objectives are reliant on IT? These may be the areas most vulnerable to an IT risk in your business.

Wider impacts of your IT failures

You may prefer an alternative definition of IT risk:

An IT risk is something that can go wrong with IT and cause a negative impact ~~on the business~~.

This definition recognizes that in addition to the business risks of IT there are wider risks to users and societies from your IT behaving badly.

Table 3.1—Business impact examples attributable to IT risk causes

Impact	IT risk cause and examples
Financial	A costly IT project fails to deliver and the investment is written off. Example: Sydney Water spent A$60 million on a customer information and billing system project that was cancelled in late 2002 (NSW Auditor-General, 2003). A major outsourcing deal blows out. Example: UK magistrates court Libra contract costs have nearly doubled (*IntoIT*, 2003). Misuse of systems to perpetrate crime or fraud. Example: Kidder Peabody suffered significant loss with the illicit trading activities of Joseph Jett who fabricated profits of approximately US$339 million, perpetrated through insider abuse of trading and accounting systems (Dhillon and Moores, 2001).
Reputational	Major business processes visible to the public grind to a halt because of an IT service outage. Example: Extensive Bank of America ATM outages in January 2003 caused by corruption of their database servers by the SQL Slammer worm (*Infosecurity*, 2004). Sensitive customer information is disclosed resulting in fraudulent misuse. Example: Softbank in Japan reported the leakage of 4.5 million customer records in February 2004 and attempted extortion (Softbank, 2004).
Regulatory or legal	Integrity of information resulting in a penalty for breach of legislation Example: AT&T incorrect billing resulting in successful legal action by the State of Florida in 2004. Failure to comply with legislation. Example: 14 years after legislation required the coastguard to develop a vessel identification system, no such system exists (GAO, 2002).
Customer	Customer service is significantly impaired. Example: *Cigna HealthCare's $1 billion IT overhaul and CRM initiative went live in a big way, with 3.5 million members of the health insurance company moved from 15 legacy systems to two new platforms in a matter of minutes. The migration did not go smoothly. In fact, there were glitches in customer service so significant that millions of dissatisfied customers walked away, causing the nation's fourth largest insurer to lose 6 percent of its health-care membership in 2002.—CIO, 2003* Closing for business. Example: Early in 2004 the SCO Group was the target of the MyDoom virus that pointed infected computers at the SCO Group corporate website in a massive denial of service attack. Their site couldn't cope and was soon closed for business. Business could be restarted only at a new Internet address (*AFR*, 2004b).* Failing to deliver what the customer needs. Example: The UK eUniversity flopped after having attracted only 900 students (*Times*, 2004).
Competition	Being outstripped by a rival with a better service. Example: In a press release relating to Google's IPO, Standard & Poor's reveal that more than six out of ten Google users would switch search engines if a better service came along (Standard & Poor's, 2004).

Note: * Research from Hovav and D'Arcy (2003) indicates that in general the sharemarket does not penalize companies that are not 'Internet-specific' companies when they experience such an attack.

The risks and impact of systems failing is the focus of Peter Neumann's book *Computer-Related Risks* (1995) and a valuable on-line resource.[16] The collection and analysis of diverse failures provides ample evidence that IT risks do in practice result in actual loss events in a wide variety of applications in different industries.

This exploration of the causes and effects points to a wide range of IT risks, catalogued on the following basis:

- Sources of problems arising in system development, including: system conceptualization, requirements definition, system design, hardware and software implementation, support systems, analysis of system concepts and design, analysis of the implementation, evolution and decommission; and
- Sources of problems in system operation and use, including: natural environmental factors, animals, infrastructure factors, hardware malfunctions, software misbehaviour, communication media failures, human limitations in system use – installation, misuse of the overall environment or of the computer systems – unintentional and intentional misuse.

Importantly, Neumann sets out the system-related causes in the context of human causal factors. In most cases, computers share only part of the blame. Multiple contributing causes are also the rule rather than the exception, illustrating that a compartmentalized approach to managing IT risks is limiting.

Neumann's focus is on understanding the impact on people and society at large from computer-related failures and drawing lessons to be learned, particularly for systems designers and developers (Neumann, 1998, 2000, 2002). Others have studied IT risks as seen by the public including Internet addiction, isolation, depression and cyber-stalking (Sjoberg and Fromm, 2001).

The 'misbehaviour' of computers studied by Neumann spans a wide range of computer systems including robotics, control systems, communication networks, and computers used in planes, ships, spacecraft, nuclear power plants, etc. We focus on a narrower range of computer system, dealing mainly with commercial IT systems within two categories: applications and infrastructure.

---

[16] This topic is the focus of an online forum moderated by Peter Neumann: the Risks Forum newsgroup, or Risks to the Public in the Use of Computers and Related Systems, known as comp.risks in the USENET community, sponsored by the Association for Computing Machinery (ACM) Committee on Computers and Public Policy (CCPP), which Peter Neumann has chaired since 1985. An archival search and retrieval system is accessible at http://www.risks.org or http://catless.ncl.ac.uk/Risks/. A summary, Illustrative Risks to the Public in the Use of Computer Systems and Related Technology is accessible at http://www.csl.sri.com/users/neumann/illustrative.html.

Implementing an IT risk management capability

Given the universe of threats, the diversity of vulnerabilities and the shape-shifting nature of the IT risk landscape, how can you cope? How can you win?[17]

Is your organization crisis-prone or crisis-prepared (Mitroff and Alpaslan, 2003)? Is your organization quietly establishing man-made disasters? (Apologies to those who prefer gender-neutral language, however the field of failures in complex systems has been somehow attributed to the male of the species [Pidgeon and O'Leary, 2000].)

We've established the need for an IT governance framework and provided an overview of the integrated IT risk portfolio management approach and the loss impacts it will help you guard against and mitigate. Now you need to get moving.

An effective IT risk management capability is one that meets your business needs,[18] considering the following key design elements:

- Strategy and policy;
- Roles and responsibilities;
- Processes and approach;
- People and performance.

These elements are explored below with indicative questions and schedules that ensure that coverage is complete.

Strategy and policy

A set of IT risk management strategies and policies is required to define the overall objectives of IT risk management, establish the importance and priority of IT risk management, ensure adequate coverage of potential areas of IT risk and provide ground rules and principles for those managing risks.

Some of these policies will include the adoption of national or international standards in certain areas (such as US NIST, 2003). You may need to go further, to question whether the standards are good enough, or whether it is necessary to develop internal standards, recognizing that adoption of standards as points of reference does not automatically mean that 100% compliance is necessarily the goal.

Your IT risk management policies should be formally documented and endorsed by the IT governance team (refer to Chapter 2) and communicated actively throughout the organization, providing useful answers to questions such as:

---

[17] To keep an eye on who is winning, check the high-level scoreboards: incident statistics on attacks on US Federal Government sites are tracked at www.fedcirc.gov (one more attempt by the bad guys) and cybercrime convictions at www.usdoj.gov/criminal/cybercrime/cccases (registering the 'slam dunks' for the good guys).

[18] The requirements of public sector vs private sector organizations in managing IT risk are likely to be significantly divergent (Jordan and Musson, 2001).

- How is IT risk management integrated with wider business risk management activities?
- To what extent is decision-making with respect to IT risks delegated and what are the authorities at different levels of management?
- What are your classes of IT risk and how is each class of risk managed? Obviously we'd suggest the IT risk portfolio seven as your starting point!
- What is the company's overall risk appetite and how should all employees interpret this when dealing with IT risks?
- What are the critical potential impacts on the business from IT risks that are the primary focus for risk management effort?
- How are funds and resources to be allocated to IT risk management activities?[19]
- What constitutes a material risk that, if identified, should be reported and if so, to whom should it be reported?
- Which risks are managed proactively – that is, in advance of the defined unwanted and unwelcome event – and which risks are managed reactively, after the occurrence of one or more unwanted and unwelcome events?

Because everyone in the organization becomes a participant in the IT governance and risk management processes, it is critical that policies are promoted widely. Many organizations have IT 'fair use policies' that specify the rights and responsibilities of IT users in the organization. Generally these are extensive series of prohibitions that ensure that employees use the provided technology substantially as intended. They are seldom encouraging or facilitating, and have policing status.

Looking beyond the need to clearly articulate the edicts, there are many positive contributions to good IT governance that can be made by technology users, given sufficient guidance and opportunity. Perhaps IT risk management adoption can be adopted in a more voluntary and active fashion in the same way that many take the responsibility to be alert and aware for terrorism or security risks in their day-to-day lives with little instruction.

Roles and responsibilities

IT risk management activities must be built into people's jobs rather than left to the virtuous or diligent to carry out under their own initiative.[20]

---

[19] The objective of IT risk management cannot be to eliminate risk completely. Rainer *et al.* (1991) describe the purpose of risk management as to find the optimum combination of loss prevention and cost. Pfleeger (2000) uses the concept of risk leverage as the risk reduction delivered for a particular expenditure.

[20] Sauer *et al.* (1997) argue 'undesirable risk-related behaviours can be a logical outcome of a particular form of organization'.

Roles need first to be defined and subsequently the right people need to be selected and allocated to perform these roles. The framework of responsibilities is perhaps best first drawn up in matrix form, considering the different types of IT risks and the risk management lifecycle. We provide examples of those who may take specific responsibilities in Table 3.2.

The examples within this matrix illustrate that each IT risk class has different roles and responsibilities. An individual may 'wear many hats' in dealing with IT risks, based on the roles they hold.

Some important considerations include:

- Separation of duties – ensuring that for each class of risk an independent role undertakes monitoring and review activities;
- Balancing the need for specialist input – contributing an understanding of a process, system or specific risk, and managerial decision-making – weighing up all the factors and determining a course of action;
- Fitting IT risk management roles into existing structures where there is a natural fit. For example, risk management treatment actions would be naturally aligned with the project manager for project risks;
- Creating new IT risk management roles when required, for example, a cross-functional business continuity coordination role; and
- Allocating joint responsibilities when necessary and ensuring all slots are taken.

Processes and approach

A repeatable and predictable IT risk management capability is founded on a set of processes that are understood and followed consistently. The risk management process need not be complex. The risk management lifecycle comprises the following steps, deployed in different ways for different types of risks:

1. Identification / discovery – getting IT risks on the radar of management;
2. Assessment / analysis – understanding the IT risk in the context of the whole portfolio of IT risks and assessing the likelihood of occurrence and potential impact on the business;
3. Treatment – determining the best option from many possible courses of action for treating the risk, planning out and completing the required actions; and
4. Monitoring and review – following up to ensure what was planned was actually done and to understand any further changes in the IT risk portfolio.

An escalation process is required in cases where the normal risk management approach proves insufficient. The completion of the risk lifecycle also requires a formal closure process step (i.e. taking previously identified risks off the management radar when they are no longer significant or relevant).

Table 3.2—Risk management responsibilities by IT risk class, with possible individual roles

responsibilities	projects	IT service continuity	information assets	service providers	applications	infrastructure	strategic and emergent
Identification/ discovery	Project team	Staff involved in business processes	Information custodians and system users	Project managers, IT service delivery managers	System administrator, users, application support team	System administrator, system support and operations team, vendors	IT architects and planners
Assessment/ analysis	Project manager	Business continuity coordinator, IT service delivery manager	Security manager	Outsourcing and vendor manager, Contract manager	Applications manager, Vendor manager (if a package)	Infrastructure manager, Vendor manager	IT strategy and planning manager
Treatment (Actions assigned by)	Project manager	Business functional heads, IT service delivery manager	Business functional heads, Chief information officer	Outsourcing and vendor manager	Business system owners, Applications manager	Infrastructure manager	Business functional heads, IT strategy and planning manager
Monitoring and review	Director of IT projects, Audit	Director of IT service delivery, Audit	Chief information officer, Audit	Director of IT service delivery	Chief information officer	Chief information officer	Director corporate strategy

Other details of approach need to be considered to ensure consistency and comparability across the IT risk portfolio. Key questions relating to the information management and analytical approach are posed:

- How much information needs to be captured and documented on each risk, and to what level of consistency and accuracy?
- How quantitative and accurate must assessments of IT risks be? Is qualitative good enough?[21]
- How is the effectiveness of IT risk management capability and risk management performance to be measured?

People and performance

IT risk management is also about people and their performance. People's skills and knowledge in IT risk management need to be developed and maintained. This requires some combination of education and training dealing with IT risks, appropriate for the roles and responsibilities held.

The culture that supports and promotes effective IT risk management is determined by the management team's actions. This culture needs to align individual's efforts and embed IT risk management as part of accepted practice and develop reward systems that recognize individual contributions to risk management.

Whistle-blowing must be encouraged and managers must listen when the whistle is blown. Your two-way communication mechanisms must accommodate good, potentially bad and very bad news. Research on the willingness and reluctance of auditors to blow the whistle on failing IT projects (Keil and Robey, 2001) highlights the personal risks that the whistle-blower faces. Senior executives who fail to listen in an increasingly accountable climate can be at far greater personal risk.

Research has highlighted the importance of manager perceptions in dealing with risk (Bandyopadhyay et al., 1999; Kontio et al., 1998; Keil et al., 2000). Further research has explored the 'hidden assumptions' that if causes of failure can be understood then management can straightforwardly eliminate them (Sauer et al., 1997). The concepts of organizational learning – learning from your mistakes or even better, learning from others (Scott and Vessey, 2000) – also have a part to play, wherein acceptance and recognition of short-term failure is a precondition to long-term success.

Implementation and improvement

People won't just accept a new way of managing IT risks is necessary without having been told why it is necessary. A convincing story must address both

---

[21] NASA (2002) represents the most developed approaches to quantitative risk analysis. Rainer et al. (1991) set out both quantitative and qualitative analysis techniques and argue persuasively that a mix of both is preferable.

why it is important for your organization and why it is important for the individual.

Change will then need to roll out in a particular way. Are all IT risk areas addressed at once, or is the focus first on those IT risks most recognizable as the 'squeaky wheels'? Is the implementation of change to be rapid or drawn-out? In what order will the different areas of the business and IT be engaged?

Standard change management practices will deal with the planned change, addressing each of these elements and ensuring sufficient resources are allocated to achieve the agreed milestones.

As capability improves over time, it will be important to sustain the changes that have been achieved and redirect the IT risk management team towards further improvements.

Call to arms

We have outlined an IT risk management approach within an IT governance framework that enables your organization to get on top and stay on top of its IT risks.

To promote your implementation steps, we recap on the position you will seek to achieve against the deficiencies commonly encountered and set out in Chapter 1, some or all of which may currently apply to your organization:

- Piecemeal approaches are explicitly countered with the holistic IT risk portfolio that provides formal coverage for all of your relevant IT risks, all the time.
- Communications failures are rigorously addressed with the establishment of two-way channels flowing from and to the top of the organization.
- Surprises and reactivity, while not completely eliminated, are reduced and dealt with in an orderly fashion – IT risks won't be pushed under the carpet to be discovered late in the day, or too late – they'll be disclosed in a timely manner by those with clear responsibility to do so and appreciated by those whose job it is to listen and respond.
- Career damage to individuals will be minimized as the focus shifts to organizational learning and development of capability – the risk that was dealt with being welcomed as the disaster that didn't happen.
- Evolving, moving subjects are not furtive shapes that go bump in the night – their movements are actively tracked within and across the IT risk portfolio, specialists encouraged to provide valuable look-ahead warnings to those who can redirect the course.
- Creeping goals become clear targets and objectives – the hurdles are raised clearly and explicitly, with the need for capability development to meet the new challenges being recognized and built in to the implementation program, a 'quantum leap' in capability is recognized as infeasible and steady improvement becomes the norm.

- Consistent underperformance founded in IT failures becomes something you'll point out in your competitors and congratulate yourselves on having avoided.

Surely that is enough encouragement to get to work! The rest of the book is designed for you to 'jump' to the IT risk class and chapter of most interest. If a hot topic doesn't immediately call for your attention, start with the health checks at the end of each chapter to prioritize your reading and implementation efforts.

Health check

This section assists you consider at a macro-level the company's requirement for an IT risk management overhaul.

Is IT risk management important to your business?

- Many types of IT risks could potentially impact the business.
- There are different views about how IT risks should be managed.
- Obtaining management airtime and funding for IT risk-related activities is difficult.

> *If you agree with two or more of the three statements, then IT risk management is important to your business.*

Are you doing the right things?

- IT risks are regularly reviewed.
- The process for IT risk identification and analysis is repeatable, structured and consistent.
- The allocation of cost and effort for managing IT risks receives formal consideration.
- All stakeholders are involved in determining relative priorities and IT risk treatment strategies.
- Ongoing IT risk funding covers both technical aspects and management / people aspects.
- It is clear how different types of IT risks are being addressed and managed.
- IT risk management is effectively linked into wider enterprise risk management processes.

- IT is managed in a proactive way.
- IT failures are examined so necessary changes to policies, procedures and approaches can be undertaken as a continuous learning process.

> *If you agree with these statements, then you are doing the right things in your organization. If you disagree with three or more of the nine statements, then there is significant room for improvement in your IT risk management capability*

Do you have a good track record?

- The business has avoided being negatively impacted by most types of IT risks.
- IT judgments and opinions are trusted and valued by the business.
- When urgent action has been required to remedy an IT crisis the response has been effective (also answer yes if you haven't had any significant IT crises).
- Tangible losses experienced from past IT failures have been acceptable.

> *If you agree with these statements, then you have a good track record of managing IT risks. If you disagree with two or more of the four statements, then there is evidence of the need to improve IT risk management capability.*

Case study: European fleet management services provider

Setting up a European data centre

A world leader in fleet management and automotive services, based in Europe and employing over 7000 people, manages over 1 million vehicles with a total value of some €10 billion in over 20 countries across the globe. It has a banking licence that gives the company access to the capital markets but also places it under the supervision of a European national bank.

The company has embarked on a strategy to position itself towards its customers as a partner with a global service delivery capability for international companies as well as a cost-effective local supplier for small and medium-sized companies. IT will play a major role in this effort and international consolidation in information and communication technology (ICT) is considered a key step forward.

Both the stricter requirements from the European national bank under the Basel II agreements and the strategic imperative require a considerable strengthening of central IT governance. Unfortunately this goes contrary to the highly entrepreneurial company culture, in which local decision power is regarded as the key to business success. While all countries use the same hardware platform and share the same core application for fleet management, this application is customized by each local unit, and there is far less standardization on the hardware and the applications in other functional areas. Several attempts to strengthen central governance over the last years had met with limited success.

The company then decided to set up a European data centre that would consolidate the processing of the major applications and the management of the wide area network. The stated objectives of the project were:

- To reduce diversity in the group;
- To leverage on the global scale of the company;
- To improve security in line with the new banking regulation and with industry best practice; and
- To create a platform for the future development of ICT.

As the project moved forward further expected benefits were identified:

- The design of the European data centre and the wide area network provides the robust and common platform that will be required for making ICT a key factor in the development of the company's strategy;
- Disaster recovery is moving from a local responsibility with mixed levels of protection against disaster towards a common solution that is designed to be fail-safe;
- Data protection and retention is also organized and monitored centrally with best practice processes imposed on all organizations; and
- The European data centre will be the key contact point to ensure that all entities comply with the security regulations of the European national bank, and will support them in implementing these.

A number of additional benefits are materializing:

- The project to create the European data centre and migrate the processing from the countries to the centre has been set up completely in compliance with PRINCE2 project management guidelines. As such it is not only the showcase for this approach within the company, but it

has also provided a number of document templates and project control process descriptions that have already been used in other projects; and
- The project has generated extensive communication between the ICT management of the countries, resulting in an exchange of experience on potential application solutions and creating the first level of convergence of applications.

Printed with permission of PA Consulting Group

4 Projects

All at sea

Fourteen years after legislation required the Coast Guard to develop a vessel identification system, no such system exists, and future plans for developing the system are uncertain. The Coast Guard's early efforts to acquire VIS were unsuccessful. In the late 1980's and early 1990's, the Coast Guard undertook numerous activities to define requirements for such a system. In 1995, the agency contracted to develop the Marine Information for Safety and Law Enforcement (MISLE) system, of which VIS was a subcomponent. The Coast Guard accepted the contractor developed VIS in 1998 despite system performance problems, intending to resolve these problems as the system evolved. However, the Coast Guard later found that there was no viable way to correct these and other problems, and that the cost to populate the system with states' data would be high. In retrospect, Coast Guard officials noted two factors that complicated VIS implementation: (1) not all vessels had unique identification numbers and (2) the system depended on the voluntary participation of the states, and many states were unwilling or unable to commit the funds needed to participate. Consequently, even though the Coast Guard spent about $9 million in identified costs to plan and develop VIS, it was never implemented. (GAO, 2002)

Down the drain

Sydney Water's customer information and billing system (CIBS) project was intended to improve service to customers, to fill gaps in existing information systems and to provide business efficiencies . . .
Sydney Water had originally expected CIBS to be operational by February 2002, at a cost of $38.2 million . . .
Sydney Water terminated the CIBS project on 30 October 2002 . . .

Before the project was stopped, the budget had increased to $60 million,
with a further revision pending and the 'Go Live' date had moved to March
2004 . . . most of the $61.0 million will be written off.

(NSW Auditor-General, 2003, p. 12)

The IT world abounds with horror stories about the failure rate of IT projects
and the impact on business. It doesn't matter whether it is an academic study,
a consultancy report, government audits, or your own post implementation
reviews – everybody agrees that IT projects commonly fail to deliver. On top of
this, almost everybody comes up with a top-10 list of reasons why – they just
don't agree.

It is quite clear that implementing IT solutions to deliver business value is
difficult, and there is more art to it than the numerous project delivery methodologies imply. Worse, not only do the projects have to overcome the array
of hurdles, obstacles and traps inherent in the nature of difficult projects, but
also fear of failure means that many organizations impose additional gates and
checkpoints that often actually add risk to a project.

There are two extreme positions in the galaxy of failure capabilities:

- Your organization is inherently incapable at project delivery – even relatively
  simple projects go wrong.
- You have inherently high-risk projects and are not addressing the specific
  risks appropriately.

Most organizations wander around in the middle ground, with neither a demonstrated competency of always delivering a quality product on time and on
budget, nor a workload consisting of high-risk projects. A fundamental lack of
competency is an IT governance issue that was dealt with in Chapter 2. In this
chapter we look at the range of challenges in delivering projects, when an
effective governance structure is in place.

Whether your interest in an IT project is as the primary recipient of the solution and service, the source of funds, the manager accountable for solution
delivery, a manager of another project with dependencies or as a stakeholder
with a less direct interest, you are no doubt keenly aware of some risks and less
aware of others. From day to day, out of necessity the management of the project
is delegated. The key question remains for you: In the relatively small amount of
senior management time allotted to oversee the projects in the portfolio, what
needs to be done to get on top of the risks and make sure they are properly
managed?

This chapter sets out the generic costs of project failure and provides a framework for you to assess both issues of individual project failure and more systemic
capability issues in project delivery. An exploration of the concept of project risk
factors leads to structured suggestions about how to manage projects with a 'high
degree of difficulty' so as to reduce the likelihood and impact of project failure risks.

An overview of the generic IT project 'voyage' precedes subsequent detailed analysis of delivery assurance philosophies and considerations that should be uppermost for phase reviews of projects. Management responses, utilizing a triage model, are discussed along with considerations of alternative solution delivery lifecycle methods and the suggested risk management stance and emphasis for each.

To conclude, a project risk health check is provided and a case study reinforces some of the key lessons learned. A comprehensive checklist for those requiring immediate diagnosis or first aid is given in Appendix 1.

The impact of project failure

We have ordered the IT risk portfolio so that projects are addressed first. Research has indicated that the largest IT risks in a high-risk portfolio will be due to projects, in particular large projects (Verhoef, 2002; McFarlan, 1981).

While our focus will be on IT projects, we point to the need to consider the bigger picture, paying heed to recent advice given to UK government agencies:

> *Our most important message is that thinking in terms of 'IT projects' is itself a primary source of problems. Delivering IT is only ever part of the implementation of new, more effective ways of working.*
>
> (McCartney, 2000, p. 5)

When an IT project fails, the investment costs are typically the headline items. Certainly there is wastage – scarce resources have been working on a project that did not deliver anything of value, these people could reasonably have been working on something else – however, there are also a couple of more insidious impacts.

We'll call the first the 'lost benefit' risk. If the project was worth doing, then presumably it was justified based on the business benefits to be generated from utilizing the IT product or service – it certainly should have been!

A well-structured business case for an initiative will typically explore the 'do nothing' or 'maintain status quo' option – illustrating this option as infeasible and unpalatable – before exploring, at a high level at least, some less-favoured options, and settling on the recommended course and explaining this in some detail. An idea of the impact of the project failure in 'lost benefit' terms can be obtained by rereading this 'do nothing' section of the business case and reflecting that the business is still in this state. Of course, the original business case may have strangely disappeared and the original promises made lost in the mists of time . . . but this brings us to the next impact from project failure.

We'll call this 'collateral damage' risk. People involved in the project may be harmed, as individuals, teams and potentially whole organizations. At its worst, following a single major failure or a series of failures, it can manifest as a massive crisis of confidence – do we have the capability to deliver anything? Those on the receiving end – who were given what, after the fact, appear to be false assurances – may never again trust the delivery team's members. Naturally many individuals will want to avoid this situation and many organizations allow them to. The project ships are quietly abandoned.

Some organizations prefer to seek vengeance. Perhaps the skipper is made to walk the plank, leaving a fearful and apparently subservient crew who are strangely uninterested in the promotion opportunities to captain now on offer.

> *Frequently, abandonment decisions are so badly handled by companies, culminating in the firing and/or demotion of some key IS staffers . . . that even those left unscathed feel intimidated and so refrain from voicing their opinions.* (Ewusi-Mensah, 1998, p. 79)

It is useful to look at the partial failure cases from three perspectives:

1. Time;
2. Functionality and quality;
3. Cost.

These perspectives are sometimes depicted as the points on a triangle that a project manager must constantly manage. If something has to give on a project then it will be one of these – perhaps the sanity of the project manager could be added as a fourth!

Time

The term 'deadline' is often used. This is the planned delivery date and generally relates to the implementation or 'go-live' date. It may have a foundation in a hard and fast fixed date in the real world – the Year 2000 date change could not be postponed;[22] it may have been set as a somewhat arbitrary but challenging goal imposed on the project by its business sponsor; or it may have its foundation in a detailed work plan, estimates and schedule.

When a project slips what happens?[23] In general terms if there is a real-time constraint it will impose itself on the project participants, with a resulting ramp up in resources and costs (to a point) and then degradation in functionality and quality. The 'must do' projects – if they are indeed 'must do' – tend to get

---

[22] The Y2K issue was perceived by many as a 'necessary evil' (Gogan and Rao, 1999) and by most as a distraction from core business. A huge proportion of IT budgets were gobbled up by Y2K initiatives in 1998 and 1999.

[23] The Australian Customs' cargo management re-engineering project delays have required amendments to legislation: the system wasn't delivered by the deadline date from which businesses were required to use it (*AFR*, 2004d).

completed – with all that entails in terms of risks in operation for the solutions rushed through the latter stages of quality assurance and deployment. Other, discretionary projects typically slip. The cost of slippage is the sum of the direct costs of project resources retained for longer, the indirect costs of lost benefits for the period of slippage and various types of collateral damage, usually intangible. Dependent projects can also slip, with the wider consequences.

Functionality and quality

Missed deadlines are difficult to completely cover up. Functionality and quality gaps are easier to hide. When the required output is poorly or incompletely specified in the first place it is difficult later to fully dimension the extent of non-delivery. Some IT delivery groups play this issue on the front foot – you'll take what you are given and no complaining – while others play defensive – you'll need to explain why this is a defect and explain why it is a priority for us to fix it. It is common for delivery teams to rely on the mounting pressure that late discovery of rework inevitably places on all stakeholders. To complain within sight of the destination port that some of the goods in the hold are missing is fine – we'll make sure they come in the next shipment – but is it really worth delaying the completion of this journey to go back for them?

In general, a functionality and quality gap will amount to a lost benefits impact. For example, instead of the ten reports specified only three were delivered, making for some pretty heavy cutting and pasting duty in user land. In some cases, however, a defect in production can directly or indirectly result in a business impact that can far outweigh the project costs and the potential business benefits. For example, a nuclear power control system that aims to automate certain procedures, allowing a reduction in labour costs. A failure to deliver all of the automation features may result in a smaller than planned reduction in labour costs. The introduction of a bug that contributes to a meltdown – a human and environmental catastrophe – is clearly of far greater enormity.

Costs

The accumulated costs of 'throwing more resources at a project' can be a simple manifestation of a partial project failure. How much more was spent on this project than originally planned? This is the direct cost of failure. Perhaps in the light of the full project costs it becomes apparent that the initiative was not worthwhile, the investment not a sound one – if the full facts had been known in the beginning another course would have been selected.

However, there is an accepted practice of interpreting past expenses on an investment that can't be recovered as sunk cost that is generally the case for IT project spend. So the revelation of a cost increase late in the day typically does not kill the revisiting of the numbers – the forward-looking investment evaluation of a single project. The investment committee re-computes the (unaltered) benefits stream – which is hopefully now closer – against the remaining spend, which although increased from the original plan is still satisfactory to allow it over the hurdle.

If multiple projects overrun, and the bad news is revealed late and on an incremental basis, eventually those who put up the money undertake a rethink. The CFO will certainly seek to ensure that a systematic abuse of the investment management process is dealt with emphatically. New IT project cost estimates will be 'factored' to account for past sins. When the well-meaning project manager steps forward with an estimate the investment committee asks for it to be inflated – some refer to this as adding contingency – before the numbers are crunched. This is one of the manifestations of the rule of thumb of 'doubling original estimates' applied to IT projects.

Of course, the dysfunctional response – for those keen to undertake exciting IT projects that keep getting knocked back – can be to sharpen the pencil, whittle down initial estimates and allow the investment committee inflation process to bring the project into the expected costs range. Ultimately this simply locks in a pattern of behaviour as the now-approved project is almost certain to chew into contingency – it is only a matter of time and everyone expects it.

Systemic failures in project delivery

Some of the statistics about IT project failure are frightening (Powell and Klein, 1996). It seems that such a large proportion of them don't succeed. For organizations that are systematically failing to deliver important IT projects, what is the business impact?

The largest IT budget on the planet serves to illustrate some systemic failures that receive the attention of the US General Accounting Office:

> *Today's hearing on the government's information technology (IT) management . . . is a critical topic because, according to the President's most recent budget, the federal government spends billions of dollars annually on IT – reportedly investing about $57 billion in fiscal year 2003. Yet these dollars are not always managed wisely. For example, the Administration reported that of the $60 billion in IT investments requested for fiscal year 2005, $22 billion – representing 621 major projects – are currently on its 'Management Watch List.' This list includes mission-critical projects that need improvement in the areas of performance measures, earned value management, and/or IT security.* (GAO, 2004a)

Within such a large and complex portfolio there are the 'ordinary failures' (refer to the coastguard example at the opening of this chapter) and there are the flagship 'challenges':

One of the five priorities in the President's Management Agenda is the expansion of electronic (e-) government – the use of Internet applications to enhance access to and delivery of government information and services. To this end, the Office of Management and Budget (OMB) has sponsored 25 high-profile e-government initiatives. The initiatives were selected on the basis of value to citizens, potential improvement in agency efficiency, and the likelihood of being deployed within 18 to 24 months. In May 2002, a total of 91 objectives were set for these initiatives. At the request of the Subcommittee, GAO assessed the progress of the initiatives in address-ing these 91 objectives as well as key challenges they have faced.

(GAO, 2004a)

In the report dated March 2004 – and thus nearly two years on from the May 2002 objective-setting period – the following progress was reported:

Overall, mixed progress has been made in achieving the 91 objectives originally defined for the 25 OMB-sponsored e-government initiatives. To date, 33 have been fully or substantially achieved; 38 have been partially achieved; and for 17, no significant progress has been made towards these objectives. In addition, 3 of the objectives no longer apply because they have been found to be impractical or inappropriate . . .

For two of the initiatives – Grants.gov and Internal Revenue Service (IRS) Free File – all original objectives have been achieved, and for an additional five, the majority of their original objectives have been achieved. For the other 18 initiatives, most of their objectives are either partially met or not significantly met . . .

Given that OMB's stated criteria in choosing these initiatives included their likelihood of deployment in 18 to 24 months, the substantial number of objectives that are still unmet or only partially met indicates that making progress on these initiatives is more challenging than OMB may have originally anticipated. (GAO, 2004f)

To understand the impact of failure beyond the public sector – where blow-by-blow accounts in the public domain are far less common – it is necessary for most to consider the competitive environment. If all competitors are equally poor, then it is possible for an organization to survive, albeit with a return only on par with the similarly poor sector incumbents.

However, in the commercial world rivals will and do react. Faster, more nimble and more competent organizations will be encouraged into all but the most highly walled gardens to feed on the forbidden fruit.

In summary, for most it is only a matter of time before large-scale ramifica-tions of project failure are felt at the corporate level, the ultimate victim shareholder value.

Organizational, program and project views of risk

Getting better at delivering IT projects requires attention at three levels:

1. The organization within which project delivery occurs;
2. The program of multiple concurrent projects that are the 'balls in the air' the management team must continually juggle; and
3. The discrete projects, each of which will be at various stages of their journey.

Managing the organization for project delivery

Systemically tackling project risk requires an investment in the way projects are done; not just a single tactical 'rescue' style of intervention, but also a commitment to a capability and maturity development.

Perhaps the first important capability is the management capability to identify distressed projects early and take the hard decision – to kill or cure. If the business is not entirely supportive of the project and there is no sound investment reason for continuing, it should be killed. If it needs curing, you need to go into rescue mode and apply some specific turnaround techniques to get the project back on track. Killing projects requires a somewhat ruthless program-level role that many are uncomfortable playing. Often it is down to the CFO to take the reins on this. The benefit of clearing out the underperformers is that resources can be deployed onto the remaining projects with a consequent increase in delivery certainty.

The development of a 'projects culture' is perhaps the next most important capability. That is, a centre or centres of expertise within the organization that exist to deliver change that is credible and perceived as 'good places to work'. Many organizations aren't serious about providing careers for their better project people. Little wonder that project roles are seen in a negative light. The best you can do is deliver (and retain your place in this poorly regarded holding pen) or not deliver and be quickly booted out or marked with a 'not suitable for real work' permanent stain. More realistically, most individuals will deliver both good and bad performances on projects; despite their performance only some of the projects will deliver successful change into the organization. The key is to attract the better performers to the more valuable (and probably harder) projects and give incentives towards improved personal performance, subsequently separating at least to some extent the appraisal of individual performance from the appraisal of project outcomes.

Leading to perhaps the third most important overarching capability, the institution of organizational learning around projects. When the repeating project failures are striking stakeholders as a dejà vu experience – 'I feel like I have seen this before' – then it is probably time for a serious, multi-year, program-level looking back. What are the patterns evident in our history of failure? What are the common things we get wrong? What are the root causes of failures? What distinguishes our successes? How well are we doing compared to others? Of course there is little point asking these questions if there is no intention or ability to actually do anything different! Insights into what can go wrong as well as the potential downside impact must be captured – but this isn't enough – to be of use they must be subsequently deployed with full recognition of the different perceptions and propensities within your management team in dealing with risk (Keil *et al.*, 2000).

Despite the obviousness of this statement it does appear in many organizations that post-implementation review (PIR) activities exist principally to apportion blame or fulfil a bureaucratic need. Post-implementation reviews that subsequently result in a modification to the approaches being taken on other current projects are the most valuable through building and sustaining a project management knowledge base within the organization (Barros *et al.*, 2004).

Managing the program – risks associated with multiple concurrent IT projects

It is widely acknowledged[24] that instead of undertaking 'big and ugly' projects it can be better, if possible, to undertake a set of 'small and beautiful' projects.

Before embarking on this course it is important to understand that while each small project will score lower on most risk factor assessments, additional risks are introduced because of the new program management challenges:

- Keeping the projects lined up and linked up – as each project charts its way through the IT project lifecycle it will be necessary for points of dependency to be fulfilled.
- Maintaining consistency of design principles – an end-to-end perspective can easily be lost and a number of incompatible point solutions can arise; particularly important is the system interfaces, end-user appearance of the whole and non-functional issues (Can the combined system function in the same way that the pieces are able to on their own?).
- Containing overheads – as coordination activity increases this can distract delivery team members from the task at hand and consume a large proportion of the IT staff time.
- Managing contention on shared resource base – if multiple projects require the services of scarce technical specialists and delivery people a queue can form, with priorities applied to determine which goes first.

[24] The *McCartney Report* (*McCartney*, 2000) stresses the importance of incremental project delivery and the Clinger-Cohen Act considers grand projects anathema.

Managing the project – generic voyage risks

Having dealt with organization and capability questions we now move into the context of an individual project. If the analogy is for our IT projects to be considered boats on the sea – headed toward their destination – then our perspective as managers is not an on-board perspective. Other literature serves as sufficient guidance for project managers as to how to handle a project. We take the perspective of the admiral in command of the fleet.

Managing IT project risks is not just about setting up projects the right way, but let's start there.

- *Design the project structure* – the right vessel. A fit-for-purpose project structure will accommodate all of the dedicated crew comfortably and within a clear command structure. Specialists will be sought to fulfil particular roles – e.g. adviser on security issues, specialist for data migration – and these must be clearly specified especially when they are contributing for only one or two of the project phases.
- *Select and allocate people* – the right crew. The required project roles must be identified and then filled with capable individuals who are provided with clear role definitions they understand and accept. The key roles and the relationships between some of the crew may also need to be formally described and communicated across the team, particularly if any ambiguity is likely to arise.
- *Develop a plan* – a high-level map leading towards the destination with at least the first leg of the journey fully mapped out. As the saying goes, if you don't know where you are going you probably won't get there. While planning in detail to the end of the voyage is impractical, it is necessary to set out a clear plan for the first leg. This promotes the formation of a strong team focused on the priority tasks at hand.

En route the following become important:

- *Regular communication* – contact with the fleet at sea, copies of the ship's log in port. With constraints that limit direct observation of day-to-day project activities, it is necessary for management information to be provided in a format that can be digested quickly and effectively by a range of stakeholders. A common saying is that a project runs late a day at a time, so regular communication is important. This is not all one-way; if new information comes to hand that may have a bearing on the project it should be communicated at once to those on board.

    So-called 'dashboard reporting' is most common, with a standardized pro forma completed regularly (e.g. monthly) for major projects. Most suffer to some extent or another from 'sunny side up' reporting influenced by a self-assessment and self-reporting regime, the most commonly accepted practice.

- *Tracking of progress against plan* – checking that it remains on course. The three dimensions of cost, functionality and time should be regularly checked, even for those projects with a high degree of autonomy and delegated powers. Most actions are invariably assigned back to the project team – so visibility to the micro-level is not desirable or valuable. When action is required (whoever is to deal with it) this should be unambiguously communicated.

At the destination:

- *Accepting deliverables* – unloading the hold to assure you have got what you wanted and didn't get something you can't cope with. As the project reaches the destination, the quality assurance (QA) activities ramp up and the user acceptance milestone looms. Key here is to identify anything critical that is missing or any defects that should prevent the implementation because they cannot be feasibly worked around. Many projects get bogged down here seeking perfection rather than a working solution. Most solutions generate a splash of change requests immediately after deployment that require a 'point release' soon after, and often the project team remains on hand 'just in case' during the post-deployment period, presenting an obvious opportunity for tidying up loose ends with minimal incremental cost.

Decision-making and control over time, functionality and cost

In terms of IT project risks there is an immediate trade-off at the project level in terms of time, functionality and cost.

Paramount is the initial establishment of goals for the project. Not everyone will have the same view so in most organizations this project definition will necessitate stakeholder identification – including the search for the elusive sponsor.[25] The business case is the typical formal artefact for the IT project that brings together and establishes the objectives relating to time, functionality and cost. While initial estimates are always imprecise it is universal that the more you want the longer it will take and the more it will cost – trade-offs are inevitable. The responsibility for making these trade-offs and establishing the risk profile of the project lies with the managers who are overseeing the project and should not be left to be defined and interpreted by the project team. Lyytinen (1988) established the concept of expectation failure: the beauty of a project is in the eye of the stakeholder.

[25] The Government of the United Kingdom now requires the identification of a senior responsible owner or SRO to take accountability for delivery of each major initiative (*McCartney*, 2000). The RiskIT methodology emphasizes the importance of clear goal identification and stakeholder engagement as preconditions to effective project risk management (Kontio *et al.*, 1998).

Subsequent to the initial set-up, some organizations choose to delegate completely the flexing of the three dimensions of time, functionality and cost, within pre-defined thresholds, to project-level management, requiring escalation only where trade-offs within the immediate context of the project cannot remove the pinch.

Others hold the reins firmly and require even minor variances to be reported and escalated. Contingency reserves might be eked out – more time, more funds begrudgingly allocated – de-scoping allowed only after formal change request evaluation. Of course the drivers of the project team and their effort and risk aversion (Phelps, 1996) should be considered: highly risk averse teams are likely to build large contingencies into their plans. This complicates the concept of project success – when success to the agents (carrying out the work) looks entirely different to success as perceived by the sponsor.

In general a multi-level approach to managing IT risks is required. A risk should be understood by all parties as a threat to one or more of the project goals (Powell and Klein, 1996). What is material and not resolvable at project level should be escalated. In practice, a complete IT risk register must be maintained within the project team, with only a 'short list' of probable high-impact risks being summarized in the management report.

For those relying on upwards reporting from the project team, you should consider the shortcomings in project-level risk management identified as commonplace on UK government agency IT projects: a too-narrow focus, tabulating numerous risks without prioritizing, failure to understand what risks can be transferred to a partner or supplier, failing to understand boundaries of responsibilities, depending on the contract or its penalty clauses to mitigate risk and failing to monitor effectiveness of risk management actions (*McCartney*, 2000).

Understanding IT project risk factors

When we look within the project context at the causes of IT risks it is necessary to sort out an important term. Project risk factors have featured prominently in the literature.[26] The following are typically included on these lists that can run to many pages:

---

[26] Stark differences between different risk factor lists exist. Lack of top management commitment to the project rates as number one for some (Keil *et al.*, 1998; Schmidt *et al.*; 2001) and is completely missed from Boehm's Top Ten. Wallace and Keil (2004) list a total of 53 project risk factors. Some attempt a link between discrete risks and the application of specific prescriptions or controls, although these can drift into neatly categorized statements of the bleeding obvious (for example, Addison and Vallabh [2002] identify 'Developing the wrong software functions' as a software project risk).

- Project size – a big project is a risk factor – variously measured in terms of how 'big' the delivered solution is to be (say, measured in terms of functionality) or how many resources are being allocated to complete the planned tasks;
- Organization impact – a big organization impact is a risk factor – typically from a user base and business process perspective; for example, a whole-of-organization user base application that reshapes multiple core business process is described with a higher risk factor than say a local user base application that addresses only a single, non-core business process;
- Project complexity measured from the perspective of its dependencies with other projects – more dependencies is a risk factor; number and types of technologies being used – more technologies is a risk factor; amount of customization being undertaken – more customization is a risk factor;
- Team skills and capability, a poor capability is a risk factor, encompassing experience and track record;
- Types of technologies being used – using new and untried technologies on projects can result in difficulty in estimating project effort and a 'trial and error' approach to design.

In many contexts the implication of highlighting these many and compounding risk factors is to set forth how 'big and ugly' IT projects have been allowed to become. The IT project risk factors are degree of difficulty factors. The initial simplistic prescription of many is simply not to design IT projects that way – or not to allow projects scoring high on risk factors to proceed.

The problem is that many firms simply must undertake projects that score highly on a number of project risk factors. In these cases a large number of 'small and beautiful' projects are not a feasible alternative to the one or few 'big and ugly'. Earlier we explored further the non-trivial issues associated with the management of multiple concurrent IT projects.

In other cases for firms confronting a high-risk factor project, there may be choices, but these choices are trade-offs. If your sights are lowered you'll never hit the higher target.

- Can the project size be reduced? Yes, but the project will deliver less functionality.
- Can less of the organization be impacted? Yes, but fewer users will benefit.
- Can better people be used to improve the team's capability? Yes, but with a higher cost and only by taking them off other valuable work or paying more for experts from outside the organization.
- Can project complexity be reduced? Yes, but only by avoiding a best-of-breed technical architecture (that is, using fewer technologies and from one, perhaps proprietary source), reducing customization and the potential for differentiation, limiting dependencies on other projects and creating a new technology silo and so on.

Understanding project risk factors is important primarily because it helps systematize the recognition of the characteristics of different projects and ensure the management regime applied to each one is appropriate.

> *Barki et al (2001) applied the concept of 'risk exposure' – the collection of risk factors which are a set of situational characteristics likely to influence the project outcome (including the summarised risk factors set out above) – and evaluated the performance of projects with different 'risk management profiles'. The three key dimensions on their 'risk management profile' were the extent of formal planning, internal integration and user participation. They found that project performance is influenced by the fit between the project risk exposure and its risk management profile. Specifically, on high-risk projects, meeting project budgets calls for high levels of internal integration and high levels of formal planning. With quality as the performance criterion, successful high-risk projects had high levels of user participation.[27]*

Key risk factors to manage

The key question then becomes, for different projects, and specifically for those with high-risk factors, how should we manage them differently, so as to reduce the likelihood and impact of risks? And how can we use the project risk factor analysis as a tool in our risk management arsenal?

Making size count

The correlation between the size of a software development project and the chance of failure is widely recognized (Verhoef, 2002).

Although project size may be typically measured in output terms – such as function points or lines of code – we perceive this risk factor hinges on the understanding that, although temporary, projects are nevertheless organization structures. They will suffer many of the same issues as are covered widely in the literature on large vs. small firms.

Large firms are often depicted as lumbering entities. Once moving, able to maintain that momentum efficiently, but not able to turn corners quickly, move off the designated tracks or stop and restart quickly. Small firms are typically depicted as more agile and nimble, able to turn, stop and start with ease and minimal cost.

---

[27] The longitudinal study approach adopted by Barki *et al.* (2001) provides some interesting data on IT project performance in Quebec at that time: of an initial sample of 120 ongoing software development projects, two years later only 75 completed projects were studied, 15 were still in development, 19 abandoned and data on 11 projects could not be obtained for various reasons. Of the 75 that completed, more than 50% were over budget and 42% were over their estimated duration.

There are benefits in larger structures principally in the areas of control – through the imposition of a clear hierarchy or chain-of-command – and efficiency – through specialization. If these are significant – and they are for many large organizations' core system IT projects – then it suggests the potential downsides of large projects must be managed.

As senior executive time is a scarce resource, it can be useful to have it focused on areas of greatest value. A role on the steering committee for the few 'big and ugly' IT projects that may be underway at any time is such a useful allocation.

Within large projects it is highly desirable that a form of divide-and-conquer strategy is adopted. The organizational form beneath the project manager will typically be based on work type and/or solution-component. For example, there may be a 'lead' business analyst who heads up the effort associated with defining business requirements and maintaining a coherent set of requirements throughout the project lifecycle.

The major size-related risk is, put simply, that the project becomes larger than desired. Relatively small percentage variability in size can be material. This suggests a stronger control mechanism over managing variances against plan than is the norm.

In summary:

- Large projects should be established when efficiency and control are important and issues of agility less so.
- A large project will act as a focal point for management attention.
- Control of large projects is enhanced with a divide-and-conquer strategy and a supporting cast of team leaders beneath the project manager.
- Strong financial controls oriented around the management of variances against plan should be imposed.

Impacting the organization in the right way

The adoption and exploitation of IT moves through stages. This can be informally articulated as 'crawl-walk-run'. Let's start with the 'crawl'.

When the business has only a limited understanding of what IT can do it is perhaps best to conceive of an initial project as research and development (R&D). Funding provided to this initiative might be more in the style of 'seed funding'. Radical business change enabled by IT might be perceived as possible and desirable within the small confines of a 'pilot' user deployment. Harnessing the creative energies of a team who are excited about the potential for IT to add step-change value requires a manager with particular skills in encouraging and nurturing the exploration of new ideas in a teaming 'concept and feasibility' phase. Prototyping and rapid revisions of a loosely controlled, largely disposable code base might be an appropriate development practice.

Now on to the 'walk'. When the business knows what it wants the IT solution to deliver, and is able precisely to define requirements (with appropriate assistance from those skilled in business analysis) then it is important correspondingly to alter the delivery model. If cross-company deployment is planned then it is important that no one user community or interest group overly skews the specifications, but a solution that meets enterprise needs is defined. Issues must be confronted and resolved early – skills in bringing together multiple constituencies and negotiation come to the fore. As the mooted solution looks ever more likely to become a permanent fixture on the IT landscape, so to the importance of 'building in' all the non-functional requirements that will make for a long-lasting and durable solution that can be cost-effectively maintained, enhanced and upgraded. Delivery teams comprising IT infrastructure and operations specialists must be formed to build a solution that is fit for 'handover' when the project is finished. A significant 'change management' component is generally appropriate to raise awareness of the change in advance of solution deployment and to ease its introduction with familiarization and training sessions appropriate for each of the target user groups.

If a package solution is to be deployed widely across an organization a variant of this model, which aims for 'minimal change' to the basic package, may be adopted. This requires even more active stakeholder engagement and expectation management. The message of 'You will be getting something standard' and 'I know this is not the way you do it and have always done it' can be hard messages to both give and receive.

Quality assurance activities need carefully to engage all the necessary stakeholders without allowing point agendas to dominate. Defect classification systems can be abused and system 'acceptance' withheld on spurious grounds. 'I don't like the system the way it has been delivered' is an entirely different objection than the more legitimate, 'Our business will be severely hampered by the solution in its current form'. However, sorting the wheat from the chaff is non-trivial, particularly when the users are the subject matter experts and the IT delivery team may be exposed on earlier process faults; for example, the familiar 'We never signed off the specs' dispute.

And now to the 'run'. When the project aims to deliver change into an established systems environment a different model is suggested. The existing systems will to a large extent constrain the viable solutions. Business requirements hopefully will be framed within the context of an existing system 'philosophy', 'architecture' or 'paradigm'. Thus any resultant changes may not require a detailed level of specification – a nod to existing system features and a 'make it work like this' instruction can be sufficient communication between the business and IT specialists with an excellent combined understanding of how to make the existing systems sing. Many of the non-functional requirements should have been 'built in' – or it may be accepted that they do not exist and cannot feasibly be retrofitted – and the infrastructure and operations specialists already know how the solutions run so need little involvement. A regression test base may exist which will allow for rapid and effective quality assurance to a 'standing' test plan, rather than a QA approach developed from scratch.

Deployment of change into the business environment can follow established channels. Existing user champions, experts and 'user group' members will be the logical path for developing and 'cascading' the user-oriented education and training around the new 'releases' of system functionality and the related business process changes.

At this 'run' stage it is important to maintain a minimal level of control that is prudent and to avoid 'single point' exposures in the delivery chain. A large retailer, long since in the 'run' stage, surprised one of the authors with a response to a standard question about system environments. It became apparent that two senior and experienced programmers had local development environments – in which software was developed and trailed or unit tested – and then migrated new and changed software directly into the production environment. There was no test environment and no independent controls over the migration of software. In addition the programmers had unfettered and unmonitored access to the production databases, which together represented a significant and uncontrolled set of risks.

In summary:

- *If technology and its impact on the firm is not known* then a pilot should be undertaken, potentially using an R&D model. R&D projects should be set up to impact on a small pilot section of the organization and be managed in line with capped 'seed funding' and a creative management style with intense 'teaming' of business subject matter experts and IT specialists.

- *Effective widespread adoption and exploitation of a technology that profoundly impacts the firm* requires a high degree of user involvement. Marshalling the wide stakeholder group and harnessing the skills of a 'wide and deep' IT solution delivery team requires excellent management, communication and negotiation skills that relatively few possess. The necessary business process perspective may run counter to an IT systems-centric view.

- *Changes in an established systems environment* call for a lighter set of management controls and a greater reliance on the in situ specialists correctly to specify the necessary changes. Imposition of management controls in the assurance and testing phase – prior to implementation – are perhaps the focus. Deployment via established channels in the user community should be a relatively straightforward matter.

Specific challenges associated with introducing change into existing system environments are addressed later.

Managing complexity

Perhaps the main prescription here is to introduce project complexity only through necessity. Avoidance of undue complexity is an extremely challenging task made the more difficult because accepted practice and IT staff recommendations may point towards complex solutions and complex project structures. Relatively rare solution design and architecture skills are necessary to propose and carry the simplest of all possible solutions from the concept drawing board to the production environment.

The second prescription is: if complexity exists, manage it intelligently (RAE, 2004). Many projects at inception might point to a number of other concurrent initiatives and suggest some form of dependency (or interdependency) exists. A typical response might be to appoint one or more interface, integration or coordination roles into the project team, through which dependencies are to be managed. Often the person in this role is relatively junior, inexperienced and lacking in content. The role in many cases is poorly defined – attendance at meetings perhaps being the primary expectation – and objectives and outcomes vague.

Intelligent management of complexity is primarily the job of the project manager. All key dependencies with other projects must be managed formally and with a degree of rigour appropriate to the outcomes at risk should the dependent project fail to deliver. Within the project any 'divide-and-conquer' strategy must be appropriate and any 'matrix' formation within the team supplemented with cross-team working practices. If the project manager isn't on top of these areas it is highly likely the complexity is not being adequately managed.

In summary:

- The concept of project complexity and how to manage it can be extremely challenging.
- Having made the project only as complex as it needs to be, the project manager must actively own the ongoing management of complexity, particularly in relation to dependencies with other projects and complexity arising from divisions within the project team structure.

Understanding your project's 'degree of difficulty'

Is it appropriate to use a project risk factors methodology to gauge relative project risks? Given the qualitative nature of the individual risk factors it is not feasible to add them up, however, it is useful to aggregate them and represent a single IT project risk measure of High, Medium or Low (for example) and understand this as a measure of the 'degree of difficulty' of successful execution, primarily as an aid to senior management reporting.

Barki *et al.* (2001) take this one step further and utilize a straightforward method of determining 'Project Risk Exposure' as overall uncertainty (an average of their 23 major risk factor variables after conversion to the same scale) multiplied by the magnitude of potential loss (an average of the 11 items comprising this variable).

We argue that the averaging of potential loss items across the Barki *et al.* (2001) list[28] may lead to a misleading conclusion. Many organizations would be better to take the most significant potential loss item rather than an average, and to be extremely cautious in attempting a meaningful conversion of the two dimensions of exposure and impact, recognizing they are qualitatively derived averages.

Commonly misinterpreted project risk factors

Having explored some extremely useful project risk factor examples, it is worth exploring others that are not inherent project characteristics and are more beneficially framed and managed in different ways.

Often the following risk factors, or similar, are suggested:

- Stability of requirements;
- Skills and experience of the project team; and
- Number and type of technologies used.

We suggest that for each of these factors a flexible stance across the project lifecycle and beyond is required to mitigate and contain potential risks to the organization.

Stability of requirements – getting the degree of flex right

While scope creep is implicated in a wide range of IT project failures it is worth first pondering the alternative of an inappropriately frozen scope. What would be the point of a delivered solution that met the original specification but no longer met business needs?

It is useful to identify and articulate the precise risks – for example, that due to project scope creep the whole project is delivered late and at an increased cost. Then it is necessary to develop, in the context of each specific project, an approach to managing requirements and scope throughout. This is 'bread and butter' stuff to the IT project manager, although challenging questions from project overseers will help to make this transparent.

Typically a 'more analysis up front' prescription is suggested as a way to avoid later scope creep. However, a contrary view is plausible: that an actively engaged user base will continue to conceive of improvements to any given specification to the extent that they are given a voice.

Commercial IT solution providers do not conceive of scope creep only as a risk, but also as an opportunity. The 'fixed price' part of scope can be delivered

---

[28] Magnitude of potential loss indicators: 1. customer relations; 2. financial health; 3. reputation of the information systems department; 4. profitability; 5. competitive position; 6. organizational efficiency; 7. organizational image; 8. survival of the organization; 9. market share; 10. reputation of the user department; and 11. ability to carry out current operations (Barki *et al.*, 2001).

and then the bow-wave of prioritized change requests can be addressed, and the profit margin widened. From a different perspective an opportunity to leverage off an established system with a rolling program of releases that delivers more 'slices' of functionality of value with only incremental investment can be hugely valuable to the business.

In summary:

- Scope creep is not necessarily a bad thing.
- Visibility over the impact of scope change across the project lifecycle is important and this will follow some generic patterns, although the specific approach to managing scope should be tailored to each project.
- The opportunity of scope creep – that the solution will do new and different things that are of value to the business – must be set against the costs.

Skills and experience – relying on the A team

From the perspective of an individual project that is seeking a short-term outcome of successful implementation it may be self-evident that the A team must be secured (Jiang and Klein, 2000). They must be appropriately cajoled and cosseted until the solution is over the line and then 'set loose'.

From an organizational perspective this is less obviously the 'correct solution'. Certainly not every project can have the A team. Also today's A team will presumably burn out, leave or be ready for promotion to higher duties in due course and what will happen then?

It is necessary to have project teams that absorb the average performers – after all, on average our team members are average performers – and for these project teams both to utilize them effectively and efficiently and to fulfil a valuable train-and-develop function.

And for the new and untried employees of course a 'risk' is taken when they are deployed on projects – in contrast to the 'tried and true' incumbents. But these are the resources with new insights that can offer radically different solution options in the exploration stage, development experience in other environments that can be leveraged to advantage, skills with new technologies that might be important to leverage and so forth.

In summary:

- The A team won't be available for all projects.
- Project deployment offers a wonderful opportunity for on-the-job training and development for tomorrow's A team.
- New skills require new blood.

Number and types of technology – the devil you know

Similarly to the skills and experience factor addressed above, there is a strong preference from a 'risk checklist' standpoint to minimize the use of new technologies deployed on projects. After all, new technologies are not known, may not work as expected, etc.

However, it is also self-evident that, over the long term, new technologies must be brought into an environment if it is to avoid increasing operational risks – e.g. platforms unsupported.

The challenge is to balance this as a creative tension and to seek a blend of the new and the old that allows for a predictable solution delivery path with options for direct exploitation of new technologies and a 'fallback to old' scenario available.

When considering how many technologies should be deployed as part of a single solution it is paramount to consider compatibilities and interoperability. It shouldn't be taken as a given that a multi-vendor solution set will 'play' when 'plugged' together. Indeed, multiple solutions from a single technology vendor may be plugged with cross-product 'gotchas' and 'glitches'.

As a general rule, early releases of technology products should be avoided, as should those that are based on standards that are described as 'emerging'. That said, within an open systems environment it may be appropriate to have around ten different technology solution components all performing their 'best-of-breed' functions as part of one integrated solution whole before you have even started. For example: a three-tiered Web solution 'stack' may have the following components:

- Front end – distributed client presentation module or thin client 'browser' (1), centralized server presentation module or 'web server' (2);
- Application logic – customized application logic conforming to the J2EE specification (3), third party and open source software incorporated into the solution (4) hosted on a commercial 'application server' (5);
- Data management – relational database management system (6);
- Security infrastructure – firewalls and intrusion detection and monitoring (7);
- Management reporting tool (8);
- Systems management tool (9);
- Back up and restore utilities (10).

All of these components are in turn potentially hosted on different boxes, each running potentially different operating systems. Behind the scenes there may be adapters and middleware layers to enable coupling and interfacing with other systems.

And all this complexity is not necessarily a bad thing! The resulting solution can have radical improvements on previous (monolithic single component) solutions in terms of scalability, integration and future portability.

Perhaps the one major warning point in relation to new technologies is in order: many IT professional's enthusiasm for new technologies has little to do with the business benefits from their adoption and application. For every wave of new technologies there is a limited window of opportunity for a small number of IT professionals to become 'experts' ahead of others and thereby advance their careers and pay packets. This may involve taking the 'early adopter' organizations down a trail fraught with 'trial and error' to the point where the individuals can claim the relevant 'expertise' and in a CV full of acronyms will hit the market and be poached away at a premium.

Alternative delivery models and their risk characteristics

Two of the most common delivery models in use today are the 'classic' waterfall method (e.g. Structured Systems Analysis and Design Methodology and variants) and the more contemporary iterative solution delivery method (e.g. Unified Process and variants). Each has different risk characteristics and suggested points of management review and intervention.

The 'classic' waterfall method approximates a production line, where there is a definite 'upstream' and 'downstream' relationship between tasks. Downstream tasks wait until upstream tasks are completed. Any defects introduced upstream flow downstream. Rework cycles are typically long, tedious and costly. On the positive side, it is relatively easy to locate blame for any errors (back to a specific phase at a minimum) that are discovered, although difficult to break out of the sequencing dependencies, which create specific time-to-market challenges. Late and nasty surprises – including show-stoppers – can occur in the waterfall model and although the blame is generally clear, the 'fix' is sometimes not.

Obvious points for management review and intervention are at stage completion (exit criteria) checkpoints.

The more contemporary iterative solution delivery methods have regular 'loops' built in. 'Slices' of the solution are analysed, designed, built and tested – and then assembled. The complete and definitive analysis and solution design isn't required before solution build can commence, although on the 'last loop' the sequencing of dependencies as per the waterfall model is typically introduced. In theory the tough parts of the solution should be iterated first – and if necessary, remain unresolved for longest – with the simplest solution components being added on the last iteration. Solid delivery estimates can be difficult to obtain early under this model although greater delivery certainty arises with each iteration. Late and nasty surprises – particularly show-stoppers – should be generally avoided in the iterative delivery model. The main risk encountered is continual iterations wherein the work is always 90% done.

Points for management review and intervention are less obvious, although logically should occur after set-up and then at the end of each significant iteration as well as the end of acceptance testing of the solution as a whole.

Beyond development – enhancement and upgrade projects

Most of the literature on IT project risks focuses on new software development. However, in most large organizations the more common projects are those that modify existing systems, perhaps with a relatively small amount of new software being developed. So how does the risk profile for enhancement projects differ?

Enhancements

Leveraging existing systems can minimize many risks associated with IT projects – the technology is known and familiar, specialists are on hand. It should be easier to estimate the time and effort required making the changes and there may well be established testing methods and practices to leverage in quality assurance activities.

However, the following risks become more acute:

- Risk of disrupting the business currently running on the systems being enhanced through the introduction of defects.
- Risk of 'over-enhancing' the current system and causing it to become less flexible and harder to change over time, as band-aids accumulate.

As yesterday's architecture is adapted to build today's solutions, further issues can arise. The proportion of time and effort involved in changing interfaces and dependent software across a suite of interrelated legacy systems can dwarf the actual changes of functionality. A cleaner, more modular and loosely coupled architecture, a common contemporary focus, will result in a predictable and better ratio of direct functionality change effort to total effort.

Upgrade and replacement

Perhaps the least attractive IT projects are those that appear to deliver few or no additional benefits but are somehow 'necessary'. Why do we need to do IT projects that deliver no business value?

Taking a one-sided view of business value – considering benefits alone – upgrade and replacement projects appear to offer no benefits, but detailed consideration of the 'do nothing' option readily enforces the 'risk-based' nature of the business case. We are doing this project because otherwise our business will be increasingly put at risk from IT failure.

The typical rationale relates to the age of – and difficulties obtaining reliable support for – the system or some of its components. An integrated IT system is as strong as its weakest link. Occasionally the system will have reached the 'limits of growth' and projected business volumes may no longer be able to be processed within acceptable response time parameters – and the system may have been also 'tuned' to the limit.

For all systems, a whole of lifecycle perspective can in theory identify the optimum point at which break–fix maintenance should give way to rewrites, where the accumulated 'band-aids' are pulled off and replaced by a 'new limb'. Often the perspective and insights needed to identify this point and the appetite and funds for the renewal of systems are absent. As a consequence many organizations defer these activities and 'live with' the impacts. Typically a gradual step-up in the total costs per change is made, often ending in a 'hands off' edict being issued by either IT or the business. After this point investment continues around the now obviously architecturally constrained legacy system.

A business case based on risk management in the systems portfolio will help the much-needed IT renewal activities gain business buy-in. A quick look in the executive car park can be a good place to start when building this case. Most cars will be less than five years old and most will be replaced at least once in the next five years and not because they have ceased to function!

Of course there are differences between cars and IT systems, not least of which being that a 'used car market' exists to trade in, whereas an old system that is 'retired' when replacement occurs is most likely to be simply destroyed or kept much as an artefact from a bygone era might be retained in a regional museum by those who had formed an attachment.

This 'status quo' option in the business case must capture and incorporate business impact of IT risks and the probability of loss to promote active thinking and decision-making on IT investments. Thereby the incremental change in the business risk profile will be captured as a benefit from change. If an accurate assessment of the increasing risks from 'doing nothing' can be communicated then the importance of 'doing something' can at least be shared, shifting the focus to when and what exactly should be done.

The answer to 'when?' must take into account the lead-time associated with the proposed change. As described extensively earlier in this chapter, the time dimension of projects can be subject to significant variability.

Ideally an extended period of stability will allow the existing system to be 'locked down' or 'frozen' while the replacement / upgrade project delivers.

There are two broad strategies:

1. Minimal change or 'like for like' upgrade with the exception of those features that necessitated the change (e.g. a new database version that is supported).
2. System transformation – where the change project is a 'double banger' to the extent that it sweeps away some IT risk nasties and delivers a radically different functionality set.

The straightforward 'like for like' option is most easily positioned – there is only one reason why it is being done – but must be correspondingly robust from a business perspective. Unless there is 'real and present' danger in the 'do nothing' option – and this is expressed in business terms – then this option won't fly or may be shot down in mid-flight.

The combined upgrade and transform option will give rise to a mixed business case that can be confusing for some stakeholders to understand. Communication is important to avoid the perception that IT is 'overloading' a business project with an IT agenda. The business and the IT agenda both find it convenient to align for the purposes of 'shared funding' of the project. Many Y2K-related enterprise resource planning (ERP) implementations failed to deliver the anticipated benefits, illustrating that mixing 'must do' and beneficial change together can prove an uneasy mix that needs active management.

The IT risk portfolio structured risk assessment framework can be usefully applied in the context of the upgrade and replacement project.

Alternative philosophies for delivery assurance

Without actually doing the work yourself, how can you be sure the project is on track to deliver the right outcomes? The key here is to understand the range of delivery assurance philosophies and to 'mix and match' the right approach for each project you are seeking to assure.

Outputs and deliverables

The first and most obvious model of assurance is one of inspection and control of work products – outputs and deliverables. Early solution lifecycle activities generate documents, while later activities generate working solutions. Each can be inspected, tested or assured in some other way.

The so-called 'V model'[29] is a useful reference model for anyone attempting to introduce a whole-of-lifecycle quality assurance regime rather than the more common testing-phase quality control regimes (predominantly oriented around 'bug catching' prior to go-live).

Early identification of rework is preferable – as shown in numerous studies which trace the cost of a given defect discovered in early phases vs. late phases of a project – and key is to ensure sufficient well-scoped reviews of early phase deliverables are occurring.

People

Lauer (1996) emphasises the importance of understanding individual – in particular the project manager's – stances toward decision-making under risk. Individuals

---

[29] The V Model provides a framework for incorporating assurance and testing into the software development lifecycle rather than treating it as an afterthought. The V shows the typical sequence of development activities on the left side and the corresponding sequence of assurance and test execution activities on the right side. The V Model emerged in reaction to some waterfall models that showed testing as a single phase following the traditional development phases of requirements analysis, high-level design, detailed design and coding. The phases used in this book should not be taken as support for the common and mistaken impression that testing is merely a brief but necessary step at the end of the 'real' work of solution delivery.

differ in their choices made in the face of changing risks and this can dramatic-ally influence the project's outcome. Do you have a cowboy in charge? Lyytinen *et al.* (1996) establishes the importance of different types of risk-generating con-texts – it matters not only who is on the team but how these people interact with the structure, technology and tasks within the system, project and management environment.

Reliance on people is not simply about trust in the delivery crew. Also important are the qualities of the people who are supporting the delivery crew, the management team and anyone engaged in an independent capacity to review in detail the performance of the project. If you are to rely on the findings and observations of an independent specialist it is important that you understand their perspective and trust their judgment – at least to the extent that you are confident they will judge the materiality of potential issues against an agreed standard.

So often one of the root causes of project underperformance is 'the wrong people'. If you have misgivings, investigate further.

Methods and standards

The third delivery assurance philosophy is a reliance model based on repeatable processes, common methods and standards.

This philosophy is grounded in a belief that projects applying 'best practice' approaches to delivery have an improved chance of delivering successfully and that 'best practice' standards appropriate for the project can be objectively ascertained.

One branch of this philosophy holds that compliance to discrete and detailed methodologies is preferable as a 'pure' form of 'best practice'. More common is to take and adapt approaches from a variety of sources (some industry practice, some home-grown) and assemble a 'workable' rather than 'pure' set of methods and standards.

For the uninitiated the task of selecting a methodology or set of methodo-logies can be daunting. For example, there are specific project risk management methodologies such as RiskIT (described in Kontio *et al.*, 1998), general project management methodologies such as PRINCE2 (UK OGC, 2001), overarching software development capability maturity models such as CMM and CMMI (developed by the Software Engineering Institute at the Carnegie Mellon Univer-sity), ISO and IEEE standards on specific aspects of the IT development journey (for example, the ISO software quality model [ISO, 1998]), older industry methodologies such as Structured Systems Analysis and Design Methodology (UK NCC, 1998), the more current Unified Process methodology (Jacobsen *et al.*, 1999) and in addition every vendor or service provider has at least one if not multiple variants.

While some research has indicated performance improvements occur with the application of methods and standards,[30] in the main empirical evidence is lacking.

Rather than project-level compliance monitoring – is everything being done in strict accord with standard X or Y? – it is more usual for general alignment questions and assessments to be considered at phases of the project or by high-level checking of project artefacts against 'templates' of required content expected or required under the selected methodologies.

Identifying, reporting and managing project risks

With recognition of Drummond's findings from the Taurus project[31] ringing in our ears:

> *Acceptance of risk, it is argued, is ultimately something determined by the balance of power between decision makers. Moreover, risk analysis and other techniques of management may actually compound the difficulties by fostering an illusion of control.* (Drummond, 1996)

We now move to look at the managerial role in overseeing an IT project and playing a part in actively managing its risks. The discovery of project risks – anything that has a probability of occurring and resulting in project objectives being missed – can be via three routes:[32]

- Audit / health check;
- Self-assessment;
- Project gates.

It may be useful to establish all three mechanisms for major and high-profile projects, to ensure no risks that could reasonably be discovered are going unaddressed. On minor projects the overhead of all three discovery methods would not be warranted.

---

[30] Jiang *et al.* (2004) survey of software engineers indicates that the CMM software process improvement maturity Level III, once achieved, results in improved project performance.

[31] The Taurus project was cancelled by the London Stock Exchange in 1993 after the Stock Exchange had spent over three years and £80 million and the securities industry over £400 million (Drummond, 1996).

[32] In addition to the 'always on' channels that will be flowing and monitored as part of your organizational commitment to IT risk management!

Audit or health check assessment requires an independent and objective party to review the project against the set of objectives. The benefit of this approach is that risks may be identified that the project team were unaware of. Issues with this approach relate to the difficulties in bringing a reviewer up to a requisite level of knowledge about the project to be able to make accurate and valuable judgments and the impact this can have on other project team members.

Self-assessment requires a knowledgeable participant within the project structure to respond to some form of survey or questionnaire that draws out an assessment and articulation of major known project risks. This can draw out a clearer summary of the risks appropriate for consumption – and hopefully action – at more senior management levels.

A project gate or checkpoint can require some form of additional disclosure and discussion, most often active and wide-ranging, requiring the participation of the project manager and potentially various specialists involved in the project.

Committee oversight

A generally recognized good practice relates to the formation of a committee to oversee an IT project. It is important to recognize that steering committees on projects will really deliver additional value only if the following are achieved:

- Business representation is real rather than notional – that is someone who cares about the project outcome and is personally at some risk if project delivery does not go to plan.
- Real issues are discussed rather than offering a simple forum for polite discussion.
- Alternative points of view are sought and obtained other than being wholly reliant on sanitized project manager progress reports.
- The project manager delivery accountability is supported rather than over-ridden or interfered with.

Alternative management responses

When bad news comes to light there are broadly three responses, corresponding to the project triage analogy:

1. Dying – a project has gone past the point of no return and the possibility of saving it has passed.
2. Living – the project is generally progressing well and tinkering does not clearly serve to improve the condition of the project.
3. Walking wounded – the project is distressed and in trouble and apparently unable to recover on its own, the time for intervention is now.

In general the dying should be either left to die or hastened along the way. The earlier a project that will not ultimately deliver is stopped the better.

In general the living should be left to get on with delivering the results.

The main focus for management attention should be the walking wounded projects. Action may include: injection of funds, more resources, change to scope, redefinition of roles or project structure, escalation of vendor or service provider delivery issues, etc.

Extensive research has been done on why runaway IT projects are allowed to continue (Mahaney and Lederer, 1999; Keil *et al.*, 2000) or are abandoned only late (Addison and Vallabh, 2002). The irrational concept of 'escalating commitment' – commonly known as 'good money after bad' – has become well-known (Drummond, 1996). If your management team are in this trap you'll need a circuit-breaker before a change of personnel becomes necessary.

What to look for at each stage of the project

Aligning with more of the 'classic' waterfall delivery model, the following section sets out some multidimensional 'checklist' questions that might be utilized in a review of project at a stage gate or checkpoint.[33]

The stages that we describe are generic and so may not represent any specific organization:

1. Concept and feasibility;
2. Requirements and architecture;
3. Build;
4. Testing, acceptance and implementation;
5. Post-implementation.

We first discuss the rationale for each of these stages and then look at the management team's set of reasonable expectations. Specific items that contribute to the risk schedule and help identify issues at each stage are included in Appendix 1.

Concept and feasibility

Good ideas can fail to get effectively addressed and many do not proceed beyond the initial ideas phase because project outputs are not sufficient to justify a management decision to release funds and allocate resources to the project.

---

[33] While we recognize the dangers of relying on checklists (i.e. leave your brain at the door) the research of Heemstra and Kusters (1996) found that in the context of IT projects the use of a short and structured checklist eases the identification and discussions about risks. They also suggest explicit use of a group-related approach and involvement of a neutral process risk advisor to increase reliability and acceptance of the results. Of course, items not on the checklists should also be considered.

Alternatively, we sometimes see that funds are committed and a project commences without addressing the critical questions.

Adequate concept and feasibility effort will result in adequate definition, justification and buy-in, and a clear basis on which to make the 'go' / 'no go' decision upon completion of this phase.

At this stage we are expecting to find:

- A clear business rationale and clarity of concept;
- A focused and effective assessment of solution and delivery options to confirm feasibility;
- Clarity of commercial value and demonstrated achievement of mandated investment criteria;
- Appropriate consideration of wider organizational impact, stakeholder engagement and business process changes; and
- A mobilized and effective project team working to accepted standards.

Requirements and architecture

Many business projects can become IT projects at this stage. The focus on specifications, analysis, technologies and the need to increasingly communicate in IT rather than business terms, can result in a loss of business support.

Detailed requirements definition often 'blows out' the original expectations of project scope. The link back to business priorities and objectives can be lost and a suboptimal solution specified.

Vendor selection can be an extremely drawn-out and costly process – often exacerbated for government organizations by procurement and probity requirements.

Lack of rigour in project start-up may take its toll here as poor control over project costs and timeframes becomes more visible to management. Unplanned risks and issues emerge to thwart progress.

At this stage we are expecting to find:

- Continuing relevance of the project to the business community that will benefit from its completion;
- An optimized technical solution and vendor delivery commitment in line with acceptance criteria agreed with the business;
- Commercial arrangements that tie solution delivery partners to meaningful milestones and business achievements rather than technical deliverables;
- A more closely calibrated business case underpinned by detailed estimates and quotes for the technical solution and vendor delivery approach;
- A basis for ongoing and tight integration with the necessary business and organizational changes that must accompany the introduction of the IT solution; and
- A combined business, IT and vendor management and delivery team that is performing well to agreed standards and staying on top of emerging issues and risks.

Build

Whether a buy or build project, this is the project phase where the service provider responsibilities dominate. Project activities can become 'bogged down' in technical issues and details.

Further drift from the original business objectives can occur. Suppliers focus on delivery to defined statements of work and must continually be drawn back to focus on overall project intent.

Interim milestones are frequently missed or 'passed on a technicality'. Suspected rework can build up – waiting to be revealed during testing. Confidence in the ability of the supplier to deliver to the original budget and timeframe weakens.

Often the parallel business activities to equip the organization in readiness for change become misaligned with the IT work stream.

At this stage we are expecting to find:

- Continuing business support and involvement in the project and continuing relevance of the initiative to the business it will enable;
- Confirmation of the solution as fit-for-the-purpose in all dimensions spanning the full scope of functional and non-functional requirements;
- An agreed and suitably detailed test plan that, when executed, will underpin achievement of the agreed solution acceptance criteria;
- Service provider and vendor delivery against commitments;
- Tight management of project costs; and
- Continuing high performance of project teams.

Testing, acceptance and implementation

Nasty surprises are typically 'discovered' late. This is often the case during acceptance testing where the full solution is assembled and real-business scenarios are executed for the first time.

True defects are difficult to sort from the mountain of test incidents that are generated. As the rework cycle takes its toll an adversarial mindset can develop: the solution provider is 'guilty until proven innocent' and tasked with the enormous burden of fixing functionality only fully specified when the detailed test case was written.

Ambiguity around acceptance criteria and disputes over late and undeclared changes to the agreed functionality surface and prove difficult to resolve – for whether borne by supplier or customer there is significant cost involved.

At this stage we are expecting to find:

- Active involvement of business representatives to bring rigour and relevance to the testing activity and assist in readying for implementation;

- Demonstration of the solution as fit-for-the-purpose in all relevant functional and non-functional dimensions;
- Clear management of service provider and vendor outcomes through to release from obligation in line with achievement of meaningful milestones and acceptance criteria;
- Application of commercial rigour to drive delivery in line with forecast costs – without pushing costs and pain into the post-implementation period;
- Organization readiness for change associated with system implementation; and
- Effective teamwork across organization boundaries towards a shared and clearly articulated set of goals.

Post-implementation

With a sigh of relief the project is typically declared over when the systems go live.

Despite the attention to detail in the formulation of a benefits realization plan, the reality is that the project team is often disbanded and insufficient resources and attention allocated to driving out the planned benefits.

An independent project review can help focus the project team on achieving:

- Business ownership and attention to follow-through on the implementation of business changes that will realize benefit;
- Active measurement and monitoring of solution performance to ensure agreed service levels are met and service provider and vendor commitments under warranty are met;
- Satisfactory progress towards a 'business-as-usual' state in the operations, support and maintenance activities;
- Closure of project accounting and a 'ruling off of the books'; and
- Identification of lessons learned and incorporation into a revision of guidelines, principles, methods and approaches.

Appendix 1 provides terms of reference for health checks that would be commissioned by a steering committee or governance body towards the goals above. Additional issues, risks and stakeholder concerns that are specific to the initiative would also shape the scope, approach and detail of each review.

Health check

This section assists you consider at a macro-level the company's IT project risk health, for input into the IT risk portfolio assessment.

Is this important to your business?

- A large proportion of your discretionary investment funds are spent on IT projects.
- The delivery of IT projects is an important part of your current strategic agenda.
- Your competitors have a credible IT project delivery capability.

If you agree with two or more of the three statements, then IT project risks are important to your business.

Are you doing the right things?

- A structured risk management process is built into each major IT project.
- Project risks are assessed – as well as costs and benefits – when projects are being selected and initiated.
- Different types of projects are managed differently – corresponding with their relative 'degree of difficulty' and other unique characteristics.
- Project progress is regularly and accurately reported.
- High-profile projects are reviewed independently at defined checkpoints.
- IT project success / failure is judged after the fact – for example with post-delivery reviews.

If you agree with these statements, then you are doing the right things in your organization. If you disagree with two or more of the six statements, then there is significant room for improvement in your IT project risk management capability.

Do you have a good track record?

- IT projects generally deliver the targeted functionality on time and within the planned cost.
- Benefits are realized from the implementation of IT solutions and services.
- Defects are found before solutions go into production.

If you agree with these statements, then you have a good track record of managing IT project risks. If you disagree with one or more of the three statements, then there is evidence of the need to improve IT risk management capability.

Case study: Agility

Successful delivery of a strategic IT initiative through an assurance program

Agility is a wholly owned subsidiary of the Australian Gas Light Company (AGL), Australia's leading energy company. Agility provides a suite of infrastructure services across the gas, electricity, water and telecommunication industries. Agility's core capabilities span across 'high-level' strategic asset management, construction, operational and maintenance services. Across Australia, Agility manages and operates over 7000 kilometres of high-pressure gas transmission pipelines, 23 000 kilometres of gas distribution networks, and 950 square kilometres of electricity distribution network for AGL, associate and third party entities.

With the background of a rapidly changing Australian energy market, Agility has successfully pursued a strategy to transform itself from being part of a vertically integrated energy business into a world-class, service-oriented infrastructure service company.

Agility had embarked on a restructure of all its SAP platforms across the business, which was in its project definition phase when the new strategic direction was finalized. Although originally viewed within the limited scope of a systems project, it was soon realized that the SAP project needed a substantial review if it was to provide an optimal system solution in support of the service-oriented strategy.

The timely completion of the SAP project was seen as critical to Agility's ability to realize strategic intent. Consequently, Agility decided that it was prudent to appoint PA in an external advisory and assurance role.

Clarifying the strategic context and setting the new direction

A rapid review of the SAP restructure project, establishing an accurate view of the current status, identified perceptions within important stakeholder groups, and helped to crystallize the role of the project in Agility's business strategy.

The project had become the key enabler to most of Agility's strategic initiatives (in particular the simultaneous cultural change and performance measurement initiatives) and the cornerstone of a complex organizational change program. This insight enabled a rapid redefinition of scope and direction and the swift revision of the project leadership and governance model, which was implemented soon afterwards.

An innovative assurance program was set up that provided guidance for the full duration of the project. Unlike traditional audit approaches focusing on compliance against pre-defined process standards, PA applied a flexible and pragmatic 'low intervention / high-impact approach' combining audit and coaching.

This approach identified key risk areas and provided support where needed while ensuring the full ownership by the Agility team for the execution of the whole project.

Assurance program activities included regular 'health checks', support and coaching of project manager and key staff, and a comprehensive 'go-live' readiness review providing assurance that the project was prepared for the critical data conversion and cut-over activities.

Ensuring successful project delivery and increasing business benefit

Confidence levels within the executive team rose quickly and regular reviews provided a clear picture of key risk areas and mitigating actions. PA assisted Agility to change direction faster and with more confidence to achieve successful delivery. The high level of alignment of the system with the strategic intent has already delivered a substantial business benefit to the organization.

The ongoing assurance and coaching role also prevented the project and leadership team from getting too close to the detail of day-to-day issues and activities. This 'non-executive director role' not only created external pressure to keep up the fast pace required to bring the project to a successful conclusion, but also provided the required support when issues were encountered.

The long-term nature of the engagement over the full project lifecycle meant that the consulting team gained a detailed understanding of the issues at hand and could provide realistic and balanced recommendations. Agility achieved a successful delivery of a critical project that has acted as one of the key enablers for Agility's strategic transformation initiatives.

> *. . . there is no doubt that bringing in PA Consulting Group was a good decision. It provided the independent project assurance that we needed to ensure the project was kept focused and on track.*
>
> (Norm Pack, Chief Financial Officer)

Printed with permission of PA Consulting Group and Agility

5   IT services

Under fire . . .

In February 2004 the SCO Group was the target of a denial of service attack linked to Mydoom, one of the fastest spreading email worms in history. The SCO website was rendered inaccessible and the site taken down. The company changed its domain name and moved to a new IP address. (AFR, 2004b)

On fire . . .

Bankstown City Council's Civic Centre was devastated by fire, the General Manager Mark Fitzgibbon completed an assessment of the damage, the response and the lessons. We extract the IT-related elements of the story:

For us the problem was that although we had the physical data files, we had nothing on which to run the data. Our mainframe was destroyed during the fire by smoke and water and there simply wasn't another machine like it in the country to read or convert the data. In fact we ended up having to import a second hand machine from France! Similarly we had to procure new file servers to recover a mountain of data contained on our office network such as all word processed documents.

(Fitzgibbon, 1998)

Closed for business . . .

Trading on the London Stock Exchange was disrupted for nearly eight hours by computer problems on Wednesday on what should have been one its busiest days of the year . . .

The tax year expired on Wednesday and it is usually one of the exchange's heaviest days as thousands of retail investors buy and sell shares for capital gains tax purposes. But the Inland Revenue said it would not extend the tax year by a day to compensate for the exchange's problems . . .

The breakdown coincided with news that the exchange had re-opened talks with Deutsche Börse, operator of the Frankfurt financial markets, on a possible merger of their operations. (*Financial Times*, 2000)

. . . and powerless

The central business district of Auckland, New Zealand, was paralysed for a period of six weeks when the power supply was broken (NZ Commerce, 1998). An overload and breakdown on one cable caused another to break down, to the extent that all of the lines eventually collapsed. In the short term, businesses were able to survive only if they had generating capacity immediately available. With the entire central business district without electrical power supply, there was an immediate shortage of supply of generators. For the financial institutions in the business district, this translated into a dramatic performance differential between the one organization that continued to deliver services to their clients, and the rest who were completely shut down.

The long-term impact was quite a different story. As the period of alternative service provision continued for many weeks, it became increasingly difficult to provide those services from a remote location. The New Zealand staff were accommodated in Sydney, Australia, and so had to work New Zealand business hours when living in a different time zone. Routine matters such as hours of work, rates of pay and leave arrangements became increasingly fraught and challenging.

Initially the problem of lack of electricity meant that the issues of lighting, air conditioning and the operation of lifts were those that affected staff safety, but as soon as standby facilities were arranged the critical business issues of delivering service to customers became paramount. At this point staff discovered which computers have uninterruptible power supplies (UPS), which servers were unaffected, and which of their external critical business connections were still operational. After a short period of time, generators needed to be started so that continuing operations could be established. So very quickly there was a transition from issues of safety to service delivery.

In the development of IT strategic plans it is common to take the major activities of the firm and to consider the degree to which IT supports or enables the business process, to look for opportunities where IT could better support or enable the delivery of that process and the process outcomes.

Where IT makes a strong contribution to the critical business processes this is considered a 'good thing' from an IT strategy point of view. IT is relevant to the firm because it supports the central activities and core functions.

However, from a business continuity point of view, the greater the degree of reliance on IT the greater the degree of vulnerability that business process has on failures in IT.

This chapter sets out the considerations you should address in developing and implementing an IT service continuity risk management capability.

IT service failures that impact your business

Mitroff and Alpaslan (2003) in a study of Fortune 500 companies distinguish the crisis-prepared from the crisis-prone. The crisis-prepared suffer from fewer calamities, stay in business longer and have better reputations; however, these are in the minority – so statistically speaking you probably don't work for one. What distinguishes the crisis-prepared? They plan for trouble, developing plans to handle more than just what they have experienced in the past, and create strategies to lower their vulnerabilities. They exhibit the characteristics of learning organizations and encourage the flexibility to envisage 'abnormal crises' – the ones most of us don't expect.

Watkins and Bazerman (2003) point out: 'The signs of an impending crisis often lie all around us, yet we still don't see them. Fortunately, there are ways to spot danger before it's too late' (p. 1). Their suggested model is for business leaders to recognize – through scanning the environment for emerging threats (a topic we take up again in Chapter 10), prioritize so that the most likely failures with the highest impact are anticipated, and mobilize the workforce in advance.

Service performance

Many IT functions have not adopted an 'IT services' model and retain their traditional focus on infrastructure, applications and systems. The mapping of services to systems and facilities is seldom complete. This means that the impact on a service of the failure of a system will not be known. Operations staff see themselves looking after equipment (infrastructure) and systems, rather than providing IT services. One system may provide several services, not all of which have the same priority or importance, but operations staff will not be able to distinguish between them.

A key activity in IT service continuity planning is the definition of a maximum tolerable outage (MTO) for each service.[34] This specifies for how long the particular service may be unavailable before the crisis or disaster status is declared. In practice an organization would not wait for those hours to elapse (one would hope) but would anticipate that a fix was unlikely in that timeframe.

Business continuity management is typically the responsibility of the chief operations officer or other senior operations staff. Examination of business processes identifies the IT services that are underlying and that are required for

---

[34] The more colourful 'mean time to belly-up' is used by Rainer *et al.* (1991).

the execution of the process. At the same time, the maximum tolerable outage of the business process can be identified.

Planning rules OK

Much of the work involved in IT services risk is in planning. In principle, all threats to essential services will need to be identified, assessed and managed.[35] However, these could be so numerous and have impacts across many services that an alternative approach may be more effective. A single threat, or a collection of threats, may be dealt with by using a scenario. A small collection of alternative scenarios may be invented that together represent all of the important threats. Rather than having Plan i for Threat i, where i could be a large number, a set of plans is created for the different scenarios.

Resilience is one of the main objectives in planning for continuity so that services can take specified levels of outage and still maintain targeted performance. This is accomplished through intentional redundant resources and selection of fault-tolerant equipment. Resilience is not able to be produced in response to a crisis, it is built in through planning. At this point priorities are established so that reductions in capacity are passed on to those services that are least critical. Again, these need to be determined in advance. The other principal objective is building recovery capability – that is, the ability to recover when a crisis takes place.

Recovery capability is partly built through careful selection or enhancement of equipment, but the action dimension is equally important. By creating a range of test scenarios and working through these with the staff who will be involved, a realistic capacity to respond can be built. Replicated resources, hardened equipment or alternative, standby facilities are approaches to enhancement of the infrastructure, that can be selected based on a trade-off between costs and risks. However, this is of little value if staff are not trained and tested regularly.

Disasters and crises

Disaster recovery planning (DRP) deals with the situations where business continuity remediation cannot be achieved in an acceptable timeframe. For example, if an organization has a maximum tolerable outage of a key business service of two hours, and it appears that the current situation will lead to an outage of more than two hours then the disaster recovery action team needs to be advised. Clearly major disasters such as fire, flood and road closure will be part of every organization's DRP. Similarly when emergency services such as police take over

---

[35] Suh and Han (2003) set out a detailed quantitative approach that assesses the business value of each IS asset from the viewpoint of operational continuity although for most organizations this approach may be impractical.

the situation then the organization's management may be unable to take any action, even to be able to enter the buildings. When emergency services withdraw, business continuity plans can be put into operation to restore the business to full functioning in as short time as possible, with the previously established priorities.

The terms 'emergency', 'crisis' and 'disaster' are defined precisely by some organizations but weakly by others. Typically a crisis is defined as having an acute impact on the financial stability of the organization or on the lives of personnel, and will require an immediate, formal and public response by management.[36] Usually, such a public response will come from the public relations (PR) or marketing teams, even though the crisis may have originated in IT, finance, product quality or staff misbehaviour. Emergencies involve public emergency response services and will likely have a declaration by an outside organization. If IT service failure is causing serious public brand damage or shareholder losses, PR, the CEO and the board may well be involved.

Information asset impacts

There is a natural connection between information asset management and IT service delivery. All kinds of IT services are delivered using information assets whether these are the computer databases or systems and applications. Requirements for confidentiality, integrity, availability and compliance can be determined by examining the information assets as well as the IT service. Some business users may be able to determine the needs for service delivery or the protection of the assets that are fundamental to their business unit's success.

In many cases a loss of connection is not damaging the asset; however, the asset achieves its value by being available, and it is the availability that is now lost.[37]

Managing system failures

It is typically at the system level that service failures are detected. The helpdesk staff gets a call that the customer quotation system is down. The included services are not apparent to the helpdesk person and so system level procedures will be used. Every failure must be treated as an incident. Formal incident recording, tracking, management and monitoring will be needed if an organization is to be

---

[36] The US General Accounting Office review of continuity of operations efforts focus on human capital considerations (GAO, 2004b) in terms of employee welfare in a time of crisis and employee contribution to continuity efforts.

[37] Besnard and Arief (2004, p. 258) describe a potential security measure for a server: 'Not plugging it into a network is a relatively secure condition but the service will not be delivered.'

able to understand its current performance level and also develop the potential for long-term improvement of its incident management. Only in the case of life-threatening, hazardous situations should incident recording not be commenced immediately.

Historically IT staff have been disproportionately involved in service continuity as they were the suppliers of IT services that were particularly unreliable. Now that IT hardware is much more reliable, the emphasis has changed to focus on the complexity of the IT installations and the dependence for these services within the organization.

The majority of incidents will have an established recovery approach that has been pre-designed, pre-planned and pre-approved. Staff will have been trained in the appropriate recovery actions and will then complete the incident record. In large installations any incident that exceeds the defined specifications that have been part of the standard training is then quickly escalated to a specialist team that is able to investigate, request additional facilities, and work towards developing a solution.

All the defined incidents will have an incident level that establishes communication channels and priority. Incident notification can be generated by all members of the organization directly through the IT helpdesk. Additional incident notifications will be generated by the IT staff themselves.

Higher levels of criticality will invoke the business continuity plan or the crisis management plan. IT staff will need to know the escalation plan, contacts and urgent actions that they must carry out. The complementary situation arises when a business continuity failure in another part of the organization leads to special, additional requirements on the IT facilities in this location.

With critical incidents the focus is on restoration – the challenge of finding the root cause of the problem will have to wait until appropriate resources can be brought to bear and priorities determined.

Complex scenarios

There are myriad things that can go wrong. Compiling an exhaustive 'laundry list' of components, facilities, systems and utilities that can fail in different ways only creates a very long list. This is not very effective for training or planning purposes. It is simpler to envisage four or five comprehensively described scenarios where several contingencies occur at the same time. In the training setting, teams of staff can read the whole scenario and determine what actions they would need to take. The necessary actions can then be compared with those that are incorporated in whatever plan is currently existing.

Scenarios can range in severity from minor to extreme, with impacts on different business units, and involving different facilities. The business continuity team and IT continuity team can creatively invent new scenarios for testing, as can crisis management team members. Of course, it is not anticipated that a particular disaster will match any of the prepared scenarios, but simply that we are prepared for the complexity of interacting demands and follow-on impacts.

Planning and preparation

Given that planning and preparing comprise the dominant activity for continuity assurance, how do we start? The challenge for most organizations is the first step. Too often there is an attempt to work out all the threats and risks – but this detracts from the driving issue, which is the business impact. The approach that follows works in three stages:

1. Carry out business impact analysis.
2. Set disaster avoidance–disaster recovery objectives.
3. Match the disaster avoidance–disaster recovery activities to the objectives.

Business impact analysis

If the achievement of your organization's business objectives can be impacted by the failure of IT services to deliver as and when required, then there is a clear business impact and service continuity is an important undertaking. As more organizations link their systems to their customers and suppliers, the IT service continuity priority increases. When using a third party provider, the service levels become explicit but when these services are provided in-house too often there are no such definitions.

Starting from scratch on IT service continuity requires the definition of the services that are provided. In some organizations this will be more clearly indicated through business processes, rather than IT services. For each service or process, the consequences to the business need to be worked out. What is the significance of not being able to process an inventory receipt for one hour, four hours, 12 hours, etc.? What if we can't update a customer's service requirement record within a day? The business impacts don't have to be worked out in money terms if this is not obvious, but qualitative assessments are sufficient.

The critical issue is to work out which services or processes have what impacts on the business performance so that they can be given the proper level of attention. The important processes or services need to be examined carefully to determine their component activities and the resources that they draw upon, because it is disruption in the supply of resources that eventuates in a discontinuity.

Business impact analysis does not examine the triggering threats or their likelihoods, but is driven by the consequences: What will happen to the business? It then establishes the recovery priorities for the organization. If we have to move to a hot site, what is the first business application that we need to get working? What else is on the recovery list and what is omitted?

Disaster avoidance–disaster recovery

For each resource disruption threat that an organization faces, it can plan for two categories of response:

1. To take avoidance or mitigation actions to build up its resilience should the threat arise; and/or
2. To take actions that build a recovery capability, so that when the threat eventuates, impacts are expected to be within acceptable levels.

That is, to reduce the risk of the event or to reduce the consequence. It is, however, possible that the risk is simply accepted, that there is no response. This should not be the default position that is the 'accidental decision' derived through neglect, but one that is taken actively through a realistic assessment of the business impact.

In some organizations the decision that the risk and its consequences will be accepted may cause harsh reality-checks for the affected staff. It may come as a surprise to find in the event of a disaster that the inability to recover within one month is acceptable.

But the decisions about whether, or how much, to avoid or to plan for recovery are not binary. We suggest that there are five levels that organizations can decide upon to ensure that business impacts are tolerable.

Levels of assurance

There is a propensity for the leader of every business unit to have an inflated sense of the criticality of the systems, services and contribution of their area. In order to sort out the priorities it is necessary to determine a level of assurance that is appropriate. An organized, defined set of assurance levels can be developed in terms of the following five standards, with a rough correspondence to maximum tolerable outages:

1. Platinum (five stars) – maximum tolerable outage less than hours;
2. Gold (four stars) – maximum tolerable outage up to one day;
3. Silver (three stars) – maximum tolerable outage up to one week;
4. Bronze (two stars) – maximum tolerable outage up to one month;
5. No standard – no defined tolerable outage.

In practice an organization should define its own standards, although it may be guided by service providers if any are involved.

The important management responsibility is to match the level of assurance to the business impact, so that funds and priorities are allocated properly. The standards are elaborated as shown in Tables 5.1, 5.2, 5.3, 5.4 and 5.5.

Table 5.1—Platinum (five stars) standard

disaster avoidance	*disaster recovery*
Highest level of availability, reliability and data integrity. Proven, mature and effective operation and support model, spanning all process areas, operating 24/7. No single point of failure vulnerabilities in IT infrastructure. Highest level of physical and logical access controls. Regularly audited and reviewed. All elements of the system supported by a highly skilled team, backed up by contracted vendor support with challenging service-level agreements.	Rapid restoration (measured in minutes) of service for a wide range of loss scenarios, including primary site loss. Typically uses a 'hot' site approach. Production system features and functionality able to be delivered from DR platform. Little degradation of performance. High degree of confidence in ability to execute an effective DR response, supported by recent tests of a formally documented plan. Good integration / alignment with user community's business continuity plans.

Table 5.2—Gold (four stars) standard

disaster avoidance	*disaster recovery*
High level of availability, reliability and data integrity. Mature and effective operation and support model, particularly problem and incident management. Typically 24/7. Designed to avoid single point of failure vulnerabilities in IT infrastructure. High level of physical and logical access controls. All elements of the system supported by adequately staffed internal team, backed up by current vendor support and service arrangements.	Rapid restoration (measured in hours) of service for a wide range of loss scenarios, including primary site loss. Typically uses a 'warm' or 'hot' site approach. Production system features and functionality able to be delivered from DR platform. Acceptable degradation of performance. High degree of confidence in ability to execute an effective DR response, supported by recent tests of a formally documented plan. Good integration / alignment with user community's business continuity plans.

Table 5.3—Silver (three stars) standard

disaster avoidance	disaster recovery
Good level of availability and reliability. Occasional unplanned outages and service disruption for users. Good level of data integrity, some tolerance for information errors. Operation support model is adequate but may have some known weaknesses in problem and incident management. May be offered mainly on a business hours basis with limited on-call support after hours. Designed generally to avoid single points of failure vulnerabilities, but likely to have some. Adequate physical and logical access controls. May be some security process and control weaknesses. Support team in place and staffed, but may be issues such as a reliance on single individuals with specialist knowledge, capacity of the team, vendor support for some components.	Planned, although lower-priority, approach to restoration of service for a limited range of loss scenarios, including primary site loss. Restoration period measured in days, typically uses a 'cold' site approach. A limited range of production system features and functionality able to be delivered from DR platform. Significant degradation of performance / change in usage required (e.g. fewer users). Reasonable confidence in ability to execute an adequate DR response, supported by a formally documented plan. Roles and recovery approach may be a bit unclear. Limited or no testing / rehearsal. Some alignment with user community's business continuity plans.

Table 5.4—Bronze (two stars) standard

disaster avoidance	disaster recovery
Variable level of availability and reliability. Unplanned outages and service disruption commonplace. Data integrity not paramount, tolerance for information errors. Operation support model has known weaknesses, particularly in problem and incident management. Generally no support after hours. Single points of failure exist in the production system, some weaknesses may exist in physical and logical access controls. No dedicated support team, roles and responsibilities may be unclear. Gaps in knowledge and skills highly likely to impact the response to things going wrong. Poor vendor support for some components.	Lower priority to restore. Restoration period measured in weeks. May not be restored at all if limited available staff resources are all assigned. DR plan is informal or high-level only. What will really happen in disaster scenarios has not been thought through in advance. DR platform may be extremely limited in capacity or not established – i.e. may need to be acquired in the event of a disaster scenario. Low level of confidence in ability to execute an adequate DR response. No testing / rehearsal has been done or is planned. Confidence in back-up procedures involving proven secondary media, stored off-site.

Table 5.5—No defined standard

disaster avoidance	*disaster recovery*
System essentially provided 'as is'. No formal systems management, administration, operations or support. Typically poorly documented from administration and operations perspective.	No formal DR provision. Possible ad hoc back-up / restore capability, not centrally managed, no formal off-site storage of secondary media. Low level of confidence in ability to restore from any loss scenario.

Implementing IT service continuity

Key implementation considerations for IT service continuity are:

- Setting the budget and spending the right amount;
- Matching your IT service continuity approach to the risk context of your organization;
- Designing-in the necessary capability;
- Managing stakeholder buy-in; and
- Measuring and managing performance.

Budget setting

One of the continuing sore questions with service continuity is: How much to spend? What is the right budget and how do we justify it? For any expenditure on such insurance activities there are many attractive alternatives that may enhance the organization's sales or profitability. So priorities need to be established in a way that permits some buy-in. Furthermore, services that are critical to the organization but provided by champion-less functions will have to be evaluated from an organization-wide perspective.

But some services are absolutes – there is complete consensus (or firm mandates from regulators) that recovery time must be measured in minutes or that full duplicate systems with real-time mirroring needs to be the goal. Such services are not the challenge in terms of definition or agreement; for them delivery is the requirement. This may be especially difficult if a service provider is responsible through an outsourcing agreement. In the typical contract the service provider will be guided by *force majeure* clauses, that allow all sorts of get-outs, as well as international agreements (such as the Tampere Convention for telecommunications[38]). In such cases 'disaster recovery' to you may not mean disaster recovery for the service provider.

[38] The Tampere Convention on the Provision of Telecommunications Resources for Disaster Mitigation and Relief Operations (1998) uses international definitions of 'disaster' to override other contracts.

Regulators are increasingly getting involved in business and IT service continuity. The Malaysian central bank, Bank Negara Malaysia (BNM), mandates that all banks have business continuity plans, that they are lodged with BNM, that every test is reported to BNM, that every outage that triggers the plan is reported to BNM – with a performance assessment – and that the plans are tested at least every year. If the regulator requires an action, increasingly organizations need to follow. Historically lax supervision and control in many jurisdictions will move from being the 'good old days' to the 'bad old days' as organizations realize that it is good corporate governance. For example, in April 2004 the Securities and Exchange Commission introduced rules which require NASD and NYSE members to develop business continuity plans that establish procedures relating to an emergency or significant business disruption (NYSE Rule 446).

There are four dominant factors that determine the level of activity for IT service continuity:

1. The risk context of the organization;
2. How much resilience and recovery capacity is designed into your systems and organization;
3. How much appetite for risk your organization has and whether this is a matter that all your staff will take on board; and
4. The performance indicators that the organization sets in this area, and the achievement against them.

Risk context

Each organization faces a unique risk context where the industry-wide generic factors combine with those unique to the organization to create a level of risk that drives the planning activity (see Table 5.6).

These environmental factors show clearly that the retail banking industry will face a much greater environmental threat for IT services than bus transport, for example.

Table 5.6—Environmental or industry-wide risk context factors

source	threat example
Stakeholder expectation	Conflicting stakeholder groups
Regulators	High level of regulation and control
Governance	IT risks can impose severe risks to the business
Suppliers and customers	Laggards or leaders
Products and services	Customers' dependencies
Nature of the industry	Rate of change, investment level in IT
Environmental security	Unique security hazards
Complexity	Internal or external complexity of relationships

Table **5.7**—Organization-specific risk context factors

source	threat example
Internet security and vulnerability	Threats to assets, customers or suppliers
E-business	Openness to the Internet, partners' dependencies
Board skill	Challenges dealing with IT issues, role of oversight
Pervasive technologies	Knowledge management, intranet, workflow, call centre
IT governance	As an organizational capability or liability

The factors shown in Table 5.7 distinguish between participants in the same industry, so that those with higher exposure to Internet-based systems will have higher threat levels.

The uniqueness of the risk context for an organization suggests that a 'vanilla' or off-the-shelf business continuity plan is not a solution. Business impacts of outages will be meaningless if they are coming from a cookbook.

Designed-in

Building in resilience or a specific recovery strategy is always going to cost less than bolting it on as an afterthought[39] – although it may meet only the targets that were valid at design time, and they may appear quaint in the rear-view mirror. Many universities relied on Internet protocol on their campuses, on the presumption that if it was good enough for cold war resilience, it'll be good enough to deal with localized campus disruptions.

Organizations with very high levels of resilience defined into their organization goals will naturally design resilience into their systems.[40] Do they get it at the right level? This is a matter of technical skill and aptitude rather than fighting for organizational priorities and budgets. Of course, their systems may be over-engineered, but the risk has been moderated.

---

[39] Although it will usually come with a higher up-front cost than neglecting recovery and resilience all together!

[40] SWIFT, for example, exchanges millions of messages valued in trillions of dollars every business day and proclaims its 'five nines' availability (SWIFT, 2002). This is 99.999% availability – which translates as no more than approximately 50 minutes per year of downtime. For SWIFT, IT service continuity is core business and managing IT risk a core competency that is loudly proclaimed. We take up the SWIFT relationship with Global Crossing as an example of a service provider risk in Chapter 7.

Buy-in and appetite

Gaining buy-in across the organization to the business of service continuity can take significant leadership as well as a specific target. For some organizations their resilience may be a badge of honour that is shared by all staff. Other organizations may need to achieve a specific level of resilience and recovery in order to be accepted as a supplier or contractor. Certification is creeping in, with widespread adoption of ISO17799 in the UK, Hong Kong and Singapore, among others. ITIL adoption will also encompass IT Service Continuity and will be promulgated widely with BS15000 and its international equivalents.

The Australian National Audit Office, in a recent business continuity and emergency management review of a major agency (ANAO, 2003a), in evaluating the IT-related aspects relied on their own *Better Practice Guide* (ANAO, 2000), COBIT, ISO17799 and ITIL Service Management guidance. In another review at around the same time (ANAO, 2003b) the Audit Office referred agencies to consider 'relevant guidance' from Emergency Management Australia (EMA, 2002) and the Business Continuity Institute (www.thebci.org). Fortunately most of the advice is reasonably aligned. All require regular testing and rehearsal of continuity and recovery plans.

Unfortunately, as surveys and reports have shown[41] many organizations don't have plans. Many of those who have plans don't test or rehearse them.

How much testing is too much? There are practical limits in most organizations to the testing and training for IT service continuity that is attempted. Relocation exercises are difficult to plan, expensive to conduct and may deliver mixed messages in terms of capabilities. Was this test a failure or was the 'underperformance' a useful and beneficial discovery? Must every test be successful?

Another dimension of appetite is the organization's risk appetite. There are some organizations for which any expenditure on risk mitigation is regarded as a waste – hanging out in front of the wing of the aircraft is where it wants to be. But most organizations will exhibit some discrimination between the areas of risk that they want to take on board, and those that they need to moderate.

Performance indicators

We have referred several times to two key performance indicators: resilience and recovery (Jordan, 2003). Before we explore these in more detail, there is a third

---

[41] Musson and Jordan (2000) survey findings revealed that only 9% of businesses have authorized and tested recovery plans for their business including IT. A survey by the Business Continuity Institute in February 2003 of Chartered Management Institute members in the UK found 55% rehearse their business continuity plans at least once a year.

that is elusive yet valuable. There is the possibility of 'right now' benefits – that are obtained during the process of planning and designing for service continuity. For many organizations, the discussion of which are the critical processes reveals some erroneous assumptions on importance in the organization, as well as over-provisioning by IT on selected systems. More than this, when trying to determine how to provide recovery facilities for a service, some re-engineering may take place that creates a more efficient, more resilient service. The service continuity perspective may produce a refreshing view or review of the way in which the organization's IT services are delivered and assured. Clearly it would be unusual to set targets for such serendipitous gains but the gains can be chalked up.

Resilience and recovery are dimensions that also make sense in our personal health and safety domains – have you had all your shots, checked your risk factors, ensured that your vitamin levels are good, got the resilience to miss the cold that 'went round the office'? How long did you take to get over your last cold or throat infection? Did you really get knocked flat by that little bug? Recovery could do with improvement.

Resilience deals with the expectation or probability that untoward events will not strike at the service delivery. A performance target may suggest that degradation in bandwidth of 50% will not cause noticeable response time delays for online customers, or that loss of one data channel will not prevent email being delivered within timeframe. How many hits can the system take and still deliver service with a service level that is acceptable? Some dimensions of resilience can be tested directly but others will have only a qualitative assessment. Resilience is the only outcome that we directly build.

Recovery depends on the specific event which may be outside all of the envisaged scenarios and only modestly represented in the team's thinking. An organization can have meticulously removed all single points of failure from its systems, but the terrorist strikes at the multiple nodes simultaneously. The only recovery possible may take months involving a complete rebuild of the hardware layers with newly sourced equipment – and this assumes that the precious data and software configuration are stored separately.

In practice most organizations suffer many minor and moderate outages and disruptions, and for these recovery statistics can be compiled. It is a common-place however, that if an arm's-length service level agreement is not in force, the consequential impacts on business services arising from technological outage or malfunction will not be recorded. The network manager knows only that the network went down to 20% capacity for 90 minutes, not what this represented in terms of customers waiting for responses or staff not being able to access external information repositories at critical moments.

So the twin gods of resilience and recovery are both goals and performance measures. The organization can assess its current achievements, set new targets and then work toward their achievement – and a few 'right-now' benefits on the way won't hurt.

Health check

This section assists you to consider at a macro-level the company's IT service continuity risk health, for input into the IT risk portfolio assessment.

Is this important to your business?

- Your core business processes are highly reliant on IT systems.
- You have a low tolerance for IT services unavailability and system outages.
- Customers and stakeholders expect you to continue to operate and deliver services through adverse circumstances, such as natural disaster.

> *If you agree with one or more of the three statements, then IT service continuity risks are important to your business.*

Are you doing the right things?

- The availability of our key systems is measured and managed.
- Systems are designed to be resilient and dependable.
- A crisis management structure is clearly defined and includes or interfaces with the team responsible for IT service delivery.
- Disaster recovery plans have been developed and are maintained for critical applications.
- Disaster recovery plans line up with business continuity plans and expectations.
- Disaster recovery plans and capability are regularly tested and reviewed.
- Where third parties are used for IT services, responsibilities for service continuity, including through disasters, are clearly defined in the contract.

> *If you agree with these statements, then you are doing the right things in your organization. If you disagree with two or more of the seven statements, then there is significant room for improvement in your IT service continuity risk management capability.*

Do you have a good track record?

- Core systems are available when required and periods of extended unavailability are rare.
- When IT services do fail they are restored within an acceptable timeframe.
- Your capability to respond to crises and recover your IT services has been assured through real incidents and/or through testing and rehearsal.

> *If you agree with these statements, then you have a good track record of managing IT service continuity risks. If you disagree with one or more of the three statements, then there is evidence of the need to improve IT service continuity risk management capability.*

Case study: Police service

Developing a disaster avoidance–disaster recovery strategy

One of the largest police services in the English-speaking world, with over 13 000 sworn officers, embarked on a major information and communications technology renewal program. As part of this renewal program, a radically different approach to delivering robust and resilient IT services was sought. A disaster avoidance–disaster recovery project was initiated to identify DA–DR gaps in IT systems and management capability and subsequently develop and implement a strategic response.

To scope out what needed to be done, business system owners and key members of the IT delivery and support teams were engaged to:

- Define the business criticality and maximum tolerable outage of each application by establishing the implication of an unplanned outage on police business objectives;
- Identify single points of failure within the IT infrastructure and supporting facilities by mapping end-to-end transactions for each application; and
- Review the strengths and weaknesses in management capability and preparedness to enact crisis management and disaster recovery responses.

Scenario planning methods were used to sharpen the DA–DR planning activities, through:

- Identifying all relevant threats to IT service continuity – environmental, deliberate and accidental;
- Reviewing the impact on IT elements that are essential to IT service delivery – including computing nodes, data network, voice network and people – under different threats; and
- Defining IT service outages for which a prepared response is required, both disaster avoidance measures – designed to address existing vulnerabilities – and disaster recovery measures – aimed at service resumption once an outage has occurred.

The police service is now moving ahead with a clear picture of the priorities for investment based on a comprehensive understanding of the business impact of system outage. Systems understood as critical and designated as 'Premium' will receive proportionally more attention and effort from IT staff throughout their lifecycle to ensure effective DA–DR capability that meets business needs is built in from day one and maintained in operation.

Printed with permission of PA Consulting Group

6 Information assets

Opening salvo . . .

CD Universe had about 300 000 customer credit-card records stolen by a hacker who then attempted extortion. When the hacker's demand was not met, the hacker posted about 25 000 of the credit-card details on the Internet (*AFR*, 2000). Those customers then had to cancel the cards and face significant disruption.

Without examining the details of that particular case, it raises many questions for you and your organization. Just for tasters:

- What is the chance that this could happen to you?
- What sensitive data do you have? Is it attractive to outsiders? What if it is broadcast?
- What percentage of the affected customers would you expect to lose permanently?
- How much security have you got? Is it enough?
- What laws would you potentially break?
- What's the cost of the fix after the event compared with before, if indeed it can be fixed?

One of the outstanding features of such examples is that the relationship with a key stakeholder – here the customer – can be seriously impacted by a technical inadequacy deep in the techie's mystery zone. How can management deal with this?

The next example shows that it's not just the Internet that creates information asset issues, it can be quite mundane.

. . . and while you're down . . .

A local government organization transferred a database from an old system to a new system, but the data became corrupted. Unfortunately the corruption was not immediately detected, which made restitution very difficult. In this case the customers were asked to send in their copies of records so that the database could be rebuilt.

This case exhibited one of the common patterns; several errors and failings took place together, exacerbating the situation. This raises some additional questions.

- What procedures do you have to ensure that real, live data is not corrupted?
- How is the production environment separated from the development environment?

The last of these vignettes concerns access to important or sensitive data.

. . . you get kicked some more

An innovative electronics company lost the complete design plans for a market-leading new product when R&D staff disappeared, along with the hard disk drive from the design lab server. A substantial extortion demand followed.

- Could disaffected staff take or damage your data stores?
- What separation of data exists? Can you make sure that staff have only part of the picture?
- What classification of data exists? Do you have 'restricted', 'secret', 'confidential' labels that are used?

While the standard literature refers to 'information security management' as the way of dealing with risks to information assets, we will be more precise and use the term 'information asset management'. We will argue later that standard approaches under the information security management banner are a mish-mash of asset protection, governance and service provision.

The CIA triple – confidentiality, integrity and availability – are the mantra when managing information assets, so we first explore the loss of these attributes. This enables us to summarize our asset protection objectives. The chapter then looks at valuing information assets, as without some approach to valuation we are never going to get protection right. The key material follows – establishing the basis for information asset management.

Accessing your information assets

An information asset is: 'An off-balance-sheet asset derived from the accumulation of, and power to use, information for the organization's advantage' (Jordan, 1994).[42] Information assets have similarities to and differences from other assets. The

---

[42] This is similar to Strassman's Knowledge Capital (Strassman, 1997).

ownership of both types of assets generates the capacity to deliver value or benefit. But information assets can be duplicated for a negligible cost, which is where the problem starts. Valuable physical assets will typically be located in a few identifiable locations and the potential for physical access security – locking them up – is both technically and financially feasible.

The US General Accounting Office identifies information assets as critical national infrastructure (GAO, 2003). Their report highlights the considerable array of high-risk assets. The issue has become so important that the US Government has enacted specialist legislation to mandate protection of key assets.[43]

Information assets, on the other hand, will be highly distributed about the organization – every document, file and data storage device is part of the asset. Documents are readily copied – as they need to be so that people can do their work. Information assets are both key inputs and key outputs of many business processes. In many organizations, information assets are not formally recognized, evaluated, stored or managed. We need access to information within the organization to carry out business processes, but it is seldom restricted to those who 'need to know'.

The 'availability' paradox

Information assets must be available to the 'good guys' but not available to the 'bad guys'. Availability is essential but it carries great risks.[44]

We can, and frequently do, control and restrict access to information assets that are held in computer systems by simple security systems such as passwords but paper documents are seldom controlled with an equivalent rigour. Ask yourself a simple question, 'Is there a default paper document classification that is broadly known around the organization?' Do all staff know whether an unmarked (unclassified) document is for internal use only or for public consumption? What does 'confidential' mean? How about 'restricted'? But the absence of defined standards does not mean that everything needs to be made 'secure'. In the same way, data held in IT systems varies between the mundane and the most valuable. A one-size-fits-all password system is not enough.

The impacts of information asset exploitation

Information assets are developed directly and indirectly in many of the processes of an organization. They are there to be used productively for the organization's

---

[43] The Federal Information Security Management Act of 2002.
[44] Besnard and Arief (2004) research considers security and legitimate use trade-offs from a cognitive perspective. Legitimate users place a higher priority on usability than security and seek 'good enough' solutions.

benefit. Their exploitation by outsiders may be theft and by insiders may be corruption, but the impacts on the organization represent the situation that management will have to deal with. This section explores four dimensions of impacts: exclusivity, costs, replacement and confidentiality.

Loss of exclusive use

Exclusivity is an essential dimension in the valuation of an asset. A private beach is quite different from Bondi, Brighton or Santa Monica. If you have exclusive use of information you can license it and generate revenue, or choose not to license it and derive the maximum benefit for your own organization. When another organization has access to your information assets, they are able to gain benefit similarly.

With a physical asset, you should know when someone is using it or has taken it. However, with an information asset, you may not be aware that you are sharing it – in some ways this is worse than knowing.

Direct benefit of the exploitation to the perpetrator

The benefit to the perpetrator is a cost to the victim, whether direct or indirect. Advanced knowledge on company performance, mergers and acquisitions and strategic initiatives allows informed, beneficial actions on stocks and shares, for example. The benefit obtained is at the collective cost of those in the organization and others without the information. The data thief has the opportunity to make greater benefit from it than its guardians, both directly in their own enterprise and indirectly through the damage to the owners.

Time, energy, goodwill

When you realize that you've been invaded, that the assets have been accessed, at best there will be a delay while replacement assets are built. The effort that goes into this could have been put to more valuable use elsewhere. Even the decision of whether to replace or not takes some time. When the milk is spilt, a decision has to be made whether you want milk this time around.

Building a replacement information asset can be a significant effort, especially if it needs to be done in a way that cannot be plundered again. The electronics company whose R&D team hijacked an innovative product design for extortion faced the need to develop a new product as the original could now be pirated too easily. This would mean establishing a new R&D team, getting the marketing people to work with them to create a new product concept, and working through the full development cycle.

Loss of confidentiality

If you are the guardian of information that is important to others and you let them down, how can that impact you?

Even unauthorized access to read-only data by police officers destroys the integrity of the data. A valued resource becomes one that is tainted by its misuse. In this case there is no loss of data. The risk concerns the reputation of the organization that has been damaged by the breach of confidentiality.

There are many situations where our private data is given to government in accordance with its authority. The abuse of this, whether by design or malfeasance, damages the organization and persuades the clients that their trust is mislaid. Comprehensive audit trail applications are now used to capture every keystroke and mouse action in such critical applications.

'Confidentiality' is used as the generic term to describe any example where information assets are exploited by anyone other than the intended users. While in many cases the power of the law is on the side of the owners, this is of little comfort when there is little likelihood of extracting suitable compensation from the offenders.

The impacts of degraded information assets

The most obvious degradation of information assets occurs when they are totally, irrecoverably lost. It's conceivable that hundreds of laptops are stolen each week in most of the major cities of the world and quite likely that some of them have useful, valuable or even critical information on them. The value of that information to others was dealt with in the section above, but even if it is completely password-protected and encrypted, we still face a loss if there is inadequate back-up.

Back-ups have been used since the earliest days of IT, when the inherent unreliability of the hardware necessitated rigorous copying of data, and the frequent use of the back-up store in a recovery process. Now that reliability is dramatically improved, we are less likely to use the data restoration facility – which explains the common reality that restore or recovery doesn't work satisfactorily.

But degradation is not simply about loss of data; it includes the accidental and deliberate corruption of records that can take place in many ways. Degraded assets can destroy an organization. If your organization's financial records have been systematically distorted, as with Barings Bank, there may be nothing left.

You don't know what you've got 'til it's gone[45]

When data is lost or corrupted is not a great time to initiate an asset valuation process. One author recalls experiencing a home break-in and it taking days before a reasonable list of stolen items could be produced, and then discovering weeks later that some other items had also gone. Yet it is easier to deal with physical assets – we can create an inventory, photograph every item and at least debate the cost of purchase / replacement cost alternative valuations. 'Sentimental' value, however, can distort the calculations.

Information assets suffer from a greater distortion. It is straightforward to create an inventory of every file, every database that is on every server as well as all the hard disks on all the laptops and desktops. It is not even an overwhelmingly difficult task to make copies. It's the value that is not apparent. One byte is quite like another byte – there are only 256 different ones – it's what is done with them. Lost data suddenly becomes more valuable, more treasured than it was when you had it.

For those who have sweated even for a small number of hours over a document before losing it to a 'blue screen' failure on a PC this loss is quite easy to comprehend.

Loss of integrity

Corrupted or degraded data, when that fact has been discovered, can be as significant as data that is completely lost. Not being able to rely on information assets for beneficial use means that every use has to be checked and double-checked. At some point trust may be re-established, but there will remain the risk of other errors to be detected.

The situation is made worse when the corrupted or degraded data is undiscovered, that it is treated as a valuable asset, as if it has meaning and value. Staff and customers make their decisions based on the assumed validity of the data, and the consequences could be enormous. The Australian alternative medicine industry (vitamins and the like) was dealt a body blow by the failure of a key supplier to maintain quality control records. When the regulator discovered this, the biggest recall in Australian consumer experience took place. The supplier and many other industry participants, mostly innocent, suffered catastrophic losses. The whole industry is experiencing a gradual recovery but has perhaps been permanently damaged in the public mind, as the industry's standard rebadging practices were revealed, together with the placebo-status of some products. And it all started with some quality control records.

---

[45] Joni Mitchell, 'Big yellow taxi'.

Loss of integrity can occur at any stage of the lifecycle. In the State of Victoria in Australia the speed cameras have been proven unreliable in capturing and recording data. In May 2004 the government announced that almost 165 000 motorists caught by fixed speed cameras will have their fines waived or be paid compensation, costing the state government A$26 million (*Age*, 2004).

Somewhere in AT&T's systems, errors have crept in, manifesting themselves in erroneous customer bills. Typically, individual retail telephone customers are unable to threaten giants such as AT&T and rely on a 'goodwill' response, or quietly fuming take their business elsewhere. The state of Florida, with Attorney General Crist leading the charge, is a more effective consumer advocate. In a May 2004 media release Crist is quoted as saying, 'We will be relentless and unyielding in our fight against AT&T on behalf of consumers until all appropriate damages are recovered.' With up to one million customers impacted and up to US$10 000 restitution being sought for each allegation of wrong billing, this is a serious information integrity issue.

Repair cost

The cost of rebuild or repair to a database can be significant. A local government authority faced the cost of buying a replacement ancient mainframe computer – one of only two still in operating condition in the world – as a necessity in order to convert a back-up tape to a common format. It was not in the best negotiating position. The old non-IBM mainframe had a proprietary data format that could not be read by other machines. In order to rebuild its database of ratepayers, it needed the collection of data that was now held only on the back-up tapes. The entire computer centre – with mainframe – had perished in a major fire. If the back-up tapes had been written in another format, that dimension of the expense would have been spared (Fitzgibbon, 1998).

But, even if the rebuild is easier, a comprehensive audit is needed to establish the integrity of the data. This involves both cost and time.

Opportunity cost

All the time and expense that is involved in fixing the impacts created by the use of invalid data, finding and identifying errors, rebuilding and then validating the data, could all have been used profitably. Using up staff and customer goodwill on something as unproductive as rebuilding a database is not anyone's first choice. Even time and effort taken in filling out an insurance claim is not the best use of the organization's resources.

'Loss of integrity' is the generic term used to describe any example where information assets have been degraded, whether intentionally or unintentionally. The value of an information asset depends to a great extent on its integrity, and value can change from 'large positive' to 'large negative' with the tiniest corruption.

The dimensions of security

What is it that an organization requires of its information assets? In this section we tighten the focus onto just the information assets, as many organizations' information security policies are more far-reaching and deal with other related areas.

Objectives

The following objectives apply equally to information assets that are stored, developed and retrieved in IT-based systems and to those that exist in paper documents, informal records, or even the memory of individuals. Most of our discussion will only concern the former.

- Information assets must be accessible only to those who have the right to access them – confidentiality.
- Information assets must be correct – up-to-date, accurate and verifiable – integrity.
- Information assets must be accessible when needed – availability.
- Information asset management must meet external legal, governance and regulatory requirements – compliance.

Observant readers will have noticed that the 'CIA mantra' of confidentiality, integrity and availability has been extended. While external legal, governance and regulatory needs will generally be in the same CIA categories, the particular threats and risks under the compliance heading are sufficiently distinctive to warrant separate treatment. So we have a new mantra – CIAC.

As a perhaps cruel aside, many organizations would also aim to establish information assets that meet the needs of the organization for its operation, management and control. While it is, of course, a valid objective for the development of the organization's information assets, it is not appropriate here where we principally consider guardianship. Such objectives are in the domain of the IT application and the IT strategy.

Confidentiality

Can we ensure that only the people who are supposed to have access to an information asset, do get access? Alternative sources of threats:

- The criminal mind[46] – a comfortable livelihood can be made if delivery schedules can be intercepted, or data can be sold to competitors.[47] If you were a criminal, how many opportunities for gain could you identify in your organization? The 2004 surge in 'phishing'[48] shows that there are other objectives for spam.
- The competitor mind – imagine a competitor is walking around your organization and finds a logged-on, ready-to-go computer system, what could they do? What would be the most valuable data to them?
- The customer – privacy legislation in many jurisdictions now permits the individual customer (or client) to gain access to their own data, but sets severe penalties if others' information is retrieved. Yet information about others is potentially valuable (credit-card details, for example) or simply of enormous curiosity value. A business customer may be extremely interested to know its supplier's cost prices and discount policies.
- The employee – devil or angel, in-between, or variable? Even the most rule-abiding employee can imagine data that they would 'love to know' – their manager's salary or performance appraisal, or a flame's age, status and home address. In the normal course of events, employees seek employment elsewhere and will need to 'feather their nest' in the new job, perhaps with a customer list, price list or even new product release schedule. But aggrieved employees have many opportunities (see www.internalmemo.com, or other rumour mills for example).
- Anyone can be a 'hacktivist' – a hacker with a mission. An organization's manufacturing locations, hiring policies, perceived social or environmental impact, or pricing practices can inspire some individuals or groups to distribute the 'truth'. Moral outrage is not confined to anarchists and libertarians – passing on real data is much more satisfying than unconfirmed rumours.

This crowd of attackers will have various means and divergent motivations: some willing to die for the cause, others simply spending a quiet evening at home on a 'hobby'.

Typical approaches to confidentiality are access control methods based on need-to-know user profiles and hard-to-crack passwords, restricting data to particular computers or networks, physical access restrictions and dongles (security

---

[46] The CSI/FBI survey (2003) provides statistics on the frequency, distribution and impact of computer crime. In total, the 251 organizations surveyed reported annual losses of US$200 million. The theft of proprietary information caused the greatest financial loss with the average reported loss of approximately US$2.7 million. Virus incidents (impacting 82%) and insider abuse of network access (80%) were the most cited forms of attack or abuse.

[47] The definition of what exactly cybercrime is and how multiple jurisdictions must work together to combat it are current topics of great interest to legislators (Pounder, 2001).

[48] Seeking log-in data by creating websites that mimic others', and gaining access to their accounts.

devices attached to designated end-user devices). Systems designers typically recognize that 'prevention' measures are not 100% effective and will build layers of detection and response mechanisms for various breaches. Penetration testing using 'white-hat' hackers can be a shocking experience for any organization that wants to establish their performance in this domain.

Integrity

Can we ensure that the data is not corrupted, either intentionally or accidentally? Intentional corruption can be an alternative strategy for all of the people identified in the above section. They can achieve their objective to steal, damage reputation or whatever, by deleting or editing data.

The cases of student grades that have been deliberately, fraudulently changed represent examples of direct personal benefit. Indeed, a common approach to fraud is an attack on data integrity through changes to prices, delivery instructions, status (perfect to damaged) or payment.

Unintentional corruption or loss typically arises from the following sources:

- Computer hardware loss, damage or malfunction, such as disk crash or faulty communication channels.
- Computer software errors – such as bugs in the software allowing a delivery to be authorized twice but only one payment received, data being overwritten, data being written to one file but not to another. Faults that allow prices to be changed without records being kept of the amendments, calculation algorithms that generate incorrect values – the list is, to all intents and purposes, infinite.
- Utility failure – the simple failure of electricity supply at a critical moment can lead an otherwise well-behaved program to generate errors. Similarly for telecommunications facilities.
- User error – warning messages such as 'Do not interrupt this operation', 'Back up all data before proceeding', 'Press *submit* after making changes' and so on, are certain to be broken at some time. If data integrity is threatened, the process must be carried out differently.

Typical approaches to ensure integrity are fault tolerant systems, imaged disks, back-ups, system logs, control totals, audit trails, recovery testing. Intrusion detection is another critical component of integrity assurance, although re-establishing a 'record of truth' once integrity is lost can be a painstaking and expensive endeavour.

Availability

Imagine the hostile crowd of users, megaphones blaring, demonstrating outside the IT services department while their systems are down:

What do we want?   *Information assets!*

When do we want them?   *Now!*

Unlikely, yes, but users facing increased performance monitoring and reliance on IT to do their work can become seriously aggrieved when they are prevented from performing well. Meeting the needs for confidentiality and integrity gives no assurance for availability, although discovered failures of confidentiality or integrity will lead quickly to *un*availability.

Can we ensure that our information assets are readily provided to those who need to use them at the time that they are needed? What are the key threats to availability? Hardware, software and utility failure mentioned in the section above are significant culprits in this area too. Additional threats arise from:

- Natural disasters – forest fire, flood, storms and the like. These threats can be to your facilities, to access to your facilities, to key staff or to utility services.
- Deliberate damage – arson, terrorism, vandalism. In this case there is the potential that the damage strikes at a particular vulnerable part of your organization, if the antagonist is well informed.
- Supplier or partner IT failure – while a contracted service provider may offer some assurance of availability, if your bank's e-banking is not operating, you may have no redress. If you are relying on this to authorize shipments, business operations may be limited.

Typical approaches to ensure availability are duplication and redundancy of resources, including computers, networks, power supplies and physical locations. The removal of identified 'single points of failure' enhances the overall availability of the whole system. Recovery strategies are dealt with in Chapter 5 under business continuity and IT service continuity.

Compliance

Legislators around the world now address information asset security explicitly and empower regulators to police them. The UK Data Protection Act 1998, EU Directive 2002/58, US Sarbanes-Oxley Act, US Federal Information Security Management Act (2002), various Australian privacy Acts, all address the issues of confidentiality, integrity and availability of records. Failure to follow them is typically a breach. Penalties vary enormously but the worldwide corporate governance movement is placing pressure on controlling board members to take individual, personal and collective responsibility for the defaults.

The decisions about the information assets that are retained and how they are safeguarded are effectively out of the hands of management. Controlling boards will need to be assured – typically through the audit or risk function – that legislative, regulatory and 'corporate responsibility' standards are being met, whatever they are.[49] It becomes quite inadequate to say, 'We have an email policy and we can retrieve any records for due legal process' as organizations are expected to be proactive in seeking out inappropriate use across a broad spectrum of illegal use and could be seen to be negligent if taking a minimalist approach. But the strong-hand supervision of email could easily open up claims of breach of confidentiality. Perhaps the availability paradox suggested above is in effect a dilemma, where both alternatives are unattractive.

Compliance is different from confidentiality, integrity and availability – it specifies the form of the information assets that we must keep and aspects of their guardianship.

Culture

It is fine to set confidentiality, integrity, availability and compliance as our objectives but it is hoping against hope to expect an organization to change to suit this new approach, just because some new directives have appeared. Unless the security of information assets is part of the way of thinking and behaving inside the organization, the level of breaches will be probably unknown and probably too high. So while the key performance indicators may be confidentiality, integrity, availability and compliance, the mediating influence will be in a myriad of organizational attitudes, behaviours and practices, that we conveniently label 'culture'.[50]

Introduction of policies to safeguard information assets needs to be carefully thought through. Clearly in disciplined forces or organizations where security is part of the culture, information asset management will be seen to be part of the framework in which the organization is operating. But other, more open organizations may demonstrate much resistance to change in this area.

The objective is that everyone in the organization will have a response towards information assets that is consistent and positively engaged. If all employees see the benefit in knowing that information assets are confidential, accurate and available when required, they should be more positively disposed towards playing their part. In the same way that building security is everyone's business and occupational health and safety concerns are widely observed, information security has the potential to become 'part of the culture'. Thus a change in the organizational culture should be seen to be one of the objectives of the introduction of information asset management policies and practices.

---

[49] For some these will be imposed, for example the Federal Information Security Management Act of 2002 applying to US Government organizations.
[50] Straub and Welke (1998) identify the importance of formalizing security management, with attention to planning and education. The OECD (2002) set out a far broader set of requirements in their call for a 'culture of security'.

Justified countermeasures

If an asset hasn't been valued, why protect it? How much protection is needed depends on the value of the asset to the organization, both positively and negatively. Assets that have a great worth and those whose loss would be most drastic warrant the greatest attention. We now look at alternative approaches to valuing assets, for the sole objective of deciding how much security they deserve, recognizing that holders of the corporate chequebook require a justification for the (perceived) 'discretionary' spend in the security arena as for other investments.

Very few information assets are formally classified as on balance sheet items. Patents, trademarks, protected intellectual property and licence revenue generating assets can be widely recognized as exceptions.[51] If an organization has a collection of patents that attract substantial fees or allow proprietary products to be marketed, clearly they need protecting. These information assets may well be stored and accessed through non-IT systems. A patent application specifies, in the public domain, the details of the patent, and legal sanction is the principal protection that is afforded. Similarly the intellectual property of movies, music performances and software is protected. Such items are not hidden away behind firewalls, encryption and passwords; on the contrary their existence is proclaimed.

Legal restraints may prevent the use or copying of these assets, although it also makes sense to act appropriately so that illicit use or copying is not easy to do. Ensuring that users have unique identifiers or must register their usage are simple approaches that can be used.

In considering 'prevention' as a response it is salient to reflect that virtually every encoding and protection mechanism for distributed copyright material has been hacked.

A secondary protection mechanism applies through international pressure to ensure that other countries enact suitable legislation – and enforce it – to protect the assets, or more specifically to support the prosecution of those found guilty of unauthorized copying and distribution. Another secondary mechanism involves the licensing of the IP to potential predators.

Looking internally, at the information assets stored on your file servers and databases, it can appear an overwhelming task to distinguish the important from the irrelevant.

The accountancy profession has been exploring ways of representing the value of information assets to the organization. Approaches such as off-balance-sheet-accounting, triple bottom line and balanced scorecard have been widely reported and adopted. However, mainstream international accounting standards require organizations to expense efforts to collect, maintain, enhance, protect and preserve information assets. It would be considered 'creative accounting'

---

[51] Although this area is not straightforward to address from a managerial perspective either, see for example the difficulties encountered within the Australian Commonwealth agencies (ANAO, 2004).

indeed to capitalize even the most obviously valuable information assets held in corporate information systems.

However, with this accounting 'discipline' view acknowledged you can't simply say that information asset value lies in the eye of the beholder. The resultant mish-mash of policy and procedure and corresponding mismatch in security investment priorities would be suboptimal – and potentially severely so – at the enterprise level.

Fortunately the goal of determining the level of security that is needed is much less onerous than the need to justify a precise monetary value to be used in financial records. The 'downside' valuation method is probably the simplest and perhaps the most obvious way to resolve this impasse.

For many information assets it is easier to estimate the cost of a loss than the value of the entire, untainted asset. On a conservative basis the value of an information asset is the cost of rebuilding it, if it were lost or destroyed. If all digital media are lost and assets need to be rebuilt from paper records or archives, there is normally a significant expense, but also a significant delay. It is appropriate to 'count' both.

For some classes of information asset – such as a university examination paper ahead of the sitting, or an organization's branding and marketing strategies for the next year – the rebuilding approach cannot be replication. The cost to consider is recreation from scratch of an alternative.

Using the 'downside' perspective of information asset valuation, the goal is not to settle on a dollar value, even approximate. The accounting fraternity has little interest in even the most precisely quantified historical-cost information asset valuation. For each asset you simply need to settle on a qualitative value on a simple scale, with replaceable or redundant at one extreme and critical at the other. All critical information assets must then be safeguarded by establishing an appropriately high goal for confidentiality, integrity, availability or compliance.

Implementing information asset management

Published standards[52] concerned with information assets are commonly referred to as proposing 'information security management'. While this is the standard name to cover the area, it typically assumes that the organization has no information governance processes, IT service management or business continuity management. This represents a historic reality; most organizations were remiss in these areas in the past. However, current best practices, and this book, provide a broad framework within which information assets can be managed. It does not require

---

[52] ISO 17799, for example.

an information asset management policy that sets the basic ground rules for governance, physical security, crisis management and so on.

Where does it fit in to the overall IT management, risk management and IT risk frameworks?

The core requirement of information asset management in IT terms is the need for IT staff to behave in particular ways, depending upon the importance of the assets. Other staff may also be affected, but it will be the IT staff who will have carriage of information asset management and will implement the controls.

IT operations staff, for example, need to know the relative importance of the physical and data assets that they are working with. For them it boils down to Category 1, Category 2, etc. Category 1 assets will have the highest requirements on confidentiality, integrity, availability and compliance so they must be on mirrored disk drives, with real-time data logs, maximum resilience, duplicated power and telecommunication lines, etc. For them it may not matter why these assets are Category 1 – which of confidentiality, integrity, availability and compliance were responsible – simply that their behaviours must be appropriate for Category 1 assets.

IT designers and implementers will need to build the confidentiality, integrity, availability and compliance requirements into the specifications of the systems, whether these are to be provided by hardware, software or procedures. Rigorous audit trails must be built into applications at the design phase for their greatest efficiency, so must recovery procedures. While password security and control may be implemented in the whole IT environment, special requirements may exist within some applications.

So information asset management comes down to: How does an organization set and achieve its confidentiality, integrity, availability and compliance objectives, within the context of a best practice framework for IT risk management and governance?

Components of ISO standard not included in information asset management

Information asset management covers information assets that are held on computer systems as well as paper records and archives, though our focus is on IT-based assets. Figure 6.1 shows the ISO standard (ISO 17799) control categories. Fully half of these control categories, those highlighted, are not specific to information assets – they deal with the framework within which information asset management needs to operate. The information asset management approach that we are advocating omits these components.

We think that the wholesale slaughter of an international standard warrants some justification:

- *Security organization*   IT governance is an overarching framework for establishing risk appetites, risk reporting, risk monitoring and review. Thus the

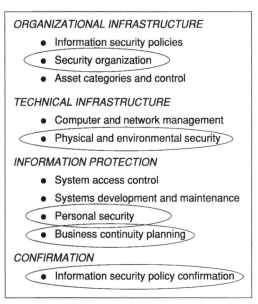

Figure 6.1—Information security management controls (ISO 17799), emphasis added

'security organization' dimension of the standards needs to be dealt with once, at the organizational level, rather than here. Security is concerned with many matters, not just information assets.

- *Physical and environmental security*   If an organization has no security policy concerning access to buildings and the establishment of safe and reliable working environments, then such controls as these need to be added. They are not intrinsically concerned with information assets as they will also address physical assets, buildings and access.

    The information asset management policy is not the place to be framing the organization's response to earthquake or Legionnaire's disease.
- *Personal security*   If staff need special clearance to work in a particular area that may be due to the information assets that are used, other assets or levels of trust that are required. This is part of HR policies on recruitment, training and deployment.

    New staff need to be trusted but part of the recruitment establishes that trust is warranted – more effective reference checks as well as integrity checks, if appropriate. Staff will be trusted with other assets – cars, product samples, inventory, etc., not just information. There is also the possibility of fraud and corruption in any position that involves money, inventory or contracts. HR staff need to be advised of 'trust level' by the information asset manager – say as part of the 'position description' – with particular reference to confidentiality, but also with respect to skills that affect the integrity of data.

Clearly there needs to be input to HR from information asset management, but this is not the place for these policies.

- *Business continuity planning* Business continuity requirements will identify critical business processes, their 'maximum tolerable outages' (MTOs) and other critical parameters, and hence the requirements for the availability of data – but not for confidentiality, integrity or compliance. Business continuity is also concerned with other than information assets – such as succession planning and standby facilities – these should not drive the information asset practices. Thus business continuity requirements are an important input into the information asset management.

  Failure in any of confidentiality, integrity, availability, compliance may be a 'crisis' for the organization, the CEO may need to hold a press conference – but this is not part of the information asset management policy. Similarly for disaster management, a disaster may impact on the organization's information assets, as well as other assets, but disaster recovery planning priorities are people, hazardous environments and contingent impacts on others. Disaster recovery planning is not part of information asset management.

- *Information security policy confirmation* Confirmation that the various policies, including information asset management, are being followed is a central component of an IT governance framework. It is critical to know whether policies exist, are being followed and work satisfactorily across the range of project risk, infrastructure planning, staff development, and many others including, yes, information asset management.

Information asset management essential ingredients

In order to achieve the information asset objectives of confidentiality, integrity, availability and compliance, a specific set of management components are described. This is not a totally self-contained approach, but fits into the governance framework and the IT risk portfolio.[53] There are needs to fit into other policy areas too. The specific components are shown in Table 6.1 and are now described individually.

Information asset policies

An overarching information asset management policy establishes the framework for creating, maintaining, authorizing, monitoring and reviewing the other policies. Organizations are able to create separate policies or to assemble them into

---

[53] Straub and Welke (1998) describe effective actions for managing systems risk through delineating countermeasures as: 1. deterrence, 2. prevention, 3. detection, and 4. recovery. These are the security-specific steps that align with the generalized risk-reduction strategies set out under the IT risk portfolio in Chapter 3.

Table 6.1—Information asset components summary

Organizational infrastructure
- Information asset policies
- Asset categories and control

Technical infrastructure
- Computer and network management

Information protection
- System access control
- Systems development and maintenance

a single volume, although workability would suggest that multiple policies are better. The overarching policy document also needs to integrate the information asset management policy with other related policies, such as HR, business continuity and project management. The key areas in which policies need to be established are risk assessment, record keeping and roles and responsibilities.[54]

Risk assessment

All information assets need to be risk-assessed in a consistent way on the four dimensions of confidentiality, integrity, availability and compliance. Typically this will involve the asset first being identified and its owner determined. The owner will have responsibility for its classification but will be only one of several sources of requirements and specifications for risk assessment. For example, the owner for an inventory price list may be the marketing director, who will be able to specify the base level of required confidentiality and availability. However, additional requirements for availability may be specified by the financial controller. Both would also have some input on integrity. Compliance requirements may be determined by the organization's legal advisers. Risks need to be evaluated according to their impact on at least a four-point scale (see Table 6.2).

The threats that impinge upon information assets are not assessed here, but they are necessary inputs. The value of the assets and the impact of their being compromised determine the security arrangements that need to be put in place. In summary, security threat plus vulnerability equals risk. Lowering risk requires attention to threats and vulnerabilities.[55]

---

[54] Hone and Eloff (2002) provide further information on the elements and characteristics of the ideal information security policy and compare this against the guidance offered by various international standards. Ward and Smith (2002) offer additional advice and example policies.

[55] Some advocate the creation of a control matrix with all threat-asset pairs considered and the strength of controls analysed against each (Whitman, 2003), although this may be impractical for larger organizations.

Table 6.2—Risk levels by impact and actions

Risk level	Impact on operations, performance, reputation or safety	Actions needed to restore or correct
Low	Negligible	Minimal
Medium	Limited	Basic
High	Significant	Major
Very high	Severe or catastrophic	Extreme

Record keeping

All information assets need to be recorded in a consistent way. Some legislation requires schedules of records to be published for freedom of information or privacy purposes but the important requirements here are for the ownership and risks to be recorded. For each information asset we can record the owner together with levels of risks posed by unauthorized disclosure or change to data, data corruption or loss, or inability to access or to meet compliance requirements.

Roles and responsibilities

Information asset management roles and responsibilities should be designed at the highest level so that implementation is consistent. The specific role of information asset manager may be carried by the chief information officer or a designated individual, such as a senior database administrator. In an organization with strong compliance requirements, the role may be better placed with other compliance functions, rather than IT.

At the other end of the scale are the responsibilities of the typical 'information worker', who will need to be aware of the meaning of the information classification framework and to operate within its specifications.

In between there will be staff with responsibilities for creating components of information assets. They may have significant discretion in the way in which they work and the ability to create new information assets during routine work processes. They have to be sufficiently trained to give the new assets a classification.

Asset categories and control

All information assets need to be classified so that protection levels can be articulated. It is easier to envisage this first for paper documents. One approach directs that for each asset, an owner needs to be identified, who will then specify the classification: public, private, confidential, restricted, for example. Typically the information asset owner is not an IT person, more likely being a business user. Documents that are intended for open access are classified as 'public', contrasting with those used internally, classified as 'private'. Within the private category, 'confidential' may mean access only to those staff who meet a particular occupational grouping.

Public, private and confidential documents may be copied by those who have access to them but distributed only to the appropriate group. 'Restricted' documents may be copied only by the owner. The policy would also state that the default classification is 'private', for example. All 'public' documents would need to be explicitly labelled as such. Controls are identified at the same time as classifications. For example, 'private' documents can be discarded in all waste facilities; confidential documents would require shredding in a standard 'private' facility, whereas 'restricted' documents would require return to the owner for a higher-level disposal.

The complication is that computer-based records contain data that is reported in all categories. From one database it is possible to envisage that public, private, confidential and restricted reports and enquiries could be made. Clearly the system designer needs to be able to identify these levels of authority as part of the requirements. Public organizations such as schools, hospitals, public utilities and government agencies may have public reporting requirements that establish a very high level of transparency – resulting in much data (or, to be more precise, many 'data views') being classified as 'public'. Organization structure, job classification, salary scales, office locations and phone numbers, may be public data, while in most commercial organizations these data are classified as 'private', 'confidential' or even 'restricted'.

The 'compliance' objective will cover the organization's own information assets that are directly affected by legislation, such as email, spam, privacy, workplace safety and financial reporting. But importantly it covers the information assets of others, for which the organization has some special requirement, for example, software licences and program source code. Maintaining registers of licences and authorizations is necessary for meeting compliance requirements.

Computer and network management

The owner of information and other business stakeholders may be able to articulate objectives and requirements for information asset management; delivering the goods is up to the IT specialists who design, implement, operate and monitor the supporting technologies. Inevitably trade-offs require consultation between the two, particularly when business enablement and protection objectives are in conflict.

In this category are the security issues of cryptography, virus checking, denial of service attacks, spam prevention, firewalls, intrusion detection and the rest. While these issues have caught significant media attention in recent times, their systematic coverage by information asset policies is often a weakness.

IT system security is only as strong as the weakest link. An attacker, irrespective of motivation and means – should be expected to be rational in their method of attack: the weakest links should be expected to be the target.

These (mainly) outside attacks can affect confidentiality, integrity, availability and compliance, across a broad sweep of assets – which may not be the specific targets and may be the 'innocent bystander' in any hit-and-run. Thus a hacker, using significant bandwidth and network processing capacity to develop a denial of service attack, may impact availability directly through the loss of bandwidth. The fileserver targeted for storing 'zombie' programs may contain confidential assets and the potential corruption of data storage areas can affect integrity and compliance.

More direct information asset exploitation – such as an unauthorized extract of your customer credit-card details – may be masked by 'general mayhem' tactics. With your crisis response team spread and in disarray the 'real' attack may be unfortunately overlooked.

Specialist texts provide detailed coverage on security topics. The necessary understanding for business managers is 'inch-deep and mile-wide'. We support this understanding with a high-level overview of the key components:

- *Building walls, doors and locks* (Schneier, 2000)—Infrastructure design is concerned with technical features such as perimeter defence through firewall and router configuration, 'hardening' of servers to leave back doors and side doors closed, the implementation of security schemes such as virtual private network and secure connections to third parties such as service providers. The segregation of technology assets into 'zones' and the use of tiers of servers to isolate customers from an organization's internal systems and encryption standards are also decided here. Information assets of different classifications and sensitivity will be stored in specific locations and the various access paths to the information will be limited and controlled.
- *Knowing what has happened*—System logging and monitoring is a basic requirement. It is important to ensure that all network access is logged reliably and the log is not simply archived or discarded. If we extend the log activity beyond log-in to include activation of 'secure' applications and functions, the log gets even larger. Clearly an organization that processes thousands of log events every day would be unable to monitor this without intelligent tools and these would need to be operating in real-time if risk levels are sufficiently high. The possibility of a manipulated log – obliterating the trails of the unwelcome visitor and unauthorised activity – must be guarded against.
- *Detecting intruders*—It is generally accepted that 100% security cannot be maintained, which means that intrusion detection systems are key tools. Regular monitoring and review of intrusion detection are essential for their operation as their main performance expectation is the amount of time saved. If catching intruders 'red-handed' is an objective then the technical and operational challenges of a real-time response capability must be confronted. It is

also necessary to monitor bandwidth use on the network as this can be a critical issue for availability of resources.

- *Responding to incidents*—When incidents occur the response needs to limit damage, thwart achievement of the attacker's goals, recover and reconstitute system and information assets and position the organization to learn from the attack and improve protective and monitoring processes and controls – in particular to avoid repeat incidents.

- *Measuring and managing performance*—Incident recording and reporting systems enable analysis of trends and issues and prioritization of adjustments to security countermeasures. The ongoing management of information assets demands that all threats are recorded, including capacity degradations, security failures and related incidents. The business or service consequences are not necessarily apparent to the network or system manager, but follow-up of incident reports can establish the full organizational implications. Managers overseeing the IT risk portfolio and responsible for IT governance are seeking to develop a sense that systems are sufficiently secure – that the cost–risk tradeoff is well balanced and will demand information to assist them understand the position (Straub and Welke, 1998; Von Solms, 1999).

- *Pursuing the guilty*—Forensic capability will enable prosecution for certain types of attack through cooperation with law enforcement agencies. The necessary quarantining of the violated elements of the network – for collection of credible evidence – will need to be balanced against the potentially competing requirements for service restoration and recovery.

- *Selecting secure products*—It is important to consider both the security features of all IT products as well as the features of designated 'security products' – an exploit at any layer of the technology stack can work. Disappointingly some of the most widely deployed IT products appear to be designed with security as an afterthought rather than built in to 'common criteria' standards (Caelli, 2002; Rannenberg, 2000). Also the greater the population of users the greater the potential damage for product-targeted exploit. Be aware then that 'moving with the crowd' on technology choice may heighten security risk by introducing the most likely exploitable vulnerabilities.

- *Patching vulnerabilities*—As vulnerabilities are exploited, IT vendors release patches. It is important to be amongst the wary and informed who take the precaution of regularly downloading and installing necessary patches, fixes and changes to configuration.

System access control

The goal for system access control is to enable legitimate use and prevent unauthorized use. Generally accepted access control principles include:

- *Least privilege*—Permission to access information assets and functionality must be granted by system administrators, the default is no access.

- *Identification*—Individual users have unique user IDs. Permission to read, write, edit and delete information assets is set against each user ID in the form of a user access profile.
- *Authentication*—A 'shared secret' is exchanged that authenticates each user when establishing a system session. Commonly this is a password, supposedly known only to the individual user (or not, as pointed out by Besnard and Arief, 2004). Additional layers of control are typical: a series of unsuccessful log-in attempts with invalid user-ID and password combinations can result in a 'lock' being placed on that user account. Biometric methods – such as fingerprints or retina scans – more accurately identify and authenticate the individual but they are not without their problems.
- *System time-out*—Logged-on sessions that are left unattended are automatically logged out after a defined period of time. Authorised users must re-establish their credentials.
- *Few 'superusers'*—People with 'superuser' and 'root' access privileges can pretty much do whatever they want. The systems administrators with the responsibility for granting others access also have a position of responsibility and trust. It is important that checks and balances are placed over these roles.

When considering access controls it is important to understand what it is you are controlling access to and whether this actually protects the information assets. For example, a typical user will need to log-on to a workstation and the network and subsequently log-on to applications. IT personnel will connect directly to application and database servers and be able to access the file systems and run-time environments. Ad hoc reporting tools can have unfettered access to large databases – for those with knowledge and ability, access to the ad hoc reporting server is sufficient to obtain a view of any record. An email can be accessed from many points, not just from the sender and receiver email application.

One of the major practical problems that organizations grapple with is the gradual accumulation of access privileges for internal users. Many 'old-timers' in user land can skip from system to system with ease. System access granted to each user is generally beyond what is really required and is infrequently revoked. So-called 'ghost' user profiles of past employees, recycled profiles (e.g. for temps and contractors) and shared user-IDs are common issues. Within the IT team – both in-house and outsourced – this is unfortunately also too common: 'I must go. Can you finish rebuilding the server? The root password is X.'

There are many weaknesses with password control – not least the common practice of jotting passwords on post-it notes around the computer (yes, in the top drawer nearest the computer is also pretty obvious). Those who click 'Yes' to the 'Remember my passwords' option are making it particularly easy for the unwelcome user!

If all else fails, simply request a password reset for yourself, learn the challenge / response method and do it to assume the identity of anyone else.

Most access control issues relate to live production systems; however, you should also consider redundant copies of data that are moved around – for example, into data warehouses – and what happens to back-up data and whether unauthorized access may be possible to these secondary sources.

> *An incident reported in February 2004 involved the leaking of personal information on over 4.5 million people from Softbank BB Corp in Japan, fortunately not including credit or security information. The investigation committee was not able to identify how the information was leaked but did state that 135 people could access the information. Elements of Softbank's response are instructive for those who have yet to experience a similar incident: strengthening of keeping logs of all access to customer information and analysis of access patterns, investment in anti-hacking measures, rigorous training and education programs for employees, service providers, agents and others, strict monitoring of the work of employees given access authority to ensure that all activities and accesses are legitimate.*
>
> (Softbank, 2004)

Systems development and maintenance

As has been suggested above, new applications need to be developed with information asset objectives in mind.[56] Integrity of data is maintained through various techniques, some of which are design features, such as audit trails, data logs and recovery / back-out procedures. Other aspects of integrity must be designed at the operating system level or at the hardware level.[57] Similarly for the other objectives. And of course the applications themselves should be built without 'Trojans' or 'time bombs' inside them. A secure application needs to be developed in a secure environment. What precisely this means in any organization is a matter for its choice and design – its absence or inadequacy will be matters for auditors. Further details are explored in Chapter 8, on applications.

---

[56] For some systems it may be desirable to develop a security plan (US NIST, 1998).
[57] Rannenberg (2000) sets out a useful structure for security functionality criteria – spanning confidentiality, fitness for use (integrity and availability) and accountability. As for the current state of play in the industry, he notes: 'If users insisted on only using certified products, they would have to do without most standard application software, in many cases, even without an operating system.'

Health check

This section assists you consider at a macro-level the company's information asset risk health, for input into the IT risk portfolio assessment.

Is this important to your business?

- You handle and process information that is sensitive or valuable in the course of doing business.
- You are the custodian of other's data that implies a duty of care.
- You need to confidently communicate and maintain secrets within your organization.
- Your business will grind to a halt if you can't get to key information (hint: if 'your systems are down' means customers don't get the information they need, then you should agree).

> *If you agree with two or more of the four statements, then information asset risks are important to your business.*

Are you doing the right things?

- Your sensitive documents are managed according to a classification scheme that staff understand and follow.
- You limit access to IT systems on a 'need-to-know' basis.
- Staff found guilty of serious security policy breaches are dismissed. (Staff know what serious security breaches are. So do you.)
- You test that data can be restored from back-up.
- You monitor your systems for attack and respond effectively.
- Your expenditure on security measures is allocated rationally and in line with the value of the information assets and the potential for loss, exploitation or degradation.

> *If you agree with these statements, then you are doing the right things in your organization. If you disagree with two or more of the six statements, then there is significant room for improvement in your information asset risk management capability.*

Do you have a good track record?

- Negligible important information assets have been lost.
- You are confident that your corporate information isn't finding its way into the wrong hands.
- Key corporate information is widely understood to be of high quality and is relied upon for management decision-making across the firm.
- Levels of information leakage, misuse and misappropriation are known and tolerable.

If you agree with these statements, then you have a good track record of managing information asset risks. If you disagree with two or more of the four statements, then there is evidence of the need to improve information asset risk management capability.

Case study: Investment management

Delivering security in a decentralized environment

As part of its aggressive growth strategy, one of the largest investment management companies in the world with over $500 billion of funds under management has acquired, and continues to integrate, a number of financial services organizations.

The necessity to integrate these organizations, alongside a heightened profile of security and operational risk, raised the implementation of a group-wide security policy to the top of the corporate agenda. Although mandated by the executive committee to implement policy, the project was to be managed by a single operating entity (OE) and channelled to the other organizations. A major complexity was that each OE retained operational management and therefore multiple levels of control had to be managed to achieve compliance. This obstacle proved to be especially challenging as it meant implementing policy into organizations with neither the power nor the authority to enforce all standards.

It was judged early that attempting to implement a 'one-size-fits-all' approach to security would be doomed to fail. To address these problems, a solution was devised to:

- Define minimum levels of compliance and rapidly bring all operating entities in the USA up to this level;

- Provide the roadmap and business case specifying alternative ways for each OE to achieve compliance;
- Achieve buy-in from all parties including development of a central governance structure and policy while retaining local ownership of solution implementation;
- Interpret the policy into the tangible work efforts that each OE could undertake while balancing technical skill levels and available resources; and
- Develop a framework to enable comparison of all OEs independent of size, capacity or business focus.

The security policy covered a number of areas including: control of information assets, management of centralized IT, network infrastructure and end-user devices, access controls, anti-virus and end-user policies. For example, a code of conduct manual with associated training was developed in a language that users could understand, highlighting the need for security and their role and ownership. On the support side, change management and data classification processes were rolled out, augmenting new and existing security technology that focused on reducing exposure at both the network and workstation level.

The result of the initiative was an enlightened senior management team, confident in its ability to create and maintain a secure environment across its North American operating entities by providing:

- Clear understanding of the current security position for each OE;
- Detailed report of existing gaps in security capability;
- Evaluation of the relative risk exposures as well as cost justified actions to mitigate those risks;
- Comprehensive and prioritized set of work plans outlining required actions and investment to close gaps and mitigate risk; and
- Fully functional security organization to implement action plans and to provide an ongoing secure environment.

The IT security organization developed its capability through the implementation activities and continues to play an active role in ongoing management of security across all operating entities.

Printed with permission of PA Consulting Group

7 | IT service providers and vendors

A bankrupt service provider

You may recall our mention of SWIFT's 99.999% availability claim in Chapter 5 on IT service continuity. SWIFT also has service providers:

> *We are closely monitoring the situation of our network partner, Global Crossing, which filed for Chapter 11 on 28 January 2002. We have taken all precautions to guarantee that there will be no threat to SWIFT's network services, whatever the outcome of Global Crossing's effort to restructure and deleverage its balance sheet. Phase 1 of our agreement with Global Crossing involved the transfer of our X.25 (FIN) network and SIPN (IP) network assets from SWIFT to Global Crossing. Should it be necessary, SWIFT can reverse this process and resume full control and ownership of both networks.* Leonard Schrank, SWIFT CEO (*SWIFT,* 2002)

A bankrupt initiative

The Libra project in the UK is an outsourcing initiative gone terribly wrong:

> *The cost of the Libra project – designed to provide a UK national system for 385 magistrates courts – soared from £146 million to £319 million. The main supplier ICL (now Fujitsu Services) twice threatened to withdraw unless it was paid more money and issued deadlines for officials to make a decision on whether to renegotiate the contract . . .*
> (*IntoIT,* 2003, pp. 10–11)

The IT service delivery value chain relies on a wide range of external service providers and vendors. The value chain is as vulnerable as its weakest link. Doing IT all in-house is not an option for any company; however, where the line is drawn in terms of what is in-house vs. outsourced differs substantially. When more dependency on third parties exists there will be a greater need for IT service provider risk management.

The key questions for those managing IT service provider and vendor risks revolve around the difficulty of achieving the right level of transparency and rigour across the management boundary.

This chapter commences with an overview of the incarnations of IT service provider failure. Key differences between in-house, external and shared services arrangements are reviewed to highlight that whoever is 'doing the doing' of service delivery or supplying you with IT products there are IT risks. A generic sourcing lifecycle provides a framework for managing risks as your relationship with a service provider emerges, develops and concludes. Contract management levers for risk management are set out – getting the 'arm's-length' aspects right – as well as the relationship management levers – getting the 'hand in hand' aspects right.

Various flavours of IT sourcing that are prone to specific risks are addressed: sourcing in a multiple provider context; offshore IT sourcing; and reliance on a 'community' support model for open-source software.

To conclude, an IT service provider risk health check is provided to help you self-assess where you stand and a case study reinforces some of the key lessons learned.

The dimensions of service provider failure

Willcocks *et al.* (1999) have collated a Top Ten list of the main reasons for failure or negative outcomes in IT outsourcing deals and refer to these as risk factors:

1. Treating IT as an undifferentiated commodity to be outsourced;
2. Incomplete contracting;
3. Lack of active management of the supplier on contract and relationship dimensions;
4. Failure to build and retain requisite in-house capabilities and skills;
5. Power asymmetries developing in favour of the vendor;
6. Difficulties in constructing and adapting deals in the face of rapid business / technical change;
7. Lack of maturity and experience of contracting for and managing 'total' outsourcing arrangements;
8. Outsourcing for short-term financial restructuring or cash injection rather than to leverage IT assets for business advantage;
9. Unrealistic expectations with multiple objectives for outsourcing;
10. Poor sourcing and contracting for development and new technologies. (Willcocks *et al.*, 1999, p. 290).

We have found this list indicates four main sources of failure:

1. Flawed sourcing strategy (item 8);
2. Poor outsourcing practice (items 1, 2, 3, 4, 10) – the converse of the risk factor is inferred as better practice;
3. Unfavourable development of the relationship with the provider (item 5 and 9); and
4. Organizational capability failings (6, 7 and 9).

You will find helpful advice in this chapter relating to each of these areas but with a different structure and coverage. We commence an exploration of the impact of service provider failure by considering four different categories:

1. Failure to deliver the in-scope / contracted service to defined service levels as part of an operational service;
2. Failure to deliver the implicit, expected or required services around a contract or relationship to make it work;
3. Failure to deliver in-scope / contracted project services in line with an agreed statement of work;
4. Failure of the service provider to stay in business.

In each case there can be serious consequences, depending on the severity of the failure. Minor failures, such as the occasional lapse in performance are commonplace and the end of service scenario – fortunately – relatively rare.

Failure to meet service levels for an operational service

An IT service provider agreement typically includes stipulated service levels that are required to be met. Failure to meet a particular service level will result in pain being experienced somewhere in your company and potentially further afield.

Service levels for an operational IT service will first and foremost specify the requirements of availability or uptime. Failure to meet this service level equals unacceptable downtime. Various other service levels are typically in place to ensure quality of service in areas such as reliability – correctly processing all requests and user sessions – and response time – performing transactions quickly.

Failures can occur across a range of severities and frequencies. Loss events will be experienced with each although this pain will be only partially reflected through to the service providers by even the best-constructed performance management regime. This is because the service provider incentives and penalties are a percentage of the contracted payments (e.g. 10% of monthly revenue by service line is risked by the service provider each month), typically bearing little relationship to the business value at risk.

Failure to meet other contract or relationship requirements

Beyond the delivery of service levels there is a set of helpful and positive behaviours that are generally expected of service providers. For example, some degree of flexibility to accommodate new and emerging requirements, leadership in the relevant IT field, a solid understanding of and commitment to industry standards, general cultural fit.

Some of these requirements may be written into the contract, although this does not provide protection in its own right. People interpret contracts – generally to suit themselves. It is thus important that key relationships are managed actively particularly in the areas that can't be nailed with service level agreements. The nature of a technology vendor relationship is normally not specified in a contract. However, most customers have an expectation of continuity of support – within a reasonable time-span – and an upgrade path to new or enhanced products. Failure to deliver to the customer expectations is far less clear to identify and very difficult to mitigate and contain. Today's Top Five vendor may be next year's down-and-out, especially as the loss-maker's cost of capital vulnerability may accelerate its demise.

So what does this risk look like when it bites? Some examples include:

- An IT services contract that has remained fixed while business requirements have changed;
- Delayed technology refresh and retention of aging hardware and software;
- Proliferation of multiple standards and unresolved legacy issues; and
- Lack of interest in adopting service improvements that might appear to be obvious 'win–win'.

Failure to deliver project services

The unsatisfactory performance of service providers is a major contributing cause of project failure on each of the three key dimensions of time, quality and cost.

- Time – a blowout against the project plan dates for a service provider task slips all dependent tasks.
- Quality – when service providers have responsibility for IT system components (application or infrastructure) both functional and non-functional characteristics of the end product (i.e. systems / solutions) and services (in operation) can be fundamentally impacted by poor service provider delivery quality. A well-managed project will seek out these early so as to reduce the downstream impact.
- Cost – extensions in time and poor quality (requiring rework) cause second-order cost implications. Difficulties in cost estimation and commercial

engagement commonly cause great variation in initial expectations / quotes and final total payments to service providers.[58]

Such outright failures to deliver lead to the obvious question: 'Don't we pick our service providers carefully and manage their project performance?'

Often IT service provider relationships commence with a relatively narrow definition of the required services. For example: 'We need someone to run our current IT infrastructure.' Only later does it become apparent that any 'build' project that requires an IT infrastructure change will need to involve the 'run' service provider and that their (operational acceptance) blessing or sign-off is necessary for new services being introduced; otherwise they will blame the project team for getting it wrong.

It is common, therefore, for IT service providers other than those contracted directly and specifically to achieve IT project outcomes to become major sources of IT project risk.

Failure to stay in business

Imagine the interest for CA customers reading this news item:

> *Beleaguered software company Computer Associates International Inc. (CA) has enough money to cover its short-term debts, it reiterated Friday morning in a conference call with investors and the press. The company also confirmed that it is under preliminary inquiry by the US Securities and Exchange Commission (SEC) and the US Attorney's Office. (IDG, 2002)*[59]

And EDS customers, reading the headline: 'Navy contract almost sinks EDS' (*WSJ*, 2004).

The paradox of contracting with a service provider who offers you an unbelievably good deal is that they may be unable to make sufficient profit to remain viable long-term.

If a key service provider goes out of business then a transition project becomes necessary. That is, a transition out of the failing provider either in-house or to another provider. Ultimately the total impact and disruption can far outweigh the gap between the lowest cost provider and the competitor who stayed in business.

Disruptions short of an outright bankruptcy can cause large ripples in customerland. Research and development efforts can be curtailed and non-critical

---

[58] ANAO (2001) reports on an infrastructure project coming in two years late and three times the budget, quality wasn't hot either.

[59] Clearly alarm bells would have started ringing for customers at that time. CA continues today (September 2004) as one of the world's major software vendors.

geographies (which you might be in!) cut back to the bone. The impact is felt in the medium term, as the overall service degrades, perhaps not severely enough to force you to switch.

Other service provider risks

With IT service providers, the main risks beyond the failures relate to:

- Finger-pointing rather than accountability;
- One-horse races rather than contestability;
- Poor value for money;
- Inflexibility;
- Difficulty integrating services with those provided by others;
- Bumpy transitions;
- Unfulfilled transformation objectives;
- Poor visibility; and
- Lack of control.

Finger-pointing rather than accountability

When each service provider is responsible for only a part of the end-to-end IT service an all-too-often occurrence is a finger-pointing of service failures that cannot be unequivocally slated back to one of the service provider's discrete domains.

Unfortunately, common in the world of IT is a multiple contributing factors problem space where all participants must cooperate to both identify and resolve underlying issues. Occasional forays by lawyers intent on contractually defining responsibilities in this space can further compound the trench warfare approach. Beware if allocating blame and responsibility is the official first step of the contractual problem resolution cycle.

Many IT service providers are organized internally to deliver services by technology silo. One group looks after servers, one local area networks, one desktops, another applications, etc. The silos are only thinly wrapped with a customer-aligned service management layer to (appear to) provide integrated services delivery. Unfortunately contracting with a single provider for an end-to-end service may not completely avoid accountability issues.

One-horse races rather than contestability

All incumbent suppliers have power. They know and understand the existing environment, they have relationships with key people on your team and they already have in-scope responsibility to leverage. They can erect barriers to entry for new players that work to your disadvantage with respect to future contestability – and not just for currently in-scope activities.

Other competitor service providers must carefully allocate their scarce sales and business development resources – any dollar spent in sales is an overhead that must be recovered from the profit margin on contracted accounts. An account that is locked up by a competitor can easily fall foul of their bid qualification regime. If a calculated probability and resultant business value of winning is low then either a 'no bid' or a notional bid may result.

You are left with an incumbent who may become lazy and unresponsive – knowing that any threat to call in competitors is an empty one. Alternatively the incumbent may take advantage of your captured-customer status by advancing their own technology agenda and increasing prices to premium levels for anything new or different.

Poor value for money

When contestability is lost, the perception of value for money is too. If every initiative or piece of work that needs to be done goes to the incumbent service provider (for better or worse) then there is no point of comparison. In such cases there is a natural tendency for stakeholders to question whether value for money is being achieved.[60]

The notion of benchmarking is an attractive one to some seeking to determine where they currently sit vs. industry norms and top quartile performers. However, service providers have perfected the art of obfuscation of benchmarking results and many will drag the anchor on any improvements that may be indicated.

Inflexibility

Many IT outsourcing contracts are established for a period in excess of three years. Typically the service provider is investing at the front end of the contract period and taking higher profits towards the back end. Generally it will suit the service provider to hold an environment stable and squeeze the delivery cost structures down over time. As a consequence it is common for the service provider to limit flexibility.

If flexibility must be accommodated it will be with significant additional cost.

Difficulty integrating services

Most service providers will attempt to operate according to some form of standard or 'cookie cutter' operating model. While there are benefits from having

---

[60] An example: 'Contracts signed under the federal government's defunct information technology outsourcing program are running at least A$750 million over budget after it was revealed that spending on the Group 8 agreement has blown out by up to A$70 million' (*AFR*, 2004f).

the service provider delivering to a tried and true formula, in adopting to fit the service provider there is often the need to disrupt your existing IT service management and delivery processes. When multiple providers are engaged this can be most acute as each (of course!) has their own 'best' way of doing things. It is important not to underestimate the effort required to integrate – even only at the interfaces between organizations – the most straightforward of trouble-ticket processes or basic control of asset and configuration data.

Bumpy transitions

Changing from an in-house to an outsourced model is fraught with transition risks, which mostly translate as a risk to IT service continuity over the transition period.

Switching or bringing a service back in-house can also be subject to similar risks as outsourcing.

Risks in transitioning to new technologies are not only about the trials and pitfalls that crop up with the component or system, but also in the learning curve in the operations and support teams and in the newly established vendor relationship. For example, how long do known defects remain outstanding? What is the frequency of new releases and how is backwards compatibility assured – that is, how do we know the new version will do at least what the old version did?

Unfulfilled transformation objectives

A contract in which the IT service is to be transitioned and a subsequent (or parallel) transformation is to occur can suffer from either of two common failings:

1. The transformation never completes.
2. The transformation occurs but is significantly biased and skewed in favour of the service provider – e.g. improvements that will benefit the service provider's cost structure are introduced without consequent reductions in service prices or valued improvements in service quality.

When confronted with this reality, many choose to strip back a core contract to the day-to-day performance of duties and separately contract for the transformation agenda. This can provide incentive in the form of revenue enhancement for the service provider hungry for the transformation pie. Unfortunately for these 'unbundled' sourcing contracts, any transformation will most typically be part revenue substitution and part risk for the service provider and may be marginally less attractive than retaining the status quo.

Poor visibility

The real cost and effort of delivering a service is typically not communicated from the service provider to the customer. Open-book accounting remains, in general, nothing more than an interesting concept and is mostly absent, other than in minority 'cost plus' deals.

It has commonly been viewed that managing IT service providers should be about managing the 'what' rather than the 'how' – that is, specifying and managing to outputs and outcomes rather than dictating the means and/or the processes by which work gets done.

This is fine when things are going well. However, when things are going wrong, as evidenced in outputs missing the mark and loss events crystallizing in your business, there is a need to get into the IT service provider's shop and develop a good understanding of the real contributing factors. This is 'dirty laundry' and any incursion will be resisted unless contractual levers and relationship development has paved the way.

Lack of control

At the heart of many IT service provider disputes is a customer's perceived view that the service in another's hands is out of control. Perhaps it is clearer to consider this as difficulty managing IT by contract. Certainly for any customer unhappy with an external IT service provider there will be another who is unhappy with their internals!

In terms of IT risk it is important to be absolutely clear what the service provider is now responsible for. Furthermore, within the agreed scope it is necessary to ensure adequate implementation and functioning of risk management controls. Recognizing the shared nature of risk management and the importance of two-way communication, agreeing to and adopting a common IT risk management model between yourself and your major providers may be an excellent start.

Alternative service delivery model risks

It is not all about outsourcing. Service delivery model risks will differ depending on where the line is drawn between in-house and third party supply.

In-house

Doing all IT service delivery in-house does not eliminate service provider risks. Lack of clarity typically abounds – it is never quite clear how 'expected', 'targeted' and 'absolute minimum' service level standards differ, partly because there is no formal contract for service. There are typically poor incentives for high-quality service delivery and in many cases an acceptance of under-performance. There may be extreme inflexibility and high-cost structures that cannot be avoided because of internal monopoly rules that are typical around IT service departments in large corporations.

Any investment in IT must be yours alone and any uncertainty in capacity over or under-provision yours to carry (Lacity and Hirschheim, 1993).

In good times in-house teams can be gutted – all of the good talent fleeing to higher-paying IT service companies and the rest remaining – and in bad times left without any 'new blood' injections. Concepts of best practice are generally absent and the importance of *demonstrating* compliance will be typically given short shrift – surely it is enough that the job is done, isn't it?

When it comes to IT risk management often there is a limited ability to question the status quo that arises from little exposure to other IT shops with different practices.

External service provider

External service providers are dancing to their own commercial tune. Customers want the best service at the lowest possible price (or something similar!) whereas the service provider has investors demanding a return.

This may manifest as the service provider striving to cut delivery costs, which negatively impacts customer service levels. Other threats exist in their potential to leverage an acquired asset as part of an outsourcing deal to provide services to your competitors – let's hope this wasn't a source of competitive advantage that you just outsourced!

It is always important to understand what the service provider will gain from a deal with your company. Ideally you can be a valuable reference site. In return for good service and a few extras you will provide some input into a case study and offer the service provider the opportunity to bring new customers through to show how great it really is. With technology vendors a seat at the 'user group' table can help you shape the direction of the product – you will of course be expected to buy it in due course, but it might be evolving into a product you want!

Shared services

The shared services model, where a separate entity is created to deliver services to a number of customer groups, contains a mixture of both the in-house and external service provider risk profiles.

There is an implied or explicit benefit through aggregation / scale that created the shared services provider. However, often this can erode customer orientation as a one-size-fits-all approach to service delivery is attempted.

An interesting dynamic can occur when one of the key customers pulls out, undermining the economics of the shared services model. This is played out in many firms with autonomous business units that seek to carve out their own IT empires. As core (enterprise) systems managed to a shared services model are deserted, their costs spiral upwards, creating a further incentive for customers to depart.

And if the shared services provider seeks to stretch its wings a further conflict can occur. The customers wanted a tame and predictable factory that is now a profit-seeking growth animal.

The dimensions of vendor failure

Your reliance on third parties in the IT vendor community who supply you with hardware and software products is similar in some ways to the service provider risks. If they go belly up you'll experience disruption, although it will be less immediate.

The line between vendor and service provider is increasingly blurring, as vendors seek to grow their service revenue and customer expectation of 'lifetime support' for products increases. When subscription models for software and on-site support for hardware are in place, vendor and service provider are merged: you depend on both product and service continuity and the entire catalogue of risks that we set out in this chapter are applicable.

Failure to support the product

Failure of the vendor (i.e. disappearance) is one risk only, failure to support product adequately is another. Even for a predominantly in-house operation it becomes apparent that most IT systems are extremely vulnerable to technology vendor service failures, particularly in relation to the 'break–fix' cycle.

Let's imagine a critical system goes down unexpectedly. The helpdesk are notified and raise an incident, while others get to work on minimizing fallout (refer Chapter 5), the internal A team is assembled and troubleshooting begins. If the problem can't be solved at Level 2 support (the common description of the internal support group with particular technical knowledge and skills) then Level 3 support must be relied on.

Obviously the dream scenario for Level 3 support is a 24/7 technology vendor contact centre that mobilizes a rapid and effective response, injecting support specialists with deep technology skills into the virtual problem management team, rapid root-cause analysis – leveraging databases of others' experiences – and insightful solutions for both interim workarounds and durable fixes. This may include the rapid and controlled assembly of a patch that can be distributed and installed readily by the Level 2 team. Only when the problem is solved and the system restored does the Level 3 support team sign off.

The nightmare scenario arises with the discovery of a technology component that doesn't appear to be working correctly and the consequent discovery that the component is no longer supported. More typically, degraded levels of support are encountered.

In understanding why degraded support is commonly encountered it is useful to consider the vendor perspective. Yesterday's technology products (the ones you bought and installed) represent good bread and butter for the vendor as long as a sufficient critical mass of customers remain on support contracts. As components age and other customers move onto newer products it becomes less feasible to assign good quality technical resources who would otherwise be working on developing the next generation of products, which are required to secure next year's sales.

Other vendor risks

With product vendors the main risks beyond the failures relate to:

1. Functional gaps opening up;
2. Aggressive upgrade cycles;
3. Proprietary solution lock-in; and
4. Unfulfilled promises.

Functional gaps open up

You review a system that meets most of your requirements and rates well against competitors. Should you acquire it?

Most product evaluation methodologies only evaluate the fit of the current product against current business requirements. An underlying risk when acquiring technology products is that the successor product may be less well aligned with emerging business requirements. This has most to do with the vendor's capability and product development track record but is unfortunately often overlooked when an out-of-the-box solution appears to offer a fast track to the desired (short-term) solution goal.

Over time as functional gaps open up, greater effort needs to be ploughed into modifying or working around the solution. The paradox is that with every modification you further commit to the increasingly ill-fitting system.

Aggressive upgrade cycles

When you are changing software because your vendor has released a new version (and withdrawn an old one) and not because you perceive any great advantage from moving, you are in the upgrade cycle. When you are changing hardware because your new software won't run on the old hardware, you are in the upgrade cycle.

If it sounds like the setting on a washing machine it can feel like one too. The main risk is that this upgrade cycle becomes an end in itself and locks out the pursuit of value-adding opportunities to enhance IT systems.

Proprietary solution lock-in

Most vendors claim their products are 'open'. Most, however, also deliberately construct their products to be differentiated from others! It is important to look beyond the veneer of openness to the underlying proprietary features and potential risks.

For example: will the data be locked into a vendor-defined world view that no others share – thus limiting opportunities for potential future migration? Are the interfaces restricted or limited so that data will not easily flow to and from other systems? Will any customizations become tightly bound into the product and impede potential upgrades? Are compatibilities assured with only a limited range of (mostly vendor produced) other products?

Committing to a 'box set' or 'stack' of related IT products is not necessarily a bad thing – particularly if the alternative is a hodge-podge of components wired up together. However, overcommitment to proprietary solutions will make you more vulnerable to an individual service provider failure or inadequacy.

Unfulfilled promises

'Vapourware' is IT terminology for a solution that doesn't appear in the promised form. Pre-emptive and premature product announcements are often made to draw the market away from a competitor offer.

The latest is always the greatest, particularly in the IT world, but this might not be the best for you. It is important first to ascertain whether you really require the features that may require you to wait and second look at the vendor's track record and discount future promises accordingly.

Managing service provider risk

Let's shift our stance from analysis to action. From here on we focus on service provider risk management as this is the most demanding. Vendor risk management techniques require a modified subset, for example, PC supply may be streamlined to 'click to buy' simplicity while negotiating enterprise software licensing arrangements might require all of your procurement and contract smarts.

Further detail of vendor-related risks and the appropriate product-based risk management approach are covered in more detail in Chapter 8, 'Applications' and Chapter 9, 'Infrastructure'.

What can be done about IT service provider risks? We'll use a generic IT sourcing lifecycle view to help you understand the possible points of intervention, which are:

- Sourcing strategy;
- Pre-negotiation;

- Evaluation;
- Negotiation;
- Transition;
- Management; and
- Review / termination / renewal.

At all points of the sourcing lifecycle there are useful risk management activities. Early on they are primarily avoidance / preventive and later they tend more towards containment. This section is oriented around outsourcing of a major IT service. For smaller and specific tactical engagement of providers these sourcing activities may not all apply. A valuable resource for further practical advice can be found in Aalders (2001).

Sourcing strategy

Entering into deals with IT service providers on a tactical and piecemeal basis – i.e. without an overarching sourcing strategy – may lock you into a cycle of surprises. No matter how much attention is brought to bear in tuning a contract (later) it cannot make up for a badly conceived deal. Multiple service providers interact and overlap and must be considered an 'ecosystem' in which any one change can impact the whole.

Development of an IT sourcing strategy is mainly a preventive risk management measure. In the process of defining a sourcing strategy, organizations must ask and answer a range of questions. Failure to do so increases the overall risk.

- How should you decompose and define the IT services you need as the basis upon which to consider alternative sourcing options? Can you match IT service requirements to those services offered by the best-of-breed providers?
- For each major IT service:
  (a) How critical is the delivery of this IT service to your business and will outsourcing reduce your ability to control and manage it?
  (b) What are the strengths and weaknesses of the current delivery model? How does the current service provider currently stack up against available benchmarks? Acting on perceptions rather than facts may spur you to pursue benefits that prove illusory.
  (c) What opportunities are available for in-house improvement? Is internal transformation a less disruptive option that could be pursued?
  (d) Does an external service provider market for these services exist and how mature is it? A narrow field of service providers competing for the work will reduce the advantages from undertaking a truly competitive process.
  (e) What are the key alternative external sourcing models commonly in use around these services and do they fit the needs of your business?
  (f) Are there any impediments or constraints to external sourcing that may become show-stoppers for you?

- Having completed some analysis, what are the stand-out candidate IT services for outsourcing and how should they be packaged to make the most sense for the IT service providers in the market? Insufficient attention to service provider motivations (e.g. term of contract, committed size of the deal) can result in poor bid responses due to the sourcing process falling foul of service provider qualification.
- How should service provider engagement processes be undertaken – timing, selective, open tender, etc. – and who should you approach? An overly formal approach may greatly lengthen the sourcing process and increases the transaction cost(s). An overly informal approach may result in probity challenges, particularly if you are in government.

The sourcing strategy supports the overall business strategy. In completing your consideration of the practicalities and the desirability of an IT sourcing approach it is necessary to understand longer-term implications. Do you want to make a commitment for an extended period of time? Some forms of service provider arrangement – e.g. outsourcing by function – can limit other forms of reorganization that may be desirable – e.g. outsourcing by business process, demerger. Do you want to foreclose on these future options? Can the process be reversed? Are specific assets in scope that might be a current or future basis of competitive advantage?

Pre-negotiation

Development of a formal request for proposal can flush out all sorts of operating details that were perhaps absent from the consciousness of the IT managers. Nasty surprises can arise – e.g. systems that are targeted for transition that are not covered by adequate current technology vendor support contracts. Any remediation that is required as part of the service provider's responsibility should be factored into the negotiation process, rather than appearing afterwards as a change to scope.

The all-important service definition must occur – without which a service provider will be happy to simply sell you what they do, or what they'd like to do. An appropriate incentive / penalty scheme will need to be developed to ensure some mechanisms exist to promote desired improvements in performance.

A competitive process will require at least two serious candidates. Occasionally one preferred real candidate and an internal 'stalking horse' will do, but in general a better commercial result is driven out when rivals are aware that each is in a race. It is thus important to attract providers you would be prepared to contract with and retain their interest, recognizing that while a sales process continues they are losing money and that each day in the game represents a bet that they will ultimately win.

Evaluation

Multiple bids are received and processed. On what grounds is a decision reached?

The various dimensions of the bids must be compared and carefully assessed. The informal aspects of service provider engagement – cultural fit, quality of communication skills, attentiveness to your requirements – should be considered along with the hard and fast – price, stability, financial strength and capability, compliance with bid requirements and completeness of service offering. Making a decision based on price alone is something you'll no doubt regret.

Many organizations employ an evaluation methodology for ensuring this process stays on track and remains balanced and free from subjectivity.[61] Particularly when outsourcing will result in internal staff losses it is important to avoid clouding this evaluation process with individual interests and hidden agendas.

Reference sites can prove invaluable, revealing the strengths and weaknesses of the service provider delivery from the customer perspective. By checking out the credentials you avoid entering into a contract with a service provider who is big on promises and short on delivery.

The evaluation team has done its job when it can recommend a preferred service provider. Key points for the negotiation team to leverage should be identified and the presence of 'show stoppers' clearly communicated.

At this point you may be able to develop your own set of deal-specific risk factors, those requirements that if not met will cause your business the most pain (Aalders, 2001).

Negotiation

The negotiation teams on both sides are looking to remove the show-stoppers and move to contract execution. However, in most other respects the motivations and intent are different. Each participant hopes to secure as much advantage as possible through the negotiation. Negotiations commonly descend into a win–lose confrontation.[62] As brinkmanship takes hold, the whole negotiation process can extend and defer the achievement of benefits that may be attached to the shift to the chosen service provider.

Both business / commercial negotiation and legal clarification and refinement are necessary. What is finally agreed must be properly reflected in a legal document capable of enforcement. This must protect the rights of both parties. However, the contract is not suitable as a management tool; therefore other documents – that typically form schedules to the contract – are developed, e.g. service catalogues, service level agreements, procedures, inventory listings, etc.

---

[61] Refer for example to the methodology suggested by Lacity and Hirschheim (1993).
[62] From the legal perspective, Burden (2004) identifies common areas of debate in IT contracts: ownership of IPR, service credits, acceptance and liability.

Divergence between business / commercial and legal artefacts is common and must be tightly managed.

Transition

It is important to manage to a transition plan, ensuring milestones are meaningful to both parties and conclude with services being delivered to the desired levels and other aspects of the service provision arrangement performing satisfactorily. Realistic transition plans recognize that service provider staff must build up an understanding of the operating environment before they can begin to operate effectively.

It is most important actively to minimize service disruption during transition. Staff with deep skills and knowledge might not move across as anticipated, but leave with their severance package. Other people impacted by the change may be operating on a below par basis for some time as they come up to speed in their new and changed roles.

Management

Ongoing attention is required to keep IT service providers on track (Kern and Willcocks, 2000). Regular performance reporting will enable you to keep an eye out for trends and major blips in service delivery. Other risks can be most effectively reviewed at periodic steering checkpoint meetings. To ensure sourcing governance forums are effective, corrective actions must be assigned to individuals and a high degree of rigour applied to ensure their timely completion.

Some choose to include a contractual obligation on the provider for a regular declaration of the provider's risk management systems relating to the services. This declaration will disclose key risks that could prevent fulfilment of the provider's obligations and describe the systems and processes that are established to monitor and manage risks. Material control issues that have been identified during the period may also be reported as part of this declaration, outlining the action that has been taken to resolve them.

Start as you mean to go on. If penalties – commonly referred to as service credits – are in order due to poor performance then it is essential to apply them. Withholding them can send confused signals to the service provider and potentially create a difficult precedent – 'But we thought you didn't care about that service level not being met.' Slippage in service performance that is not quickly and effectively remedied may set in.

Review / termination / renewal

If services are not being delivered in line with expectations over an extended period of time a 'drains up' review may be in order. Possible outcomes of a review include termination or renewal.

Termination must allow the operating services to be lifted up and transitioned to another service provider or back in-house. This can be painful and time-consuming and it may be a significant distraction. Ultimately of course if you don't have the appetite to change the service provider then it is important to have the will to jointly improve.

As blame almost always lies on both sides of the contract and relationship it is generally best in these circumstances to engage an independent third party to conduct the review to agreed terms of reference.

Risk-effective contracting

Effective management of IT risks across the sourcing lifecycle revolves around agreeing and managing to a contract. What are the essential ingredients? A solid set of service level agreements, clear rights and responsibilities, an ability to change and a solid foundation of enforceable contract terms and conditions.

Service level agreements

SLAs set out in precise form what 'good enough' is. As there is a risk your service provider will not deliver to a 'good enough' level every time, you will need both the agreement and an accepted process for identifying and discussing areas of underperformance.

Often SLAs provide the framework for contractual forms of redress, including the imposition of service credits. Most service providers give incentives to their staff toward meeting agreed SLAs too – so it is an important tool to have at hand.

If you have a critical need from an IT service provider it is worth putting the time into defining the requirement in a precise service definition and negotiating the agreed service level.

Don't expect to be able to list every possible requirement in a service level catalogue and have your service providers deliver to the target levels each and every month, with detailed reporting to prove the case. Do expect and demand to have this level of rigour for your key requirements (Aalders, 2001).

Rights and responsibilities

In an IT service provider arrangement there can be high costs of duplication and overlap and significant risks associated with gaps. These costs and risks can be partly curtailed by clearly defining roles and responsibilities.

For the simplest of arrangements this can be in list form and for the complex arrangements – such as enterprise-wide deals that involve multiple IT service providers – this may need to extend to complete process and procedures documents with associated responsibility matrices.

Ability to change

Paradoxically contracts must lock each party into a commitment, but IT contracts are also required to have some flexibility, particularly those that will last a significant period of time. To avoid the risk of contractual obsolescence, mechanisms must be built in to allow change while preserving the integrity of the contractual arrangement.

Key to this is a commercial governance forum for proactively addressing this – i.e. actually reaching agreement on changing the contract – as well as dealing with escalations and disputes.

Terms and conditions

Ultimately, if all else fails, you may need to go to court. Of course you don't intend to but must be prepared to. Perhaps the ultimate form of risk management in IT service provider relationships – when all else fails – must be legal redress.[63]

On a brighter note, the service provider also wants to stay out of court, particularly if they might lose, so a negotiated settlement in an arbitrated setting may be a better way.

At any rate, the terms and conditions of the executed contract become vital in such a worst-case eventuality. The enforceability of provisions that relate specifically to transitioning out of the service provider relationship becomes important.

Let's review a best-practice IT service provider contract and some of the key terms and conditions that you may need to rely on as a risk management tool of last resort:

- Step-in rights allow you to take over and perform the service the provider is failing to perform, with the provider's assistance and (in theory at least!) at the provider's expense;
- Replacement of subcontractors on reasonable grounds, such as in the case of a failure to comply in any material respect with obligations under its subcontract or performance that is materially deficient;
- Obligation on the provider to return data and information that is confidential or proprietary;
- Termination-for-cause provisions allow the contract to be terminated, generally if material breaches have occurred or if the provider has become insolvent;
- Termination-for-convenience provisions allow the contract to be terminated for other reasons with defined penalties setting out the sole remedies for the provider in such a case;

---

[63] The Royal Automobile Club of Victoria took Unisys to court and was awarded A$4.65 million after it was found Unisys failed, twice, to deliver a computerized claims management system that could process documents in the two to four seconds in the original contract (*AFR*, 2004c).

- The provider can be required to offer personnel used to deliver the services for employment, offer assets used to deliver the services for sale (at market value or written-down book value) and offer an opportunity to take over any premises used to deliver the services; and
- Disengagement obligations set out general requirements and standards of behaviour to apply during an unexpected or expected transition-out period.

Managing the relationship towards lower risks

Having the contracting essentials in place – getting the 'arm's-length' aspects right – is half the risk management battle. The relationship management levers – getting the 'hand in hand' aspects right – is the remainder. You must position and invest in the relationship and then measure and manage performance actively.

Positioning the relationship – contractor to partner

There is plenty of talk of IT service providers being partners with their customers.[64] Before dismissing this as mere marketing and sales hype it is important to recognize how long you plan to have a relationship with your IT providers and thus why you need to worry about the softer stuff.

Most IT services avoid categorization as commodities and therefore disallow the straightforward substitution management ploy common in other contractual relationships. Most are not transaction-oriented so a form of ongoing dependency exists.

So you need to deal with people – as well as the machines they build and run for you – and work through those normal, thorny people issues. What sort of sales targets does the service provider have for your account this year and is this measured quarterly? Are incentives being offered to you so you can try their new products and become an early reference site? How do staff bonuses get calculated and does your assessed 'satisfaction' have any relevance for the pay packets of the delivery and account team? If your service provider's customers were queued up in their priority order, where would you be?

Investing in the relationship

So if managing service providers effectively requires the development of a relationship, how much time and effort do you need to put into this?

Not necessarily that much and not necessarily on a one-on-one basis. One firm in Australia calls in their key IT service providers a couple of times a year and provides them a joint briefing about the business strategy and the major IT implications arising. Service providers are asked to nominate their interest in the

[64] Zviran *et al.* (2001) chart the development of a relationship into a strategic alliance.

initiatives that they think can add the most value and to suggest areas that might be lacking.

Where critical, high-volume or high-value IT services are being delivered under contract, daily contact of one form or another may be required. This should be more than exception-based; because otherwise the service provider will be wincing every time they hear from you! Ideally, rather than being the 'nagging customer' you should encourage the service provider to call you with potential problems before they have occurred and impacted you.

Measuring and managing performance

If you have got service levels that you absolutely must have met then frankly you probably don't need to wait until the end of the reporting month to find out how the service provider believes it performed on them – your staff and customers will tell you! However, this regular reporting process is important to manage gradual, incremental and long-term change in the right direction. For example, if the top three endemic issues are reviewed and actions set in place to resolve them each month, at the end of a three-year arrangement you will have got through the top 100.

Don't get lost in the metrics and measurement maze. Focus on getting meaningful reports and most importantly, improvements in the required areas.

Other performance management tools including auditing and benchmarking should be in play but will typically play a subsidiary role.

Auditing

In large outsourcing deals, regular audits are necessary to ensure a transition-out remains possible and tenable. Service provider records, documents and other related obligations – not tied to day-to-day – should be checked periodically.

Process-based compliance checking is also important in areas where output management just isn't good enough. For example, reviewing security and information management procedures to ensure sensitive data being controlled and looked after by third parties is not in danger of being exploited.

Benchmarking

Many large-scale IT outsourcing contracts include specific provisions for benchmarking. Before benchmarking you need to think carefully about what you are trying to achieve. Plenty of companies attempt to use benchmarking to beat their service providers up for a better deal. This is often interpreted from a straight cost perspective, but can also be adjusted to consider quality of service issues.

Benchmarking should provide an objective measure of performance against what would be achievable by others in the same situation. It is theoretical but should be grounded in an analytical framework with a level of accuracy substantially better than the order-of-magnitude cost or quality improvements sought through undertaking it.

You should be aware that service providers confronted with a poor benchmarking report will probably dispute it and seek to obfuscate the results. If you can cut through that, the real issues may emerge – it may be difficult for the service provider to see how their prices can be cut or service lifted without their margins being impacted.

Managing multiple IT service providers

Most companies use multiple IT service providers,[65] creating a patchwork quilt that unfortunately often evolves away from a pattern. While each service provider arrangement individually needs to be managed according to an overarching sourcing strategy (Aubert *et al.*, 2004), and through the lifecycle from both contractual and relationship perspectives (Lacity and Hirschheim, 1993; Aalders, 2001), engaging with multiple providers creates a set of additional risks that need to be managed.

The rationale behind a multi-sourcing approach is to engage with the 'best-of-breed' for each job. That is, the most capable and effective at the right price, recognizing that no one provider can be the 'best-of-breed' in each service line.

Multi-sourcing risks arise when the 'best-of-breed' benefits do not eventuate and become overshadowed by negatives, issues and overheads. These 'negative synergies' have three root causes:

1. Poorly shaped 'clusters' of IT services;
2. Misaligned technology and provider strategies; and
3. Broken processes end-to-end.

In each case it is necessary to understand and then tackle the root causes to avoid the major risks of multi-sourcing.

Shape the 'clusters' of IT services

The key principles of shaping 'clusters' of IT services are to:

● Give each service provider control and responsibility over a set of related technologies or platforms – most providers excel in service delivery on only a limited range;

[65] Empirical research of IT outsourcing deals between 1991 and 1995 identified that selective outsourcing decisions had higher success rates than total outsourcing or total insourcing decisions (Lacity and Willcocks, 1998).

- Group IT activities that relate to 'build' or 'service development' activities – those spanning the cycle from proposing a solution through to managing the implementation of a working technology service; and
- Group IT activities that relate to 'run' or 'service delivery' activities – control over day-to-day operations and service once it has been developed.

An iterative approach is required to take into account the capabilities of the incumbent and alternative credible service providers and to explore potential economies of scope or scale that may be achievable. The clusters are refined on the basis of what the market has the capability to deliver, and where there is contestability.

An example illustrates this shaping process (see Figure 7.1). Seven clusters of IT services that are candidates for external service providers are defined,

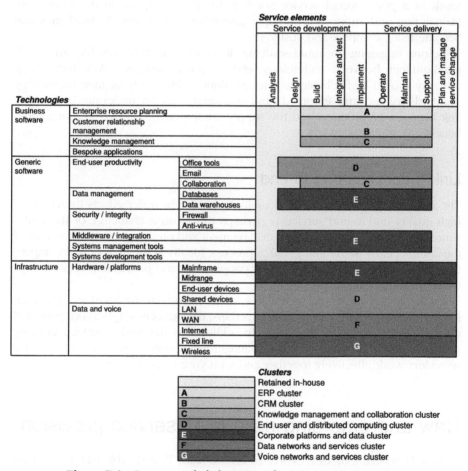

Figure 7.1—Recommended clustering of outsource arrangements

spanning all technologies and IT activities, with a significant retained function holding responsibility for those activities not suitable for external service providers.

Further complexity may be introduced into the shaping of clusters for companies operating in multiple geographies or with diverse business units each with certain unique IT service needs.

Align technology strategies with sourcing strategies

Where companies have opened up competition in IT sourcing and then taken a hands-off approach to setting the technology agenda, the result can be a large number of tactical point solutions based on divergent technologies. These may each represent individually expedient deals but, when considered end-to-end, result in a poor overall service solution for the enterprise in the long term. Maintaining and supporting multiple generations of diverse technologies can become risky, complex and costly.

Before engaging in multi-sourcing it is important to resolve any such misalignment between technology and sourcing strategies. Any technology diversity should be for business reasons alone, with clearly defined technology standards agreed and enforced, and managed with an understanding of the link between IT products and the supply community, to deliver the maximum benefits.

Link processes end-to-end

The integration and alignment of multiple service provider efforts to achieve a high-quality end-to-end service is perhaps the greatest challenge of the multi-sourcing approach. Introducing a management and process framework as part of the contract early in the multi-source process, ideally at the time of real competition, provides a foundation for open cooperation and partnership relationships (Kern and Willcocks, 2000).

Clarifying the roles, responsibilities and hand-offs at the interfaces between service providers will help to avoid overlaps, disconnects, duplication, gaps and delays in operating the processes. In addition to day-to-day service delivery processes it is important that the management layers of the multiple service providers work effectively together and with your organization.

New and emerging risks in IT service provision

As new IT sourcing models evolve so do the risks. Two notable trends in recent years have been observed:

1. The rise in the offshore IT service provider market.
2. The shift to a community-based model of support for open source software.

A brief exploration of these new and emerging sourcing models is set out below with suggestions as to how management attention may need to be heightened in each case.

Offshore sourcing

Offshore sourcing describes a model where the service provider's base (where most of the work is carried out) is in a country different from your business. Most typically the service provider will be based in a country such as India that enjoys relative stability, lower costs than most Western countries and a relatively high IT service quality reputation.

The main risks to avoid that relate to offshore IT sourcing include:

- Political and economic instability may create a relatively less secure and predictable operating environment than exists for an on-shore provider;
- Inability of both service provider and customer teams to bridge social, language and cultural barriers to interface and to work as teams effectively on business initiatives that require IT solutions and services;[66]
- Difficulties achieving redress in the event of a contractual or service delivery dispute;
- Significant 'hidden costs' in terms of management time and the two-way 'exchange' costs of travel and accommodation;
- Legal and regulatory issues and requirements that you may not be able to satisfy by having your company data stored in another country; and
- Greater potential for your intellectual property tied up in the computer systems you use to be exploited by a third party in another country without an opportunity for redress.

The areas for heightened management awareness include:

- Sourcing strategy – include offshore sourcing considerations and be wary of pushing services to where they don't naturally fit;
- Evaluation – include country-specific issues in the evaluation of service providers, specifically check: language, government support, legal and commercial environment, educational system, labour pool and skills, political stability, cultural issues and infrastructure that will support the provider's ability to deliver services over the long term;

---

[66] Lander *et al.* (2004) consider the trust-building mechanisms utilized in outsourced IT development projects.

- Transition – invest in establishing the relationships and processes, in particular the interfaces at the 'front end' of IT service development (getting the business requirements right) and the 'back end' (rigorously testing the delivered solution);[67] and
- Management – establish specific roles within the retained function to monitor review and control the performance of the service provider. Staff these roles with people skilled in 'cross-boundary' management.

Open-source software support

If managing service providers and vendors is difficult – can you do without them?

Open-source software is not owned and supported by a single service provider and there is no vendor, only the distributor. The source code (that is readable by programmers) is accessible to anyone and in theory can be supported by anyone. A so-called community model of support is relied upon for those who encounter problems. While the lock-in risks associated with proprietary IT products and services are avoided under the open-source model, there are additional risks.

The main risks to avoid that relate to open-source software support are:

- Difficulty interfacing with the open-source community for support – the process can appear complex and uncertain to those accustomed to phoning service provider and vendor hotlines;
- Difficulty securing SLAs for support of software – even when you are willing to pay;
- Uncertainty over the size of the installed and supported user base – are you part of a critical mass of customers for a software product that has real potential or do you risk being one of the few real users of what is principally a laboratory project;
- Lack of protection from intellectual property challenges brought against the user base of open-source software; and
- Uncertainty over upgrade paths and potential significant divergence and 'fracturing' of the open-source community, with each branch introducing a risk that you are left out of the mainstream.

The areas for heightened management awareness include:

- Sourcing strategy – carefully select the technologies and platforms suitable for an open-source community support (and/or self-support) model;

---

[67] Sabherwal (2003) considers the evolution of coordination in outsourced software development projects.

- Evaluation – confirm the strength of the open-source community for the products you wish to use;
- Transition – invest in building links into the open-source community; and
- Management – establish specific watching-brief roles for open-source within the retained technology strategy and planning function.

Health check

This section assists you consider at a macro-level the company's IT service provider risk health, for input into the IT risk portfolio assessment.

Is this important to your business?

- IT service providers are relied on to support the running of a significant part of your business day-to-day.
- Critical IT services are dependent on IT components that aren't fully supported in-house but are reliant on third party support.
- A material investment would be required if a single major IT service provider you rely on were to go under or a specific technology vendor discontinue a product line that you rely on.

> *If you agree with two or more of the three statements, then IT service provider risks are important to your business.*

Are you doing the right things?

- All important systems are covered by current support and maintenance agreements with vendors.
- Service providers are delivering to their service level agreements.
- Contractual disputes with service providers are resolved adequately.
- An IT sourcing strategy is agreed with the business units that rely on IT services being developed and delivered.

> *If you agree with these statements, then you are doing the right things in your organization. If you disagree with two or more of the four statements, then there is significant room for improvement in your IT service provider risk management capability.*

Do you have a good track record?

- Service providers deliver the necessary support to your major IT projects.
- Business disruption due to service provider failure to deliver day-to-day has been rare and tolerable.
- We have been able to exit and transition out of service provider agreements that were not working.

If you agree with these statements, then you have a good track record of managing IT service provider risks. If you disagree with one or more of the three statements, then there is evidence of the need to improve IT risk management capability.

Case study: Financial services

Delivering a business-responsive IT infrastructure for less

This US-based financial services business offers its clients a comprehensive array of financial products and services, including life insurance, fixed and variable annuities, defined contribution retirement plans and mutual funds.

In a fundamental re-examination of their approach to the delivery of IT infrastructure services, the options for outsourcing and the challenge of undertaking a major transformation were considered in parallel.

Their starting point was to recognize that in transactional outsourcing, the focus on 'getting the best deal' has resulted in many outsourcing failures. The consequences of 'winning' in the deal, and 'losing' in the future implementation were clearly unacceptable.

Therefore, the business sought a transformational agreement with an outsource provider and focused initially on defining a robust governance model for the current and future relationship. The governance model was developed based on an understanding of the service provider's management approach, their operating style, and their use of process standards such as the Information Technology Infrastructure Library (ITIL). It also accepted the need for organizational change within the retained IT function; a new way of interacting with the business and the need for review and development of internal processes.

With the assistance of an independent delivery partner, the business:

- Conducted a diligent assessment of the insource versus outsource options in parallel with the engagement of potential service providers, establishing a robust business case that modelled the financial and risk implications for each sourcing option;
- Came to grips with and built in the necessary deal flexibility for the impact of new technology approaches, such as utility computing, within the context of the desired infrastructure transformation; and
- Designed the necessary organizational change and established a service management organization to oversee the transition and proactively manage the third party's delivery performance ongoing, thereby mitigating major areas of operational risk.

A major agreement to outsource its IT infrastructure was executed. As the relationship emerges from transition, the business is well-placed to obtain three main benefits:

- To advance and simplify the regional technology infrastructure – improving stability, recoverability and security;
- To improve the cost structure – permitting a scaling of the infrastructure more easily with predictable cost impacts; and
- To enable the business transformation senior executives envisioned.

Printed with permission of PA Consulting Group

8 Applications

When downtime means down time

The fourth major air traffic control breakdown in three years left more than 200 000 travellers fuming, with delays and cancellations snowballing from Southampton to Glasgow. For an hour at the height of the morning peak, a computer failure left planes barred from taking off at all major airports . . .

For airlines, the breakdown left planes, pilots and cabin crew in all the wrong places, with costs running into tens of millions of pounds . . .

According to National Air Traffic Services (NATS), problems began when engineers turned up at Heathrow's West Drayton control centre before 3 am to test software which is intended to be introduced later in the summer. The 45-minute test appeared to go as planned. But when the system was switched back on to full operation at 6:03 am, ready for the arrival of the morning's transatlantic traffic, controllers at NATS' nerve centre in Swanwick, near Southampton, noticed 'errors' in flight data . . .

The spokesman admitted the system was 30 years old. (Guardian, 2004)

Lessons to be learned

In December 1999, RMIT commenced the Academic Management System (AMS) information technology implementation project. The aim of the AMS project was to integrate all RMIT's student management activities into a consolidated system to streamline processes including student enrolments . . .

The implementation of the AMS was largely outsourced and went 'live' in October 2001. Since going 'live', the AMS has suffered a number of functional and technical problems . . .

The anticipated cost of implementation of the AMS to the end of 2003 of $47.2 million represents 3.7 times the original implementation budget. The current system has not provided the functionality originally planned and RMIT faces significant challenges in transitioning to a high quality student

administration system that is sustainable in the medium to long-term,
as well as funding the activities necessary to achieve this outcome.
(Auditor-General of Victoria, 2003)

Sometimes it seems that you just can't win. New systems can be as risky as old; in-house and purchased applications both bring risk schedules, and computer-to-computer systems can be as vulnerable as those with people as users.

Further risks lie in the management of the intellectual property tied up in your applications. All software built by others must be licensed for use, any 'smarts' of your own should be protected. Underlying issues relating to preserving the integrity of the installed base are also explored.

A systems lifecycle framework for risk management is introduced. Getting things right early – in analysis and design – provides the foundation for managing application risk beyond implementation. Diligent management of all change in the operating environment that might impact the system is key to predictable ongoing behaviour. Investment in keeping a system current until the day it is decommissioned is key to avoiding end-of-life risks.

Across the suite of applications risks are reduced through investing in systems architecture and enforcing standards.

To conclude this chapter, an IT application health check is provided to help you self-assess where you stand and a case study reinforces some of the key lessons learned.

The impacts of IT application failure on your business

At the most fundamental level all systems take a set of inputs, perform some processing and produce outputs. With this view, a failure occurs when a system 'must do' or 'should do' something and in operation it doesn't.

An engineer will be primarily interested in whether a system is behaving according to a specification. A bug or defect in the system will be acknowledged when the system in operation diverges from its specification.

As a business manager you will be more concerned with a wider definition of IT application failure including:

- Information provided as output is not useful, open to misinterpretation, out-of-date, incomplete, lacking in precision;
- Users find it difficult and inefficient to operate and hard to understand;
- The system is too slow and can't handle the required transaction or data volumes; and
- The system can't be changed to accommodate new and emerging business requirements.

All IT staff, confronted daily with complaints about the systems they support will be able to add to this list.[68] However, while it is tempting to describe all shortcomings in our IT systems as failure – and risk to be avoided – we believe the search for the perfect system is an activity best kept distinct from the pragmatic management of IT risk.

We recommend keeping a focus on the *critical business requirements* that an application must meet. Your key concerns must be focused where the potential business impact of failure is greatest. This may be measured in various forms, for example:

- Financial loss;
- Reputational damage;
- Regulatory or legislative breach;
- Customer impact;
- Loss of competitive advantage.

As you can't afford to gold-plate all of your applications, you'll need to allocate limited resources to avoid failures in the most critical.

As each user will perceive the applications they rely on as critical, a consensus-based approach won't work. When evaluating IT risk on a cross-company basis it is necessary to introduce objectivity to the task of classifying applications in terms of criticality.

Continuity, correctness and tolerance

Most of the methods deployed in the quest for an optimized IT service continuity regime will focus on the definition of a maximum tolerable outage for each application. In short, how long can the business continue to function without each? This is a key topic within Chapter 5 on IT service continuity risks.

The criticality rating determined by the maximum tolerable outage (the smaller the MTO the more critical the system) will impact in the main the non-functional requirements, particularly those relating to resilience and redundancy in the end-to-end platform. Correct design and operation of the infrastructure is key to achieving these requirements. Further details are provided in Chapter 9 on IT infrastructure risks.

For now, let's assume you have a system that remains 'up' when you need it. What else could go wrong?

---

[68] Checklists of system quality (Barki *et al.*, 2001) stated in the negative will provide you with a start: unreliable, not easy to use, insecure, not easy to maintain, inflexible, technically complex, not portable, inefficient, impossible to test, hard to understand, undocumented, slow, imprecise, incomplete, irrelevant and out-of-date.

1. *The application doesn't do what it is meant to do.* This system (assuming it is able to be tested!) would fail a 'positive test'. Positive tests are designed to confirm a system produces an actual result that matches a (required) expected result. For example, calculating interest owing on an account correctly.
2. *The application does what it isn't meant to do.* This system would fail a 'negative test'. Negative tests are designed to ensure accidental, wilful or malicious operating would not violate integrity of the system and that the system only produces 'allowable' outcomes. For example, it may be a requirement that a user should not be able to delete all the data held on a particular system.

How a system handles itself in fatal error modes or when it encounters unexpected operating conditions is also potentially important in determining criticality. For example, if a system hangs it may severely impact the performance of other systems hosted on the same platform.

Distinctions should be drawn for application failures that may not necessarily have a negative impact on the business. Some application failures are tolerable and tolerated – many organizations rely extensively on workarounds for known defects on even their most important systems.

Systems in context and the extent of business impact

To tease out the potential impact of any particular failure you must understand how the system is used to support the business. How many people will be impacted if the system doesn't work properly? To what extent will this impact their business activities? How important are these business activities within your enterprise?

> For example, if System A is a local database used for back-office administration by a few users, and System B is a major enterprise platform supporting the daily fulfilment of all of your company's customer orders, clearly System B trumps System A in the criticality assessment.

From a reputation perspective it is necessary to understand which failures will be visible to your company's stakeholders and how these may be perceived. The internal IT user base may be more vocal, or their bosses more politically influential than the external stakeholders and as a consequence may bias criticality assessments.

> For example, errors in the company's Website may have broad brand-damaging consequences in customer-land that may not be immediately obvious to your CFO – who may otherwise tend to overrate the criticality of internal financial accounting systems.

How much of the responsibility for risk mitigation and avoidance do you wish to place on the system? Can you place policies and procedural controls over its use that will overcome application failure issues that may arise? Can you achieve the desired 'trustworthy operating' state through a more cost-effective investment in a mix of people and systems controls?

For example, manual reconciliation processes are typically implemented around financial applications to ensure their integrity.

When people and computers don't mix

A system adds value through its support for and interaction with people and with other systems. Unfortunately at each interaction things can go wrong: misuse, abuse or simple misunderstanding at the human–computer interface; integration and interoperability failings when computers need to talk to each other.

Unfortunately, IT often wears the blame when it is but one of the contributors to an incident. IT does not have a 'magic bullet' (Markus and Benjamin, 1997) to transform the organization. In cases where people and computers don't mix well – and unpredictable results arise – it is also likely that various other factors have contributed, for example:

- Insufficient investment in training of users;
- Poor involvement of users in solution design – leading to a design that may be functionally correct, but is not 'friendly' or easy to use, and as a consequence is open to misuse and misunderstanding;
- Unforeseen cultural or language differences in the user base that was not understood; and
- Limited, rapid or forced user acceptance testing – system features that would prove problematic in operation are not identified until too late.

Within the applications designer domain the following practices contribute to avoiding risk of 'operator error' and misuse or abuse:

- Designing applications for usability and adhering to commonly accepted interface design standards;
- Building in checks and controls at the point of data entry; and
- Making irreversible and potentially damaging actions hard for the user to execute accidentally.

However, better system design alone will not be effective in managing these risks. Further common prescriptions aimed at tackling the root cause include:

- Clearer business ownership of applications and business sponsorship of IT projects;

- Assignment of end-users to project roles; and
- Lots of education and end-user training sessions prior to the system going live.

These are all worthy of your consideration, perhaps as part of a broader 'managing organizational change' framework in which issues of psychology and politics are encompassed (Markus, 2004).

When applications need to talk and work together

Looking beyond the achievement of correctness, internal consistency and integrity within a single application – in itself non-trivial – we now consider the interfaces between one application and another.

Computers are not good with ambiguity and at the interface between one system and another there is always an opportunity for misunderstandings to arise. Because extensive 'negative testing' can never be exhaustive, in even the most tightly specified interfaces there is the opportunity for gaps to open up. As the number of applications grows, integration and interoperability issues multiply.

How can managers gain assurance of predictability and dependability in a chain of different applications that must work together to support the business?

Two applications

In considering a simple pair of applications that must work together properly, the first part of the answer lies in standards:

- Adopt a few standards for information exchange between systems; and
- Require technology products bought in and developed to adhere to these standards.

The second part of the answer lies in interface specification.

- Ensure explicit agreements are drawn up between developers of integrated systems on how the interfaces will operate;
- Make the interface specifications complete and binding – in effect a contract for the systems' behaviour; and
- Consider no question too dumb until it has been answered and agreed.

The third part lies in testing.

- When the interfaces are changed, or systems on either side go through a major change, re-test the behaviour of both systems in an integrated environment.

A suite of integrated core systems

Further issues arise when a large number of core systems are bound together – a reality for many large enterprises today. Unfortunately for many the system interface diagrams resemble a bowl of spaghetti. Every system talks to every other system and as a consequence introducing even minor change is fraught with danger. Systems have outgrown even the capacity for the archetypal systems engineer superhero to grasp in their entirety.

Principally as a risk management technique, the large and complex core system portfolio being 'touched' by multiple projects demands a management mechanism to align, coordinate and control the design, build, testing and deployment of change. Most organizations adopt a core system release program and process to manage these related projects and the delivery teams.

The main joint activity within the core system release program is integration testing, which seeks to provide assurance 'knock-on' effects are understood and acceptable and that all system bedfellows will work together as expected, particularly when transactions are run 'end-to-end'.

However, the core systems release path is not without its own pain. For many enterprises, a bottleneck is encountered by projects requiring changes to core systems or integrating with core systems. This bottleneck is most acute for large and long-running projects requiring changes to multiple core systems and manifests as:

- Alignment of projects to a centrally governed release calendar and general 'marching in step' with the dominant (typically the largest) project effecting change to core systems in each release;
- Delays being encountered when releases are 'filled up' or 'booked out' by other projects or impacted by slippage somewhere in the program; and
- Extensive testing phases consuming a disproportionate amount of total project time, often severely constraining business time-to-market aspirations.

In addition, the core systems program is costly and perceived by many (not appraised of the risk management objectives for IT) as 'overhead'.

Whether you love it or loathe it, the option of radically overhauling the entire suite of core systems is a high-risk endeavour countenanced by many but undertaken by few. This makes managing core system releases a competency worth mastering.

The evolution of IT application risk

Greater dependency

Over time organizations in all industries have become more dependent on IT. In many cases it has become literally impossible to perform manually what is now done with IT systems. While undeniable benefits have been achieved as automation and reliance has grown, so too has the risk profile due to the increase in the impact of failure. As a consequence it has become dramatically more important for business managers to control the investment in IT and the risks associated with its use proactively.

When things go wrong with your IT, it is at the application level that the malfunction becomes visible as this is where you have your greatest reliance. This doesn't mean that all protection is to be concentrated at the application level; the supporting layers may be more critical.

Greater complexity

Systems have become significantly more complex. This can be seen in various guises. For example, the graphical user interface (GUI) of today's PC is significantly more complex than the earlier text-based 'green screens'.

Commercial competitors in virtually every application area have enhanced their solutions – from early and basic functionality, in a 'Version 1', to gradually more advanced solutions aimed at securing market share and pulling customers along the upgrade cycle.

In-house application development functions looking to survive and thrive have adopted increasingly business-driven attitudes. When 'no' is a word the business owners of systems don't want to hear, to the extent that funds allow, systems are added to and adapted.

Specialization and proliferation

As a counter to the growing complexity and functional richness, new software development approaches have been applied to keep individual systems and components a maintainable size and of manageable complexity.

As a consequence there is an ever-growing menu of packaged software products – the mixing and matching of components to create a combined solution now relying on an increasingly aware and sophisticated community of buyers, implementers and users.

Within a distributed computing environment[69] systems are tiered, or broken into chunks across clients (end-user devices) and servers (back-end devices), rather than under the single-box hosting of an application in the mainframe era.

For on-line services offered over the Internet to your customers, the end-user device and their network connectivity is out of your control, and all traffic to and fro runs over the shared Internet. Application services may therefore be subject to service quality variability that you can't address.

---

[69] Refer to Chapter 9 for more information on this topic.

Defining the boundary of any individual application becomes increasingly difficult as it forms a composite part of a larger end-to-end environment. The ability to confirm a system will work correctly in advance of its deployment in a particular environment becomes increasingly difficult as the variable system 'bed-fellows' and their potential configuration cannot be easily determined in advance.

Integration and interoperability

Early functional transformation objectives were met with 'siloed' systems. Over time the boundary for enterprise transformation and supply-chain integration has required the linking up of systems across the company and with others in the industry.

Increasingly applications have needed to become aware of and able to respond to other applications in the environment – passing, interpreting and responding to messages, sharing common data, relying on shared methods of user identification and authentication, etc.

While the number and type of interfaces between systems have proliferated, potential methods for integrating systems have also grown. For example, an entire class of software 'middleware' has been created to fill the complexity of the 'gaps' between interrelated systems.

Significant additional risks arise in a suite of systems where the whole is only as strong as the weakest part. Vulnerabilities within a complex inter-networked environment are difficult to identify, understand, monitor and control.

Retained legacies

Most companies have been less than rigorous in removing old applications as new applications have been introduced. Over time there has been an accumulation of software, some of it duplicative and overlapping. The massive United States Department of Defence relies on about 2300 business systems, including accounting, acquisitions, logistics, and personnel systems (GAO, 2004c), which is unfortunately evolving without an architectural blueprint to the tune of some $14 billion in operation and maintenance costs annually.

For those companies involved in merger and acquisition (M&A) this legacy issue can be even more acute, particularly for those who have not rationalized back to a single system for the combined business in the post-acquisition phase.

The duplication has meant for many that significant pieces of business logic are physically coded in multiple places. Any maintenance and enhancement activity must faithfully update all similar pieces for the integrity of the whole system to be preserved. Needless to say, in a large and sprawling code base, often not well documented due to the natural proclivities of the IT software developer, this is a challenging task and one that almost invariably becomes reliant on individuals with the consequent increase in risks.

As every system requires at least a minimal investment in support and maintenance, many have found the growing applications suite burdensome. Mandatory
maintenance and upkeep expenses for operational systems come to consume
an ever-increasing proportion of the available funds. This in turn has shut out
further potentially valuable development initiatives.

Despite this ever-growing legacy reality being widely recognized, many organizations have been constrained from or chosen not to bite the bullet and continue
to delay rationalization. Paradoxically, a stand-alone risk assessment of a major
rationalization project will identify the project as 'high risk' while allowing the
status quo to remain unaddressed.

And of course, application legacies create risks in the underlying infrastructure
layer, a large Australian Government agency providing an example:

> *Centrelink's central data store is a Computer Corporation of America Model
> 204 database, an ageing system that runs on an IBM mainframe installed
> in the mid-1980s. So important is the Model 204 system to the agency's
> operations that while the rest of the world has moved on, Centrelink has
> built, and continues to maintain, the biggest 204 site in the world. Model
> 204 isn't Centrelink's only database. The agency operates numerous
> database platforms, including Sybase, NCR Teradata, Oracle, IBM DB2
> and Microsoft SQL on a wide range of hardware and operating systems.*
>
> (*The Australian*, 2004)

Those stuck with legacy systems are at least dealing with the devil they should know.
As will be seen, the alternative of moving to new systems is far from risk-free.

IT application risk profiles

New applications

New applications are risky for a number of reasons:

1. Projects are required to implement them – and, as discussed at length in
   Chapter 4, it is far from straightforward to deliver a high-quality system solution on time and within budget. Two further issues require specific coverage
   for new applications replacing old:
   (a) Data migration will need to occur in concert with the introduction of new
       functionality, the need to map data correctly across into a new database
       while preserving the integrity of the old and meeting the validation rules
       of the new is a particularly challenging sub-project in its own right.
   (b) Switching over from a system that is known – and hopefully trusted –
       to a new and unknown system can require a significant stakeholder

    management exercise – to build confidence – on top of the normal project load. From a risk mitigation point of view, back-out plans will also often need to be comprehensively thought through and will be 'new' rather than standard deployment practices associated with the current system.

2. New bugs as well as new features can be introduced – importantly, any bugs that make it through to the production environment will be unknown to the users who, even if well-trained in how the system should be driven, will need to operate using ad hoc and unofficial workarounds for a time.

3. Performance, particularly under load at peak times, can be difficult to predict and assure with confidence for expected volumes – this can be further complicated when the actual usage patterns and overall business volumes are difficult to predict, as in the launch of an on-line business in which customers are an uncontrollable user base.

4. New component technologies are often deployed – in a 'learning environment' for the IT operators, all idiosyncrasies and outright flaws may be difficult to detect and resolve in a timely manner.

All this adds up to create an inherently less predictable operating environment, which is higher risk for the business. The good news is if the risks are managed well as the system is 'bedded in' and the user community remains faithful to the change agenda, then these new application risks are temporary.

Whether old or new, a full understanding of application risks requires a consideration of packaged software against custom-built software.

Packaged software

The initial risk management stance for most new applications should be biased towards the selection of packaged software. Advantages are provided through the comfort of dealing with a 'known quantity' at both vendor and product level:

• Vendor track record and viability to support a product can be assured – with a base of customers to support, the core application support team can be expected to have a high level of specialist skill and understanding of the complete code base; and

• Product features can be verified, either directly through product trials and tests or through access to the existing user group for reference purposes.

The CFO will probably be more supportive of the 'buy' rather than the 'build' alternative, because the solution should be cheaper; however, it is important that everyone understands the risks too.

Buying something that others also use is fine, and notionally a lower risk, but what if it isn't what you need (Sumner, 2000)? Dell decided SAP R/3 didn't support its processes (Scott and Vessey, 2000) and the FoxMeyer Drug Corporation claims that its SAP R/3 system sent the company into bankruptcy (Scott and Vessey, 2000; Markus, 2000). Hershey in 1999 (Scott and Vessey, 2000) and Cadbury–Schweppes more recently (*AFR*, 2004a) have also experienced post-implementation difficulties that have been material. Not only is chocolate not always sweet, a number of garbage disposal companies have also 'dumped' their ERP projects (Scott and Vessey, 2000).

Let's start with the assumption that you have a set of requirements for the solution and that you have selected a product that is the 'best fit'. Even then it may fall significantly short of meeting all of your requirements.

There is a fork in the road. Many choose to abandon their specific requirements and revert to a vendor-defined view of how the world works. In doing so, many argue that business advantage available from the unique application of IT is lost.[70] At the fork in the road, others will choose to customize, thus introducing a divergence from the vendor's product lifecycle.

The two main issues that arise in a customized installation are: the limited support you will get for the customizations and the surrounds, and the difficulties of upgrading and keeping in step with the next version when it is released.

It is necessary, therefore, to justify and tightly contain all customizations – developing them whenever possible as 'configuration' of base software or as cleanly separated 'add-ons' – and to deliberately limit the extent of the core product changes you make.

All commercial systems have flaws, many of them known. The vendor's fix priorities will not necessarily match your own. As a consequence, you may be left with a reliance on workarounds for known bugs for an extended period of time. The larger and more vocal the user base, the better the bug-fixing support and it is here that moving with the crowd has its risk management advantages. Some of the users of the established ERP systems, such as SAP, are into the third generations of their software and find it stable, mature and providing plenty of functionality. Older versions remain supported almost by popular decree – or by the collective fanning of cheque-books!

Chapter 7 on service provider risks addresses problems that can arise when software product vendors are relied upon, specifically:

- Functional gaps opening up as business requirements change;
- Incurring cost and expense of upgrading software at a forced pace in line with vendor's aggressive upgrade cycles;
- Being locked in to proprietary solution limitations that restrict interoperability; and
- Relying on promises that remain unfulfilled, particularly in relation to vapourware.

---

[70] Carr (2003) argues that there is little opportunity for competitive advantage through the unique application of IT. We take up this theme in Chapter 10.

Custom-developed software

So if your assessment of vendor and packaged software risks suggests handcrafting your application is the way to go, what are the main specific risks to manage?

Despite your conclusion that your business requirements are best met by a purpose-built solution, a large proportion of your business is subject to the same rules and constraints as anyone else's. Equally, the large parts of the IT system 'below the waterline' are almost certainly very similar to others'. While reinventing the wheel is not necessarily a major risk, it is important to recognize that you can get this wrong mainly because your team has not done it before. The undesirable result is a high rate of defects in the delivered product.

As you are the only user, you are also the only 'bug catcher'. There is no vendor proactively patching the software for known bugs before you strike them. This will manifest as cost and effort in the testing and rework cycle or a more significant impact and cost of fixing the system once it is live.

Upkeep and enhancement of the system will be your responsibility and you'll need to maintain the necessary skills and application knowledge. Bear in mind that most IT professionals greatly prefer a development challenge to the maintenance and support role, and usually place documentation at the bottom of a 'to do' list.

Software assets and liabilities

Your application portfolio should, of course, be an asset. You may have capitalized past software development and deployment activity and this may represent a significant item on your balance sheet. But is your software also a liability? You have no freedom to simply junk the ones that don't work for you and risk of loss through misuses is in some cases unlimited on the downside (Verhoef, 2002).

Controlling your application assets

Understanding what you have got – establishing and maintaining a controlled register of applications and understanding where they are deployed – is a basic prerequisite.

Tellingly the Y2K project for most companies commenced with an extensive 'discovery' phase which sought out and described all of the software in the place, most of which was not catalogued. Unfortunately, since the Y2K period has passed many companies have let these basic controls lapse.

Once you know what you have got, then it is important to build effective controls around the applications, in line with the criticality of each.

Software library and version control practices ensure that you retain a tight link between deployed, executable software back to the source code – or other 'trustworthy' source (e.g. formal and unaltered software release from a vendor). Production changes must be migrated from development and test environments – and only after the change has been assured will the new software be migrated into the centralized computing production environment and packaged for deployment into the distributed computing environment.

Software as intellectual property

Many large companies invest significant amounts of money on the development of software assets[71] and then pay little attention to protecting the investment from loss or exploitation. Should they?

While undertaking the development you will, in most jurisdictions, have automatically obtained copyright protection. This makes unauthorized copying of the application software or related artefacts illegal. General employment and contractual confidentiality provisions should limit those involved in development from 'making public' or taking your application to a competitor.

In some jurisdictions, and depending on the terms of engagement, the original authors – the developers – may claim a right to assert authorship and to prevent 'debasement' of the software product, which for most is not a big deal.

However, let's not ignore the skulduggery. Your starting position should be to assume that any software developer who had access to the source code has a copy on a form of removable media somewhere – at home, under the bed, etc. And your competitor who just poached your top programmer? They probably have a pretty good understanding of your systems by now. What is the worst that could happen – they rip off your best ideas and show themselves in the market in their real 'me too' colours? As the saying goes, copying is the sincerest form of flattery.

For most it is generally not worth the hassle and effort to obtain and enforce patents. If you come across a patented area in building your applications – interestingly, and the subject of wide debate, including Amazon's business methods patent of the online shopping experience ('Method and system for placing a purchase order via a communications network', US Patent 5960, 411) – you may need to work around it – so as not to infringe it – or license it. Lawyers will advise.

Software licenses

For software that you have licensed from service providers and obtained from other sources there are two main risks:

---

[71] For example, the Australian Commonwealth agencies together report an intangible asset value for computer software greater than the total of all other intangible assets (ANAO, 2004). Unfortunately only 30% of agencies have a policy that dealt with these intellectual property assets.

1. Not having enough and incurring liabilities or penalties for being caught using unlicensed software; and
2. Having too many licenses and paying too much.

Assuming you have control over the distributed computing infrastructure (refer to Chapter 9), and have imposed administrative controls and policies in place to limit users from 'do-it-yourself' activities, managing stability in this area is straight-forward and predominantly administrative.

If the assets aren't under control of IT administrators and electronic discovery tools aren't installed, then you'll be flying blind. In such a case it may be better to carry more rather than fewer licenses from a risk management point of view.

If you are acting as the creator of software that is distributed to others, a whole raft of additional risks opens up in relation to adhering to the licence obligations for any component software that you may have wound into your IT product.

Unwanted and unwelcome software

While everyone with an external network connection is exposed to the threat of viruses and other unwanted and unwelcome software, your corporate IT software is also potentially the specific target of attack or exploitation.

The broad impact of the malicious activity of releasing a virus guarantees the headlines.[72] The localized malicious deployment of software is far more likely to be covered up by the victims.

Unwanted and unwelcome software can make its way onto your systems from many paths, for example:

- Email-borne viruses that pass through filters and blockers and exploit email software features;
- Sharing of files via removable media such as disks or USB drives;
- Inappropriate downloads from the Internet; or
- Deliberate and malicious implanted software – going by exotic names, such as Trojan horses, back doors and time bombs.

For viruses, a number of different strategies are adopted – from simple 'don't click on email attachments' advice to users through to ubiquitous deployment of anti-virus software and frequent updating of the anti-virus signatures. On the author's PC the anti-virus software lists over 67 000, last updated yesterday. This

---

[72] You may recall the 'excitement' whipped up over the Love Bug virus when it reached the Pentagon (*ABC*, 2000b). At the time Lloyd's of London estimated a US$25 billion damages bill, most of which was uninsured (*ABC*, 2000c). In 2004, although still claiming headlines, the stories are marching away from the front page and no one seems to calculate the damages any more.

is one of the most fast-moving of the IT risk categories, fortunately with a mini-IT-industry behind it in the anti-virus and network security management camp and the necessary plentiful on-line resources to keep the specialists in your team up to speed.

Making sure your core applications and production systems remain 'pure' – that is, only running the software you intend to have running – requires a range of controls that include the security 'essentials' covered in Chapter 6 and other controls aimed at avoiding dreaded 'turned insider' risks. Key to these is vetting of personnel prior to them entering the 'inner sanctum' of IT and critically examining credentials (Caelli, 2002).[73]

The lifecycle approach to managing risks

Effectively managing IT application risks requires an understanding of the lifecycle each system goes through and the key risks you can avoid, mitigate and contain at each step.

Setting the systems agenda – strategy, architecture and planning

When the system is merely a twinkle in the eye, significant risks can be avoided.

- Prioritize delivery schedules and understand dependencies – establish the capability, capacity and constraints of your IT delivery function and match this with the scope and scale of the requirements for changes to the application portfolio, prioritize and sequence your initiatives to achieve maximum 'bang for buck'; and
- Establish the architectural 'plot' – fit any new applications into the application portfolio by identifying and resolving scope and 'interconnectedness' problems, mark out the applications nearing end-of-life in order to minimize further enhancement and establish guidelines for the evolution of established applications.

The IT project chapter (Chapter 4) addresses in detail the risks of IT solution delivery and how they can be best managed. The following sections provide application risk management tips for each stage of the project lifecycle.

---

[73] The cybercrime annals on www.usdoj.gov/criminal/cybercrime/cccases highlight many criminal incidents from current and former insiders in addition to those perpetrated by hackers and outsiders.

Concept and feasibility

The main risk management objectives of this stage are first, to stop foolhardy initiatives from progressing further and second, to set the winners off on the right course with business and IT delivery efforts aligned.

- Confirm feasibility – make sure the business and IT thinking is aligned around the concept. What is it you actually want? And the solution: What can actually be delivered? Develop 'order of magnitude' estimates and ensure the price tag matches the budget or otherwise revisit scope. Use prototyping to bring the 'mock' application to life.
- Get the overarching logic right – establish where you will make additions and enhancements to the existing applications portfolio and which component of the application will deliver the required business functionality. Establish the criteria the delivered solution must meet.
- Consider all the options – consider buy vs. build and the risks of each, establishing the credentials of IT service providers who you may rely on if you proceed.

Requirements and solution architecture

The main risk management objective of this stage is to avoid rework by specifying the solution right before it is built. The architecture design in itself is a midpoint deliverable that can be rigorously assessed for quality (Losavio *et al.*, 2004) although it rarely is. You will also actively manage delivery partner contracting and technology acquisition risks during this stage.

- Prioritize requirements – refine estimates and confirm what you must have, should have, could have and won't have within the scope of the solution.
- Define interfaces – establish explicit 'contracts' between multiple teams working on different systems that must integrate.
- Choose technology components – weigh up and select the technology components that you will acquire, adapt and modify, confirming the reliability of the source, the quality of the product and the viability of continuing support.
- Achieve design completeness / cover all the dimensions – navigate and jump all the 'sign-off' hoops, encompassing business stakeholder engagement for signing off on the business requirements and IT specialist engagement for the technical solution.[74]

---

[74] Designing security into the IT system may be assisted by the functional building blocks set out by Rannenberg (2000).

Solution build, acquisition and integration

Now the coding begins for the custom-built components and the tailoring or configuration of the acquired software. The main risk to avoid is the introduction of defects in the parts and integration 'gotchas' for the whole.

- Divide and combine – the system design must be decomposed so it can be assembled by multiple specialist teams working in parallel, but it must also come back together as a whole. This task is further complicated for initiatives requiring multiple releases of software and where application and infrastructure overhauls are proceeding simultaneously.
- Stick to assurance principles – process and product assurance techniques must be applied consistently throughout this phase, for each of the application components, with focused audit for high risk modules (Sherer and Paul, 1993).

Testing

The main risk management objective of this phase is to identify unacceptable defects and confirm they are resolved.

- Confirm completeness and correctness – using both positive and negative testing to confirm the system operates according to its specification and in line with business requirements.
- Build confidence – demonstrate correct functioning of the system end-to-end for key business processes.
- Gain acceptance – provide the evidence to support acceptance of solution components from delivery partners and business acceptance of the whole.

Implementation

The main risk management objective is to avoid disrupting the business as changes in the application portfolio are introduced.

- Rehearse the day – practise the technical aspects of going live with a representative set of system users so that the timing, sequence and potential impact is clearly understood.
- Seize the day – mobilize the implementation team, follow the rehearsed implementation plan, verify and validate the success of implementation.
- Back it out – have a Plan B that is also rehearsed which returns the business to normality. You'll have to try again.

Maintaining and evolving systems

Removing bugs from an application – in the worst case to enable it to be brought back on-line from failure, more generally to prevent the recurrence of previous incidents or avoid future anticipated incidents – is a core part of 'business as usual' for the IT function.

Unfortunately, due principally to the complexity of systems and the inability to test IT systems exhaustively, fixing one bug can introduce another.

At any rate, the constant 'band-aiding' of systems will, over time, make them more fragile and difficult to fix. At some point the accumulated band-aids will need to be pulled off. This is best conceived as a mini 'lifecycle' for the renewed software.

Retirement and decommissioning

Unfortunately funding for this 'clean up' activity can be hard to secure: rarely is there money set aside for the end-of-life costs (no matter how reasonably foreseeable!) and there are no obvious beneficiaries.

Rarely is 'just switching it off' an option. Obligations to retain records for 'historical' purposes – although often poorly articulated due to gaps in electronic records management, are potentially of legal and regulatory significance.

Moving off a system that has reached the end of its useful life is ideally woven into a 'replacement' project which takes into account data migration and the introduction of 'like for like' (or better!) functionality.

Unfortunately for some with antiquated core systems that really must go, this procedure can be likened to radical organ transplant surgery – with its associated costs, risks and potential impact.

While the lifecycle approach is not a guarantee that applications will be risk-free, it offers positive steps that are distinctive at each stage. Understanding what stage of the lifecycle applies to a particular application gives you a focus on the questions to ask and the range of remedial actions that are available to you.

Health check

This section assists you consider at a macro-level the company's IT application risk health, for input into the IT risk portfolio assessment.

Is this important to your business?

- You have advanced IT applications that support your business strategy and contribute to your source of competitive advantage.
- Incorrect processing of information within your systems could cause significant cost and disruption company-wide.

- There are serious consequences of systems failing to act dependably that may include loss of life.
- You depend on more than a handful of applications to inter-operate.

> *If you agree with two or more of the four statements, then IT application risks are important to your business.*

Are you doing the right things?

- You regularly assess the functional and technical quality of your applications.
- All significant changes to applications are tested effectively before the systems go into production.
- An architectural blueprint for applications guides current and future development of interrelated systems.
- Acquired software packages and custom-developed software adhere to agreed and common standards.
- Your key business requirements for IT systems are met from your existing application portfolio.

> *If you agree with these statements, then you are doing the right things in your organization. If you disagree with three or more of the five statements, then there is significant room for improvement in your IT application risk management capability.*

Do you have a good track record?

- There have been no significant commercial losses from IT application failure.
- Systems are the source of user delight rather than complaint.
- Your applications can be changed with relative ease and a high degree of confidence.

> *If you agree with these statements, then you have a good track record of managing IT application risks. If you disagree with one or more of the three statements, then there is evidence of the need to improve IT application risk management capability.*

Case study: Leading water company

One of the world's largest water companies, servicing tens of millions of customers, provides a comprehensive range of services including water process engineering, customer services and asset management.

As part of the drive to deliver more value from the core business, the delivery of IT development and support was outsourced during 2000 to a pool of IT service companies. An independent delivery partner was appointed with overarching responsibility to deliver clear measurable business benefit through IT-enabled change.

Aligning application portfolio development to the business need

In order to meet the operations division's business needs, a program was established with a governance structure that ensured sponsorship at a senior level whilst delegating business ownership to operations managers. The coupling of the business with the IT delivery programme ensures a close fit between the application teams – resources primarily drawn from the pool IT vendors – and the business units ultimately responsible for delivering the business case. This approach also ensured the focus on benefits was achieved from application development mobilization, and not bolted on at the end of development prior to deployment.

Managing risks and delivering the business case

The operations program is responsible for the successful delivery of the portfolio of projects with their associated benefits. Within the program, the individual project teams are led by a pool partner and made up from a mixture of people from the pool partners and different parts of the user organization. In developing the pool partner project delivery approach a number of key principles were developed to manage risk:

- The pool partner's project manager is the single point of accountability for delivery of all aspects of the project, including liaising with the water company's staff to roll out the business change.
- The project embraces both the business change and the technical delivery; these are both the responsibility of the project manager.
- Contract structures are in place that apportion risk according to which party is best able to manage that risk.

- Fortnightly reporting to the programme team with regular, planned-for audits on project and technical delivery.
- Recognizing the value of offshore development but the real challenges faced in communication between on-shore and offshore.
- For offshore development projects, the project manager remains on-shore while the project focus, and the balance of the project team, typically moves on-shore (definition, outline design), offshore (detailed design, development, system test) and finally on-shore (acceptance and implementation).
- A project is not finished until the benefits are delivered.

The result has been the creation of effective project teams delivering projects, and their benefits, on target.

Printed with permission of PA Consulting Group

9 Infrastructure

Servers on wheels

In 2003, two thieves, who posed as authorized computer technicians from the outsourced provider EDS, were allowed access to a highly secure mainframe data centre and after two hours emerged wheeling two servers away. Worryingly, in the days of international terrorism, this theft was from Australia's Customs department in Sydney's international airport (*ABC*, 2003; *SMH*, 2003). It later emerged that two further computers were missing and this was not picked up for some months due to poor asset tracking.

Upgrades and merger integration don't mix

In April 2004 ANZ bank stopped a major project that had been running since 2001. The Next Generation Switching project had aimed to deploy new infrastructure technologies into the core transaction network of ATMs and EFTPOS machines. Continuing with the project at the same time as completing integration with the recently acquired National Bank of New Zealand was considered too risky (*AFR*, 2004e).

Difficulties with the US Navy fleet (of PCs)

Early in 2004 EDS realized they were in trouble on a US$ 8.8 billion contract to support the desktop fleet of the US Navy. Some of the contributing reasons include: a failure to understand how military requirements differ from the requirements of corporate customers, vast underestimations of scope and complexity and poor estimating of the cost and difficulties of servicing the fleet of 345 000 PCs. EDS project losing US$ 400 million on this deal in 2004 (*WSJ*, 2004).

While the boxes and wires are, for most of us, the least sexy part of IT, they are nevertheless prone to their share of risks. This chapter helps you divide and conquer the IT infrastructure landscape, understand the evolving nature of infrastructure risks and guide you on both keeping the lights on and successfully executing major transformation.

How IT infrastructure failure impacts your business

The delivery of IT services requires a solid foundation. Do you have adequate capacity to process and carry the volumes of data that will flow through your organization tomorrow?[75] Will systems stay up and running when they are needed? Can they change to meet evolving requirements?

If your infrastructure fails, the applications and IT services can come tumbling down like a deck of cards. In thinking through the potential impact, it is most useful to decompose the IT infrastructure landscape into five generic areas: facilities, centralized computing, distributed computing, data networks and voice networks.

Additional types of IT infrastructure are required in different industries – these are outlined here at only a high level.

Facilities

All of your physical sites and buildings are points of vulnerability. The essential ingredients for an IT installation are power, air-conditioning and physical safety and security of the installed devices and their operators.

Recent widespread power failures in Europe and the USA have illustrated the reliance many organizations have on 'the basics' continuing uninterrupted – or being rapidly restored.

While some environmental threats – earthquake, fire and flood – can dramatically strike the facilities, less dramatic but occasionally impressive impacts can result simply from a rodent's gnawing.

When co-locating you are sharing facilities with others. While risk reduction advantages due to the professional management of the facilities and the building compliance with engineers' data centre specifications are obvious, there may be a downside. More people will be coming and going and deliberate attack – from outside or turned insiders – may be more likely on the site due to the accumulation of targets.

The risk mitigation measures for facilities include: back-up sites, uninterruptible and redundant power supplies including back-up power generators, redundant air-conditioning units, bunker-like construction, access control security measures, monitoring and escorting of visitors. Managing IT risks in this space overlaps with ordinary building and facilities management, but has plenty of special 'twists'.

---

[75] The World Health Organization experienced an unprecedented spike in demand for its online services when the SARS outbreak suddenly positioned them as the authoritative source for the public. Capacity planning based on historical trends would not have been sufficient to prepare the organization and Maximum Tolerable Outage perceptions changed overnight.

Centralized computing

The centralized computers, the enterprise application and database servers, are most often identified as the heart of the IT landscape. Certainly the data centre managers would have us all think so!

Failure

If these centralized systems keel over then all hosted services go down, information processing ceases and all users are impacted. Depending on the nature of the outage, information assets are also at risk of loss or corruption.

In cases of deliberate and malicious attack on your systems these risks are heightened – if indeed the objective of attack was to damage rather than merely snoop.

Unfortunately often the knowledge of the mapping of IT services to infrastructure is incomplete – the consequences of Box A 'going down' are poorly understood and in times of crisis confusion reigns.

Here is the focus of the classic incident and disaster recovery response: bring the standby system into life, recover and restore data, bring up the systems and confirm that all is fine. In Chapter 6 on IT service continuity risks the full recovery of service to users is the objective and this step is simply one of many along the way.

We will proclaim again here – given the continuing lack of focus of organizations on these practices – it is essential these basic procedures exist in a documented form and that rehearsals and tests of the DRP are undertaken regularly.

The 'gold-plated' technology solution that many aspire to and few attain, often because of the price tag – is to have no single points of failure, full and automatic fail-over to a 'hot' standby site that is a mirror of the production platform. If chasing this technology dream, do not overlook the need to bring the right people on the journey.

Performance degradation

Perhaps the less obvious risks relate to degradation of service from the centralized computing platforms.

When the volume and timing of IT transactions is unpredictable – an increasingly common situation for all Web-based systems which cater for customers as end-users – an unacceptable performance degradation can occur with relatively little notice.

This occurred in early 2004, when Qantas announced its new bargain domestic Australian airline – Jetstar – with a fanfare offer of discounted tickets, and Virgin Blue – its competitor in the space – immediately responded with a 'see you and double' counter-offer. As bargain-hunting customers went into frenzy –

both on the phone and via the Web – those customers of Virgin Blue who had already bought full-fare tickets (including one of the authors!) were caught in 'holding patterns' on the phone and Web as the underlying systems ground to a halt (*AFR*, 2004g).

The need for tight capacity management, including proper planning and allocation of resources in advance of the demand and facility to scale (expand) the infrastructure is key to being able to avoid severe consequences from systems running 'like a dog'.

Third party reliance

As almost universally the infrastructure components are procured rather than built in house, other wider risks relating to centralized computing platforms tie back to technology vendor risks (explored in more detail in Chapter 7 on IT service provider risks):

- The willingness for vendors to sign up for a 'fix on fail' deal within guaranteed response times is contingent on you staying on the current versions of hardware and software;
- The provision of proactive patching and maintenance releases of technology products is similarly reserved for current and supported versions (Lawson, 1998); and
- Operations and integration problems in a multi-vendor environment can increasingly result in finger-pointing when failure occurs that can't be slated back to an individual product's performance.

To keep in step with vendor-supported infrastructure components you'll need to make timely decisions to migrate and bring the business community along with an appropriate justification. Many companies have found themselves in a tight spot due to hardware obsolescence and expiring vendor support.

Distributed computing

Assets in the distributed computing infrastructure – most obviously the individual user's client device such as a PC – are less important in their own right than the critical servers. Loss of a single device will typically impact only one user's IT service experience.

While frustrating for the user – who amongst us hasn't ranted at the poor helpdesk staff about PC failings! – this typically isn't a headline risk item.

The issue of information asset loss or exploitation – certainly made much easier when IT assets are portable – is dealt with in Chapter 6. The key mitigating action is to host enterprise data on servers rather than PCs, or at the very least to offer some form of back-up solution for those with enterprise data on 'their' PCs.

Sitting between the centralized and the end-user IT asset are a host of other network, access, local services and security computing assets, including for example local area network file and print servers, remote access and firewall devices. These are typically exposed to a mix of the risks associated with centralized computers (many users can be impacted when they are down) and end-user assets (they are typically easier to steal or damage than the data centre kit).

When we draw together the entire distributed computing base, a number of key issues arise:

- Viruses and other unwanted software can spread rapidly and infest a distributed computing environment;
- Attacks on the centre can be staged from an outpost;
- Liabilities for operating with unlicensed software can be significant;
- Costs can be notoriously difficult to understand and control; and
- Service delivery consistency continues to be elusive to even the specialist managed IT services providers.

Best practices in control of distributed computing assets require the establishment and maintenance of a baseline – a 'source of truth' asset register – introduction of standard operating environment and software loads, a 'lockdown' approach where only administrators can alter the base configuration and remote administration techniques. Specific products have their part to play – such as subscription-based anti-virus software.

Maintaining currency – again important for vendor support – is also often required to satisfy the appetite of increasingly demanding and IT-sophisticated end-users. However, the costs of 'refreshing' the desktop fleet can be far from refreshing for the managers who foot the bill!

Data networks

Connectivity is an increasingly important feature of the corporate IT environment. When links are down, or bandwidth constrained, IT service quality can degrade rapidly.

Network redundancy and resiliency – alternative routes for the traffic to follow – are key traditional design principles to adopt to reduce risks of individual link outages.

However, when you or your customers are using shared and public networks, such as the Internet, your business remains vulnerable to system-wide service disruptions. A key question for every business manager at risk of IT failure is:

How vulnerable is your core business to failures or extended outages of the Internet?[76]

In answering this question, consider four common IT services that are Internet-enabled:

• Customer access to on-line services offered by you;
• Supply chain partners linking with e-business applications;
• Your staff accessing on-line services for business purposes; and
• Use of email for business transactions.

In addition to Internet reliance issues, specific carrier and managed network service provider dependencies are common, along with the associated third party reliance.[77] Many customers will be subject to standard terms and conditions which are set out by the network carriers and may not truly reflect their service standards and risk management requirements; larger customers may be the only ones with negotiating strength to dictate terms.

As the world increasingly converges to Internet Protocol standards for data networks, issues of security and bandwidth management reign supreme:

• A plethora of technology products and services purport to offer at least part of the 'answers' to the continually evolving security 'problem'. These offer to authenticate and identify users, establish secure sessions and encrypt traffic, protect from intrusion, detect intrusion, gather forensic evidence, etc. However, for every new security defence there is a new form of attack, requiring the ongoing vigilance of specialists.

    Further network security management considerations are covered in Chapter 6 on Information asset risks.
• Issues of effective bandwidth management – achieving delivery and performance certainty – over mostly shared, public and packet-switched networks remain problematic.

    In the meantime the use of connection-oriented services goes on – the old 'leased line' remains the only real alternative for securing point-to-point data network performance – and this suffers from being an obvious single-point-of-failure.

---

[76] In a recent online survey (Whitman, 2003) of IT executives, 95% of respondents use the Internet to provide information, 55% to provide customer services, 46% to support internal operations, 27% to integrate value chain partners and 18% to collect orders.

[77] A telecommunications failure in Australia resulted in the loss of half of a major bank's ATMs and the Australian Stock Exchange was forced to close, suspending trade for a morning (*ABC*, 2000a).

Emerging technologies continue to offer up challenges. For example, many early adopters of wireless data networks have exposed themselves unwittingly to security vulnerabilities.

Voice networks

The integration of voice and data networks is a contemporary trend that will perhaps make this part of the IT infrastructure landscape defunct in the next few years.

For now, most companies have the 'fall back to phone' option when the computing and data network infrastructure is down. Rarely is the PABX and public switched telephony service (PSTN) down at the same time.

Those migrating to 'Voice over IP' may well benefit from lower costs, but most will have a heightened vulnerability to outage due to the consolidation of both voice and data communication over the same transport.

As the traditional voice network component is a relatively stable and mature part of the enterprise's IT infrastructure, with an acceptable performance track record, it is likely not to be the focus of risk management attention. Those with tightly integrated computer and telephony, inbound or outbound, call centre infrastructure are perhaps the exception to this general rule.

Industry-specific infrastructure and risks

The ubiquity of computing technology was highlighted in the Y2K scare which gave coverage to the risks of flaws in distributed and embedded computers: lifts not working, office building doors not opening, electricity generation and dispatch functions stalling, robots on manufacturing plants going wild, aircraft control systems failing, etc.

While the specific issue – inability to handle the date change event – is now behind us, what became obvious during the Y2K period is the high reliance on computing technologies across all spheres of human endeavour.

As an example, recent work on process control systems highlighted particular vulnerabilities in the changing risks of the industry-specific infrastructure challenges:

- Historically, process control systems were designed and built using proprietary technologies and installed in isolation from ordinary IT systems. However, recent trends have been to base newer systems on more cost-effective platforms (e.g. standard PCs).
- Furthermore, the desire for remote control and management information has led to the adoption of common network protocols and the connection of many of these systems to the corporate IT network.
- While these changes have certainly yielded many business benefits, it has also meant that control systems now possess more security vulnerabilities and are

increasingly exposing these weaknesses to the same threats faced by corporate networks – notably viruses and malicious hacking (US NIST, 2001).

IT infrastructure's evolving risks

As your IT infrastructure evolves so do the risks. Understanding this evolution will help you to frame your risk management approach accordingly.

Migration of IT application features into the infrastructure layer

Traditionally when programmers were set a task of writing a new application they started from scratch. Computers needed to be directed at a low level and in precise detail, tailored to the hardware, to perform even basic tasks – like storing a piece of information in memory.

Over time the features of operating system software grew to fill out the common requirements of managing input, output, processing and control of peripherals.

Other software was developed to handle files, databases, certain types of system operations – such as back-up and recovery – and various utilities were built to run as companion and support tools. Some were bolted onto the operating systems and others became adjuncts.

Application features that might have required laborious coding and customization many years ago can be programmed quickly now with a 'hook' to an infrastructure layer feature.

While application development has become more efficient, the reliance on the infrastructure layer has become more significant. Vulnerabilities in acquired infrastructure components are inherited by any system that is built on them.

For example, a database management system may allow 'back door' access so that data is able to be changed directly. This infrastructure element and its associated tools, such as low-level file maintenance programs, can detract from the integrity of the application. Thus critical information can be easily corrupted without the normal controls imposed by the application.

Market dynamics of infrastructure

The cost of IT progress – new IT infrastructure that is faster and better and has more features – is obsolescence. New products attract new customers – and this is where vendors fight to stay in business: growing and retaining market share. If you have chosen an IT vendor without a new product pipeline they won't be in business for long.

Most companies are better off moving with the herd and sticking with the established technology vendor leaders. In this game how good (or new) the product is – technically – is rarely the deciding pointer to the least-risk route. As a consequence it is important to balance the influence of the engineers, who have a penchant for new toys, in the buying cycle.

Why timing is important

The time value of money concepts within financial circles suggest that a dollar tomorrow is worth less than a dollar today. In buying IT infrastructure the value equation is the other way around. For virtually every IT infrastructure purchase decision being made this year, it'll be cheaper next year.

While the natural response of delaying purchases is seductive – particularly for the procrastinator in all of us – this tendency must be set against a rational appraisal of the total costs and risks of running the existing infrastructure.

In theory one could infinitely defer replacement acquisitions – running systems until they literally ceased to operate. After exhausting and failed 'resuscitation' attempts the battle is conceded and the asset is wheeled out to the junkyard.

'But what about the risks to my business?' I hear you cry!

What about the cost and impact of the 'surprise' downtime and the scrambling and unpredictable search for a replacement? What about the degradation in service performance that might occur under load in the meantime? What about incompatibilities through the infrastructure layers that might result from retaining old components?

In short, these costs and risks can significantly outweigh the differential between this year's infrastructure component price and next year's.

Significant research by Broadbent and Weill (1997) identifies the category of 'enabling' enterprises that build out IT infrastructure in advance of need.[78] Thorogood and Yetton (2004) utilize real options theory to justify the upgrading of IT infrastructure in anticipation of an organization change: the capacity to rapidly and flexibly deploy business applications has a (call option) value that justifies the infrastructure upgrade.

However, timing remains extremely important. You don't want to be the first onto a vendor's product – you'll be one of the guinea pigs – and you don't want to be the last – it'll be too soon time to change.

The emerging utility model and some risks to consider

Users of IT are extremely interested in the 'on demand' promises of the emerging utility computing model. It is best to view this as more of a direction and a trend than a destination.

---

[78] In contrast, they identify 'dependent', 'utility' and 'foregone' views of IT infrastructure that are reactive, cost-reducing and absent, respectively, in their strategic postures.

The features of a utility model for IT – in which you 'plug in' and consume what you need and pay only for what you use – can be partially achieved today and is clearly flagged by major vendors as a direction for tomorrow.

Supporting technology directions include: autonomic and self-healing computers (they manage and fix themselves when something goes wrong), grid computing[79] (delivering virtually infinite capacity on demand), Web services (network-hosted and -invoked application components), and storage virtualization (allowing effective shared use of a large pool of storage resources).

From a risk management perspective, there are a few things to understand:

- Pooling and sharing IT infrastructure does increase your dependencies on others – the extent to which you are willing to expand your 'circle of trust' should carefully consider a range of IT risks including in particular information asset and IT service continuity; and
- The extent to which your legacy IT infrastructure will be able to 'plug into' the new IT infrastructure may be constrained – as a consequence the costs and risks of changing across must be considered.

We move now from the evolutionary perspective to the here-and-now.

Moving towards 'set and forget'

Most business managers are not so enamoured of their IT installations that they could be called 'box huggers'. They are quite happy with the IT infrastructure being out of sight and – if it is working – out of mind. Their preferred risk management strategy we'll call the 'man and a dog' approach. The man is there to feed the dog and the dog is there to bite the man if he tries to touch any of the controls!

This 'lights-off' operating nirvana is elusive – even for those who chase it – and 'set and forget' a completely inappropriate management stance for enterprises reliant on their systems.

There is a wide range of capability that must be in place to actively manage, operate and support IT infrastructure. Much of the spending in this space is really risk-related and couching it in these terms is useful.

Table 9.1 draws upon the Information Technology Infrastructure Library (the most widely accepted approach to IT service management) practices and the risk mitigation or avoidance outcomes associated with each.

Other necessary practices that might be more familiar relate to basic housekeeping, administration, operations, tuning and monitoring of systems. The mundane task of archiving data from a server is seen as important only if it isn't

[79] Connecting multiple distributed computers and harnessing their combined power.

Table 9.1—ITIL service management components (UK OGC, 2001)

Why do?	*To manage risks of . . .*
Service level management	Delivering a service that falls short of requirements Failing to act on issues of under-performance
Financial management	Misallocating IT costs and over-spending
IT service continuity management	Loss of service beyond the maximum tolerable outage (refer to further details in Chapter 5) and inability to respond in times of crisis
Availability management	Unacceptable downtime and unreliability
Capacity management	Running out of headroom to cater for tomorrow's business volumes Paying for storage, processing and connectivity capacity that you don't need
Security management	Losing or compromising valuable information assets
Incident management	Impacting the business when service disruptions occur
Configuration management	Losing control of valuable IT assets High-cost and inefficient systems management
Problem management	Repeated occurrences of system failures that haven't had the root cause addressed
Change management	Defects in production systems that cause costly errors and impact users' productivity
Release management	Loss of integrity and consistency in operational systems

done – the disk will fill up and the server will be unable to store any more. The integrity of back-up copies of critical data becomes important only when you need to bring it back!

Now if you have obtained assurance and are confident that those in charge of the IT infrastructure from day to day have all this in hand, you may be able to take a management-by-exception stance.

Over and above the IT infrastructure service management responsibilities, when things go wrong and fall out of the ordinary it will be necessary for 'escalation' to occur. The business managers at risk of IT failures must be clearly 'wired in' and be ready to call the shots on restoration and remediation priorities. Bear in mind, if customers need to be told bad news it shouldn't be coming from the IT department and ditto for the press!

De-risking infrastructure transformation

If the trouble and warning signs from day to day are overwhelming and a major overhaul of the IT infrastructure is required, how can this initiative be de-risked?

We won't repeat here the project-related guidance of Chapter 4 – we'll focus on some of the top infrastructure-specific challenges.

Set direction

Even IT infrastructure projects require some form of governance. Notwithstanding the technical nature of the work being undertaken, it is important for the business goals and objectives to be established and any 'no go' zones clearly set out.

We have found the use of 'guiding principles' set at the commencement of infrastructure-related initiatives to be important.

Typically these address the following:

- Priorities of time, cost and quality of the solution – for example, must be done by X, must be done for less than Y, must not introduce high-severity defects and incidents;
- Extent of business impact during change that is acceptable;
- Expected durability of the solution expressed in terms of business growth and/or expansion;
- Stance on accommodating or freezing changes during the course of the transformation project;
- Acceptance or prohibition of publicity around the initiative;
- Service provider rules of engagement;
- Financial transparency and opportunity to control and/or audit;
- Stakeholder consultation requirements; and
- Consistency or alignment with a defined IT strategy and end-state architecture.

These principles form a frame of reference for the transformation team.

A step at a time and fall-back ready

In the GCHQ case study described at the end of this chapter, a major IT transformation and relocation was described as 'a bit like rebuilding an aircraft carrier from the keel up, whilst it is at sea and flying its aircraft operationally'.

In this project it was simply too risky to attempt to move systems, people and data in a single jump. A step-by-step approach helped reduce risk.

However, as timescales were typically tight, there was generally not the luxury of organizing this as a serial project. Multiple tasks needed to run in parallel and be synchronized with precision.

Each implementation of major IT infrastructure change was supported with a fall-back or back-out procedure that had been tested and rehearsed.

A useful analogy from rock-climbing: beginners are told to move only one hold at a time. Only once the new grip is secure will the three-point hold be released.

Health check

This section assists you consider at a macro-level the company's IT infrastructure risk health, for input into the IT risk portfolio assessment.

Is this important to your business?

- You spend significant amounts of money on IT infrastructure assets.
- Performance and reliability of systems is important to your business and your customers.
- You have a complex IT infrastructure installation with multiple network links to business partners and the Internet.

> *If you agree with two or more of the three statements, then IT infrastructure risks are important to your business*

Are you doing the right things?

- Your critical IT infrastructure components are all current and supported versions.
- Capacity management plans are kept in place for all critical platforms.
- Your disaster recovery plans and incident response plans are maintained and tested regularly.
- Incidents and problems are resolved in accordance with a repeatable process.
- Your IT infrastructure is well documented.

> *If you agree with these statements then you are doing the right things in your organization. If you disagree with three or more of the five statements, then there is significant room for improvement in your IT infrastructure risk management capability.*

Do you have a good track record?

- You have avoided significant commercial losses from IT infrastructure failure.
- Your systems run reliably and at the required level of performance.
- You consistently meet the business service level requirements for systems performance.

> *If you agree with these statements, then you have a good track record of managing IT infrastructure risks. If you disagree with one or more of the three statements, then there is evidence of the need to improve IT risk management capability.*

Case study: GCHQ[1]

Designing and managing Europe's most complex IT relocation

GCHQ is responsible for signals intelligence and information assurance in the UK, working closely with the UK's other intelligence agencies (commonly known as MI5 and MI6), the Ministry of Defence and law enforcement authorities. Signals intelligence supports government decision-making in national security, military operations and law enforcement. Information assurance defends government communication and information systems from eavesdroppers, hackers and other threats and helps protect the UK infrastructure (such as the power, water and communications systems) from interference. GCHQ is a 24/7 operation and is supported by one of the most advanced IT facilities in the world. The UK's national security depends on GCHQ's operational integrity and continuous availability.

GCHQ wanted to consolidate its operations from 50 buildings spread over two sites and move its 4500 people to a single, purpose-built, high-tech facility. The key benefit sought from this move was a change in the way the organization worked – to become more joined-up and flexible. To realize this benefit GCHQ needed both to alter its business processes and to develop new systems that could be integrated with the existing 'legacy' processes and systems. These changes had to be made whilst moving to the £337 million new headquarters, known locally as the 'Doughnut' due to its shape, which is big enough to contain the Albert Hall inside the space at the heart of the immense building.

The complexity of the relocation was increased by the scale of the IT infrastructure – over 5000 miles of communications cabling and 1850 miles of fibre optics run through the building and the fully equipped computer rooms cover an area equivalent to approximately three football pitches. Over 100 discrete systems had to be moved to the new building – each larger than the IT facilities of most UK corporations, including probably the largest supercomputer cluster outside the USA. The relocation and transformation programme comprised over 60 highly interdependent IT, relocation and change projects with a combined value exceeding £300 million. GCHQ's design authority described this complex programme as being 'a bit like rebuilding an aircraft carrier from the keel up, whilst it is at sea and flying its aircraft operationally'.

The contract to manage the requirements of this relocation implemented a systems engineering approach to designing and building complex systems. This methodology applied to designing, building and operating the 'whole system' and covered every aspect of the business, including people, operations, technical infrastructure, support and, importantly, how the overall system will evolve. Combining with GCHQ's body of knowledge a highly capable and integrated team was formed to be able to deal with the immense complexity involved.

A key element of the programme was to develop an approach that addressed the complexity and scale of the problem:

- Step-by-step approach to minimizing risk: Business continuity dictated that the systems, people and data could not be moved in a single go. Instead, the team developed a step-by-step approach that involved the re-engineering of the legacy systems, integrating these with new systems while addressing business issues, and finally moving the people.
- Overcoming the complexity of the program: Meticulous planning, issue management and dynamic testing all helped to make this complex task achievable. For example, to assure business integrity during enhancements to existing IT applications, the team implemented 'roll-back' systems. These ensured that if a change was applied to an existing service and it did not work as planned, then the service could quickly revert to its previous stable state, without any interruption to GCHQ's operations.
- Simulation models: A major part of the approach was to use computer simulations – for trade-off analysis, performance analysis, reviewing behaviour, failure mode analysis and scenario testing – to help decide on a safe course of action to support the business under all foreseeable circumstances.

The programme met the aggressive schedule within budget, delivered the benefits sought and maintained the continuity of GCHQ's critical intelligence operations throughout the move. The UK's National Audit Office Report of July 2003 commented, 'Other government departments might learn lessons from the way that GCHQ developed its program management arrangements for the hybrid change program.'

Printed with permission of PA Consulting Group and GCHQ

Note: [1] Formally Government Communications Headquarters but known only as GCHQ

10   Strategic and emergent

Degrees of failure

Although the strategic vision was wonderful: *Margaret Hodge, Minister for Lifelong Learning and Higher Education, said: 'I want the UK to become the leading producer of quality on-line higher education. UK eUniversity Worldwide is key to making that vision a reality. This joint venture creates new opportunities for many students.'* (Sun, 2001)

It has been a bad week for information technology in the public sector. The worst casualty is the Government's flagship e-university, hailed by ministers as the Open University for the 21st century. It is to be quietly dismantled after embarrassing performance failures . . . The UKeU, launched amid fanfares at the height of the dotcom boom in 2000, aimed to market and deliver British university degrees worldwide through the internet . . . But £35 million later, it recruited only 900 students. Now the Higher Education Funding Council for England says that it will 'scale down and transfer' its work. In other words, the plug has been pulled.

(*The Times*, 2004)

Enquirers looking for information about the eUniversity are now given the sad message: 'Enquiries should now be directed to the Higher Education Funding Council for England.' (ukeu.com, 2004). *And the IT assets have been put up for sale.* (*Public Technology*, 2004)

Or a competitor with a technology edge?

While it can be argued that the emergence of the Y2K problem as a business issue was the best example of an emergent risk, a more specific example is helpful. The irrecoverable loss of market share by Barnes & Noble to Amazon was a nightmare scenario for the boards and executives of mature, blue-chip companies. Their safe, established positions could be not simply eroded, but savaged by a company with a technology edge. Barnes & Noble was the time-honoured leader in the book retailing segment across North America. Yet it was unprepared, both in strategic terms and in terms of its technology development, for the Internet customer.

The message was clear and strong for many industries with fragmented markets, products that could be digitized or global opportunities. The responses ranged from prescient to comical.

This chapter opens with a discussion of the impacts on the business of IT strategic failure. Next follows an examination of the role of IT in business change and the contribution to shareholder value. We close with an analysis of the much-touted link between IT and strategic agility and responsiveness.

The impact of IT failing to support the execution of your business strategy

Just as the organization's strategy is not announced in neon lights over the entrance to corporate headquarters, the support that IT delivers to the strategy is not immediately apparent. While neither strategy nor the IT support role is highly visible to outsiders, they may not even be clear within the organization. In even a moderate-sized organization, the role and contribution of IT are often hidden by the complexity of the systems, their usage and their interconnections.

Does business strategy drive IT or vice versa? Or are they developed together? Even informed executives within an organization may not immediately agree (Clemons, 1991). For most organizations, the business strategy clearly comes first and IT needs to deliver systems, applications, tools and techniques that support and enable. However, IT may have been neglected to such an extent that it is unable to respond. Alternatively IT may have gone down a path of technical challenges that diverge from business goals or needs.

Graceful degradation

The slow, continued decline in IT capability that arises from failure to renew, refresh, retrain and reinvigorate is not apparent on a day-by-day or week-by-week scale. Even in an annual review, critics may receive harsh retaliation. External benchmarking can become unacceptably painful. On a daily basis there is no imperative for change, but if this continues indefinitely, the organization ends up with a reduced capability to envisage IT benefits or to deliver them. This is the 'boiled frog' syndrome[80] of reality denial.

Of course the opposite is no better – would we want our dilemmas to be otherwise? – the overreaching of an organization, beyond the level of its IT

[80] How to boil a frog! Place in cold water under a gentle heat; supposedly the frog does not perceive the incremental change. (No animals were harmed in the writing of this book.)

capability, leads to the myth of Icarus.[81] Many organizations have 'bet the farm' with technology developments, only to find themselves at best spending many years in rebuilding their assets.

The life experience of the professional person anywhere in the world includes several such aspects: spending enough time with the children, keeping the weight and waistline in order, balancing work and home. Nothing is critical today, but after ten years it can be too late.

Choose a grail, any grail

IT is one area of the organization that is at extreme risk of 'mantra-itis' or being driven by a fad, slogan or management holy grail. Sometimes this sounds quite respectable, such as when trying to 'align the IT with the organization' (Strassman, 1997). From the 1970s' slogan of 'better MIS with better decision-making' to today's 'agile computing', there is much risk in chasing a slogan over following a real goal that has relevance to the business.

It is going noticeably wrong when this goal is espoused by IT, but the rest of the organization is unaware. The likely suspect when talking about IT supporting the business strategy is the goal of aligning IT with the organization.[82] Almost every CIO will endorse this, claiming to have already achieved it, or to be pursuing the path. Obviously the contrary is untenable: 'No, we don't bother about aligning with the business, we're just making sure we're the best IT shop around!' But a reasoned assessment shows that concern with strategy is critical, but a direct mapping is generally very high risk.

What is needed for most organizations is the ability to respond, in a reasonable time and at reasonable cost, to strategic initiatives as they emerge. Business strategy can change much more quickly than IT. A complete IT refresh and rebuild over a period of ten years would be extremely demanding for many organizations, yet corresponding changes to strategy are feasible. Flexible IT infrastructure is much more valuable (and lower risk) than close tracking of each strategic move.

The goal that is often foisted upon IT is one of reducing its own costs consistently each year. An arbitrary percentage, such as the convenient round figure of 10%, needs to be achieved – whatever the strategic imperatives. While this can be realistic for utility inputs, such as server capacity and bandwidth, when outputs are constant, it is seldom capability-building or enhancing. It may bring about its own variety of graceful degradation, as the IT infrastructure is patched up so that more important development projects can proceed.

---

[81] According to legend, Icarus flew so close to the sun that the wax attaching his wings melted, leading to his death fall.
[82] Bergeron *et al.* (2003) in an innovative study illustrate methods for analysing and interpreting IT alignment with the business.

Diversity versus standardization

In terms of the survival of species, there is an ongoing debate whether the generalist or the specialist does better. The generalist species – with a wide variety of diets and territories – is less vulnerable to change than the specialist – which is able to flourish exceptionally in good times, but may face extinction during the bad. However, the generalist never experiences the boom, but is resilient during the bust. Similarly for IT infrastructures, there is a danger in being highly tuned to a particular environment, should that environment change. Adaptability comes through diversity, but diversity inevitably incurs additional costs. Standardization such as a 'common operating environment' for PCs will reduce total costs of ownership, but will entail higher costs should an unforeseen change be required. Higher opportunity costs if the change is not made and higher roll-out costs if it is.

It would be a disaster if a financial market player required all of its foreign exchange traders to utilize the common PC standard, and wasteful if support staff had the same facilities as the traders. Clearly mature decisions involve applying appropriate technology. This is not always as apparent as this example when looking at different support staff, for whom IT facilities may well be seen as utilities.

For most organizations, email is a utility that must be standardized across the organization. However, if one group needs secure email, it is necessary to define email out of the common core of applications that are fully standardized. In its place the organization may instead opt for two or three standards, according to real needs. It is here that much judgement and persuasion are needed, as sectional interests will always argue for special needs. As Albert Einstein is supposed to have said, 'Everything should be made as simple as possible but no simpler.'[83]

Flexibility in determining the appropriate adoption of standards is the approach when trying to avoid the risks at each end of the scale. Some small-scale experimentation with emerging standards and technologies can greatly assist in the standardization decision, but early adoption carries its own risks.

IT doesn't matter[84]

Carr argues powerfully against the perception that IT has strategic importance:

> As information technology's power and ubiquity have grown, its strategic importance has diminished. The way you approach IT investment and management will need to change dramatically. (Carr, 2003, p. 41)

---

[83] See, for example, Peter Neumann's recollection: www.csl.sri.com/users/neumann/neumann.html
[84] Carr, 2003.

The uniqueness and scarcity of a resource are the attributes that give it strategic effect, but IT is available to all, and at reducing unit costs. Thus the opportunities are available to all and at similar costs. However, the risks and hazards become proportionately larger. While organizations have obtained competitive advantage through IT, in many cases it is short-lived. Sustainability of an advantage is almost impossible, as new technologies will erode the previous advantage and the leapfrogger will eventually be leapfrogged.

The stunning, almost overnight, success of Google as the Internet search engine of choice cannot be seen as permanent in and of itself; it will require continuing development, at least. The challenge of sustainability is heightened by the fact that there is now a clear target for thousands of researchers and innovators. Eventually the barrier will be breached.[85]

The important corollary in this view is that the downside risk outweighs the upside potential: '*When a resource becomes essential to competition but inconsequential to strategy, the risks it creates become more important than the advantages it provides*' (Carr, 2003, p. 48).

When, for most organizations, IT is comparable to their competitors', with no distinguishing benefits, the danger comes from its failure. Much like the fact that most cars on the road can comfortably match posted speed limits (sometimes many times over) leads to similar journey times for beaten-up wrecks and limousines, yet a breakdown humbles even the best.

> *It's unusual for a company to gain a competitive advantage through the distinctive use of a mature infrastructural technology, but even a brief disruption in the availability of the technology can be devastating. As corporations continue to cede control over their IT applications and networks to vendors and other third parties, the threats they face will proliferate. They need to prepare themselves for technical glitches, outages, and security breaches, shifting their attention from opportunities to vulnerabilities.* (Carr, 2003, p. 48)

Yet there have been clear strategic opportunities in the past and it is obdurate to suggest that they have now all become extinct (Farrell *et al.*, 2003). It is simply that most opportunities will be short-lived, and the majority of organizations will not achieve them.

Sustainability

There is a difference between sustainable competitive advantage and sustainable competent development. The critical competency for most organizations is to be

[85] In a press release relating to Google's IPO, Standard & Poor's reveal that more than six out of ten Google users would switch search engines if a better service came along (Standard & Poor's, 2004).

able to deliver the incremental improvements in IT that are required, as Beard and Sumner (2004) demonstrate for ERP systems. An innovative application, a bold new step, can provide a strategic impetus that propels the organization's competitive position forward. At that point the benefit has been achieved, but sustaining the competitive position requires both continuous improvements, as others will be following closely, and an absence of strategic initiatives from competitors. The strategic advantage initially created through the innovative use of IT may become a strategic position based on market share or dominance. IT's role is then one of 'not messing it up'.

The counterpoint of 'sustainable competent development' merits explanation. It is here that the role of IT is demonstrated in assisting and supporting the organization in its strategic manoeuvring. Consistent competence in being able to define IT needs and then implement them will ensure that whatever the organization's strategy, IT will be able to be depended upon to play its role. This relates back to the IT governance questions that face senior management and the board. Knowing that IT can both define and deliver gives the strategic leaders the confidence that wherever the organization goes, IT will be able to play its part.

Sabre-rattling

Do you have first mover capability? Can you do 'leading edge' if you need it? These capabilities are necessary if a broad range of strategic initiatives are to be announced, even if not seriously intended. In the dot-com boom era, many entrenched, mature industry players announced broad initiatives into the e-world. There were many cases of announcements not being followed by delivery. Was it that the leading-edge or first mover capability was lacking? Or, were the announcements simply intended to deter start-ups from entering the field, letting them know that 'big guns' could be brought to bear?

Such announcements demand credibility. If an organization doesn't have the capability, industry gossip will quickly erode the perceived strategic threat. On the other hand, an organization that is known to be IT-capable, that has a track record of delivering sound IT investments, will be able to deter upstarts readily and buy themselves valuable time. In such situations, being certified as CMM level 5,[86] for example, gives significant bite to an announcement, even if it is bluster. The corollary is, of course, that organizations with a negative capability reputation will have their strategic utterances involving IT derided, further diminishing the organization's standing. Most organizations fall into the middle ground, with some successes and some failures, and a mixed credibility. In such cases scepticism dominates: 'They're going with wireless PDAs! Couldn't even get the finance system in on time!'

[86] The Software Engineering Institute's (Carnegie-Mellon University) top rating for IT delivery capability (capability maturity model).

Driving shareholder value through IT-enabled business change

With Hammer and Champy's runaway success in the early 1990s with their book on business process re-engineering (1993), the slogan of IT as an 'enabler of change' entered the business psyche (Broadbent *et al.*, 1999). Over the last decade 'shareholder value' has gained enormous emphasis. Do the two go together? Does IT enable change? Does that change add value for shareholders? The negative answers are the strategic risks, of course.

With infrastructure projects as the general exception, IT developments bring change to organizations – to the way they are structured, coordinated and monitored. The very essence of an IT project is to change the way things are done, and frequently to change the costs. Costs may be the most transparent connection with shareholder value, if the productivity or efficiency of the business is improved while maintaining or increasing revenues. Such a natural increase in 'earnings per share' is not always apparent in IT projects.

IT is the business – or not

Quite distinct differences in strategy appear for organizations where IT is the business, and for those where IT has a minor role (Chang *et al.*, 2003). When IT is the business – such as for Google, Dell and Yahoo – or the key driver of operational effectiveness and service delivery – online stockbrokers, banks, airlines, telcos, for example – then every IT project is able to have a direct impact on the performance of the organization and, hence, its worth in the marketplace. In a complementary way, many of the strategic initiatives of these organizations will contain a very significant IT component – it is hard to avoid.

But this is not the case for all organizations. Berkshire Hathaway has not made its way to a leading position of investment companies through IT. It would be an unusual investor at the annual general meeting who quizzed the board on their IT strategy. Similarly for Westfield Corporation whose expertise is in shopping centre development. Whatever role IT plays, it is expected only to be supportive by investors. Shareholders expect the senior management to spend their time thinking about shopping centres – land, buildings, tenants, demographics – rather than back office functionality. The only common expectation would be an absence of disasters.

When IT is the business, systems and technologies can differentiate the organization in its marketplace. Dell's capacity to deliver a customer-specified configuration PC in a short timeframe clearly sets it apart from the industry. That the IT is used to analyse price sensitivities to incremental system improvements, as well as to forewarn key suppliers of likely trends, show that Dell drives the organization through IT. IT risks represent risks that propel to the core of the business – as do opportunities. Each strategic initiative, or change, almost certainly includes an IT component, if not being totally IT.

A more generic indicator of the potential shareholder value of IT, is when IT competence or capacity makes it onto the list of significant key performance indicators (KPIs). The drivers of value are assessed in their contribution by KPIs. But there is no immediate connection with change in the organization. The middle ground of organizations obtains some strategic and cost benefits from IT and agrees that IT competency is a strategic necessity, rather than source of advantage.

Enablers of change

While every project brings change in some form, strategic change that has been enabled by IT may not require a fresh project. If the structure, design and functionality of the IT applications have been constructed suitably, the organization can change its complete approach to its marketplace, reinvent its customer face, or restructure its product management functions without IT being involved.[87] Many ERP systems have an enormous range of functionality built into them, to accommodate many business models and methods, yet these can be altered – in principle – through relatively simple means (Hanseth et al., 2001). Of course, if the ERP has been completely customized to fit the current organizational form, the amount of flexibility is diminished.

Internal organizational or structural changes should be within the expected capability of any well-designed system – the ability to change working groups, membership of teams, product categories is essential (Markus and Benjamin, 1997). Failure in this area makes the systems *barriers* to change, rather than enablers (Markus, 2004). It is a commonplace that jackhammers get brought into buildings to make changes that seem inconsequential – sometimes even before the building is complete. A low budget airline flying a fleet of Boeing 737s shouldn't lock out their options by hard-coding all their systems only to meet that specification or the particular seat layout currently in use. Where is the shareholder value in a locked-down system?

Another misspent change scenario exists when IT changes force changes on the organization that have no business benefits (but perhaps serious disadvantages, costs or consequences). The expiry of an equipment lease or IT outsourcing agreement may mean that a wholesale replacement takes place with disruptive effects and negligible gain. Similarly if some vendor software, that is performing completely satisfactorily, becomes an unsupported version. The risks are now so high that a new version must be implemented, but there may be enormous transitional costs, changes in business processes and disruption all around.

However, there are many clear examples of systems enabling organizations to make change that wouldn't be possible, or feasible, without technology. To

---

[87] Yusuf *et al.* (2004) illustrates an emphasis on organizational change in ERP implementation.

restructure the world's 'car boot sale' / 'yard sale' / 'garage sale' disaggregated activity into a thriving single marketplace would have been unachievable to eBay without the Internet and the World Wide Web. But a mundane empowerment of change through technology is the simple workflow implementation built upon email, www and intranet, that enables Corporate Express and other office supplies companies to engage directly in their customers' internal business processes.

Engine room efficiency

This is the very essence of IT's contribution to most organizations: the engine that powers the transactions and customer service that are the central activities of the organization. And as with real engines, efficiency is the KPI that matters most (after reliability). When corporate data centres are significant IT assets for the organization, ensuring that they are efficient, and becoming more so, is essential. Competitors and peers will be in a similar situation and, to avoid a competitive disadvantage, it will be necessary to pursue evolutionary developments in efficiency. It is one of the common benchmarks used by stock analysts to assess competitors in an industry.

So, every year we need to be able to find achievable improvements in efficiency in many areas of IT. This is not the same as routinely cutting the budget by 10%. Obviously data centres with their transaction focus will be a target – but historical improvement track records going back over the years will mean that all the obvious savings have been made and progressive improvements become more challenging. Other areas where utility models are appropriate – telecommunications messaging and routing, batch document printing, data storage and archiving, for example – will similarly be readily available for incremental efficiency gains.

The risk is, of course, not being able to deliver these improvements in efficiency. Is it strategic or emergent? Actually it's both. The basis of competition will be eroded as your organization's efficiency falls behind industry norms, and the dieback is so insignificant in the short term that the difference is not immediately apparent.

The other risk is to regard activities that aren't 'engine room' as if they are. Knowledge management systems are unlikely to have KPIs that refer to transaction efficiency. Being able to find the knowledge required and to deliver it to those who need to know are much more critical. Having the knowledge that enables the organization to win the contract or to deliver its outcomes vastly outweighs the transaction time or message speed.

What matters in terms of shareholder value? Clearly areas where efficiency is a valid measure need to be posting consistent, measurable improvement that at least matches industry benchmarks. But equally importantly, shareholders would want to know that management are able to distinguish between 'engine room' and the rest.

The influence of your IT capability on business capability

Dell has established an astounding leadership position in the PC market with clear advantages in speed to market, agility and responsiveness, overwhelmingly delivered by IT. Its make-to-order model dramatically reduces the volume of product in the supply chain and ensures that new models can be brought in more quickly than competitors as well as reducing the risk of obsolescent inventory filling up the channels. The intellectual property incorporated into the configuration tool, which allows the prospective customer to examine alternative components, enables Dell to determine the price elasticity of individual components as well as correlations between products – whether the customer goes ahead to purchase or not. If the 60 GB disk option is turned down by more than a critical percentage of tyre-kickers, Dell can turn to their suppliers and drive immediate bargains – before a single machine is delivered. The potential customer need not know whether the offering that they are receiving is test marketing, a leading edge 'special' or overpriced to buggery (to use a technical Australian term).

Those that don't have Dell's capability face the strategic risk, where their IT does not enable equal market facing competence. Of course, not all organizations need to be able to perform at this level, but the risk is that your organization's IT doesn't deliver the agility, responsiveness and speed to market that is demanded of the strategists.

IT as turbo booster / brake

The capability that is needed for speedy responses to market conditions needs to be built into the architecture of the IT.[88] It is as if a turbo booster is designed into the systems so that management can simply hit the button to deliver extra power on demand. If this is missing, all you have is a brake, which may not be apparent. Rapid response capability is designed in; although the responses themselves may be unpredictable at design time.

For many organizations a strategic decision to start 'bundling' products, so that customers buying two products or services received a special pricing package, would require re-engineering of conflicting software systems (and perhaps restructuring of the organization) to present a unified view. In some cases such future scenarios could not have been reasonably envisaged by developers – and shouldn't strategists have put that potentiality into the system specifications, anyway? Other organizations are effectively boxed in by merger and acquisition activity conducted by senior management with only a cursory nod to IT during due diligence. A post-merger force-fit of architecturally dissimilar applications achieves little – and may drive your best IT staff to seek more meaningful employment elsewhere.

---

[88] Weill *et al.* (2002) argue that strategic agility can be created through designing the 'right' IT infrastructure.

Too often IT capability is thought of in terms of the skills and achievements of the IT function, when the underlying architecture is critical, and harder to change. Flexible architectures with broad adoption of standards facilitate change and responsiveness. Risk is measured in terms of non-standard platforms, high levels of specialist support requirements and high levels of customized applications.

Emerging technology

Any examination of responsiveness includes forward scanning of environmental changes, and in this context that represents emerging technologies. Each new technology may enable a significant market-facing response, from you or your competitors. But in scanning the horizon there are two dimensions – breadth and depth. We must work out what range of technologies is to be monitored and the detail level of each that is needed. Given that many technologists get great pleasure and satisfaction from exploring anything new, constraints need to be imposed, but they need to do justice to the business.

As Segars and Grover (1996) point out: *'Reacting to the "technology of the year" bandwagon can be myopic and expensive'* (p. 381).[89] Breadth and depth are interrelated as a 'field of vision' view would suggest that mainstream technologies are the focus and need to be studied carefully, while fringe technologies, that may never achieve business functionality, need only be put on a watch list. Clearly core, currently employed technologies that are becoming post-mature will need to be replaced at an appropriate time and brand new technologies may need to be adopted rapidly should a competitor get in with an innovation.

Timescale is deceptive, and it's painful to say that on this subject Bill Gates is right! He said that what can be achieved in three years is nowhere near what is generally supposed or estimated. On the other hand, our view about what will be the state of affairs in ten years' time is hopelessly inadequate – today's barely emerging technologies may well be widely distributed, substantially developed and maybe even hard to comprehend. A glance back to the Web of 1994 shows that it revealed almost nothing of its power to change the way the world communicates and does business.

But there is another risk here. If technology scanning is the responsibility of the IT function, how will they identify the business opportunities or threats?[90] In many organizations IT can spot the upcoming technology but what it means to the business is not known to them. Involving those business leaders with some interest or motivation in IT in the blue-sky parades from vendors and developers

---

[89] Segars and Grover (1996) identify IT strategic and emergent risk factors at the conceptual level: lack of concrete or understandable strategic plan, no ongoing assessment of strategy, lack of interest by top management in IS planning and lack of skills or methodology for constructing enterprise models. These overlap substantially with our IT governance concerns set out in Chapter 2.

[90] An example is highlighted by Bell (2000) in an analysis of emerging technology and its potential to aid corruption and fraud.

can encourage mutual exploration of the possibilities. It does require intense communication between IT and business leaders to identify those new technologies that will make a difference to the business.

Delivery

In the end, we may be able to spot the technologies that are emerging and make the appropriate strategic decisions at the right time, but cannot deliver. This originates from two distinct IT weaknesses – existing IT assets may not be malleable enough, or IT staff may not have the specific capabilities. The latter is particularly common for new technology but it is not an insoluble problem. The necessity for flexibility of the underlying IT architecture has been mentioned several times but this is where it is felt most keenly. Many organizations were particularly fortunate that their preparations for Y2K required the replacement of obsolete systems; their replacements just so happened to be flexible to accommodate the immediately following needs for e-business.

However, other than the direct failings of IT, it is a commonplace that the IT development can be done but the organizational changes are too challenging. More systems fail through non-acceptance by the business than by failure of IT to deliver. We can see the drastic nature of organizational changes through the corresponding social ones. Technology-based services lead to closing bank branches, but it is not easy to implement. There is difficulty in getting widespread adoption of electronic tags for toll ways or acceptance of road pricing – the technology is the easy part, getting the business or society to change is the challenge.

Health check

This section assists you consider at a macro-level the company's IT strategic and emergent risk health, for input into the IT risk portfolio assessment.

Is this important to your business?

- IT is a driver of value for your business today.
- Achievement of the targets in your three-year business strategy is heavily reliant on IT.
- Your use of IT enables you to be differentiated in the eyes of your stakeholders.

If you agree with two or more of the three statements, then IT strategic and emergent risks are important to your business.

Are you doing the right things?

- IT constraints are factored into your business strategies and plans.
- A current IT strategy is developed and agreed with the heads of the business.
- A target systems architecture guides application and infrastructure component selection.
- Your 'preferred' systems and technology direction is clear.
- Candidate business and IT initiatives are evaluated for their fit against the IT strategy and target systems architecture.
- You maintain an IT service provider and sourcing strategy.

If you agree with these statements, then you are doing the right things in your organization. If you disagree with three or more of the six statements, then there is significant room for improvement in your IT strategic and emergent risk management capability.

Do you have a good track record?

- When strategically important IT initiatives come along they are delivered.
- Your resources aren't squandered on IT initiatives that are poorly aligned with the needs of the business.
- Your IT capability can be 'flexed' to meet changing requirements that may emerge.

If you agree with these statements, then you have a good track record of managing IT strategic and emergent risks. If you disagree with one or more of the three statements, then there is evidence of the need to improve IT strategic and emergent risk management capability.

Case study: Egg

From infrastructure reliability to system delivery and operational performance

Egg has been at the forefront of delivering innovative financial services, marketing across multiple technology channels. With the Prudential as its majority shareholder, one of the largest life insurance and pensions companies in Europe, Egg has led the way in providing an intuitive, customer-friendly and robust service. Initially a telephone banking operation, Egg made an early entry into the Internet environment and has established itself as one of the leading providers of on-line financial services in the UK.

Prudential first launched Egg in 1998, 'a radically new direct financial organization, designed specifically for the digital age'. The timescale demanded a leading approach to program organization and management, backed up by project coaching and working within a progressive culture.

Egg achieved on-time launch, meeting five-year targets within the first six months, establishing the brand as a UK household name and attracting more than ten times the anticipated number of customers. Following this success, Egg quickly realized the competitive advantages of exploiting Web-based technologies to design an organization 'specifically for the digital age'. To achieve this goal, Egg needed to provide customer value over and above expected banking transaction processing, which in itself would mean a huge reliance on IT systems and support. Any systems architecture developed would have to be capable of dealing with massive transaction volumes that were hard to predict. Specialist knowledge and expertise was necessary to ensure that issues related to infrastructure and related platforms were addressed, including:

- Developing an architecture based on the optimal mix of 'best-of-breed' e-commerce systems solutions that would enable on-line trading, and would anticipate the development of a financial portal and the building of virtual communities.
- Establishing a stable technical environment in which multiple development projects could work effectively;
- Introducing an integrated process that brought the development, operations and support functions together to ensure accurate release deployment and maintenance of service integrity; and
- Proactively managing capacity and network planning capabilities.

Overall the robustness of IT infrastructure and performance has meant that services have been consistently reliable, providing the customer base with fast and seamless transactions. Egg was one of the first companies offering personal financial solutions that made comprehensive use of the Internet on a fully integrated basis. Egg has grown to be arguably the most visible Internet financial services company in the UK.

Printed with permission of PA Consulting Group and Egg

11 IT and other enterprise risks

Having established the need for IT governance, the benefits of proactive management of the IT risk portfolio and having explored each of the seven classes of IT risk, we now turn to examine other enterprise risks and the relationship with IT.

You can't put a fence around IT risk and separate it from the remainder of your organization's activity. IT is intimately associated with a range of business activities that are sources of risk and, as such, has a key part to play in the control environment. IT risk managers must team with those managing enterprise risks from other perspectives – in their line roles or as functional specialists – to ensure IT risks are given the right priority and that opportunities for IT systems and services to assist in managing risks of different types are leveraged.

Furthermore, at a general level, IT can facilitate the wiring-up, locking-down and constant surveillance of your business, and specifically in the domain of risk management information systems, IT will be relied on for advanced risk analytics and reporting.

Finally we examine IT risk management reliance on a range of other organization capabilities for effective preparation, defence and response: from the strategy-setting role of the business leaders to the physical security role of the building and facilities staff – down to and literally including the janitor!

Divergent perspectives are healthy and ensure completeness in the coverage of enterprise risks, as part of the risk management process is to have more than one layer of control. Guidelines are provided in this chapter to help you manage the linkages and dependencies between IT risk and other risk management activities across your enterprise.

Relating the IT risk portfolio to other types of enterprise risk

It is too easy to refer to IT and 'the business' as if somehow IT isn't a part of the business. Our exclusive focus on the IT risk portfolio needs to be balanced with a consideration of other enterprise risks.

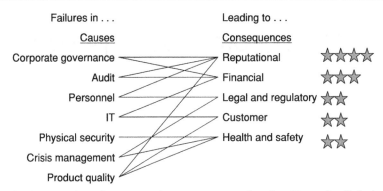

Figure 11.1—Mapping of causes and consequences, showing illustrative links between the multiple causes (of a specific set of events) and their collective consequences

Rating IT risk alongside other risks

Do IT risks rate as one of the top risks in your company?

Let's establish a framework within which to answer the question:

- For consistency of language, we say that (risk) causes lead to (risk) events that then have (risk) consequences;
- Failure within the IT risk portfolio is one of many causes of risk events within the enterprise – one of the many areas in which things can go wrong that can lead to a negative consequence for the business;
- Other risk causes may be totally unrelated with IT risk, or closely related with IT risk – this is known as inter-risk correlation; and
- The consequence for the business will not always be quantified. When measured reliably, it will be available only for past actual loss events and will typically be focused on the normal range of losses or 'expected loss'.[91]

Within this framework we can create an illustrative ratings table of enterprise risks, illustrating the top risk causes and the major risk impacts or consequences, experienced within a given period (see Figure 11.1). The focus here is on the major 'hits' taken by the enterprise and the contributing causes.[92] The lines joining the causes and the consequences indicate the major relationships evident in the risk events experienced within the period. For example, failures in

---

[91] 'Unexpected losses' are those typically large consequences that are outside the normal range.
[92] This approach is similar to the approach taken by the World Health Organization in the World Health Report 2002 (WHO, 2002), in describing the major burden of disease. The leading ten risk factors and injuries are set out with causal links indicated, for example, between alcohol and road traffic injury, tobacco and lung cancers.

corporate governance led to reputational and financial loss. The number of stars is indicating the qualitative or quantitative assessment of the consequence. Note the big 'hit' to reputational loss also resulted from personnel and product quality failures that were contributing factors in the risk events.

In this illustrative example, IT ranks fourth behind failures in corporate governance, audit and personnel as a major cause of negative enterprise risk consequences, for the specific illustrative set of events.

Quantified loss and qualitative loss data should be normalized against the expected losses (normal range) in each category. While 'plain sailing' is desirable, it is not anticipated in any category of loss. Figure 11.2 illustrates this concept. Outcomes range from better than expected (one star), expected (two stars) through to catastrophic (five stars).

Comparability of losses in different categories may be attempted, but will remain open to the charge of subjectivity and may be considered insensitive (e.g. three deaths in our refineries is considered equivalent to how much in fraud-related loss?).

Where quantitative data is available – say, quantified total loss distribution represented as an aggregate annual loss – it may be translated as shown in Figure 11.3. This approach to rating IT risks alongside other enterprise risks reflects the reality that in most organizations priority funding will go towards patching today's gaping holes.

If IT doesn't rate as one of the top priorities then it won't get the priority funding.

To the extent that the top risk causes don't mop up all available funds and attention, management discretion will dictate how the remainder will be shared out amongst those areas most likely to negatively impact the business in the future and look with favour upon those offering cost-effective risk management options.

If you are operating in such an environment, IT risk spend needs to be justified and cannot be taken as a given. The pragmatic questions to ask cover a range of assessment tools:

- Actual loss experience: What are the major 'hits' you are taking? How did the 'things go wrong' and which risk portfolios do the things going wrong lie in?
- Control assessments: How effective are the existing controls and how can they be improved? Where are the most sensible, actionable and preventive risk treatment strategies directed?
- Key risk indicators: Do you have a set of indicators across all the risk areas that are effective in identifying deviations from the expected norms?
- Scenario analysis: For a broadly defined collection of scenarios, how well does your organization respond? Given that the scenarios cut across risk areas through multiple contributing causes, how should your limited risk treatment spend (mitigation) be allocated to ensure maximum effectiveness?

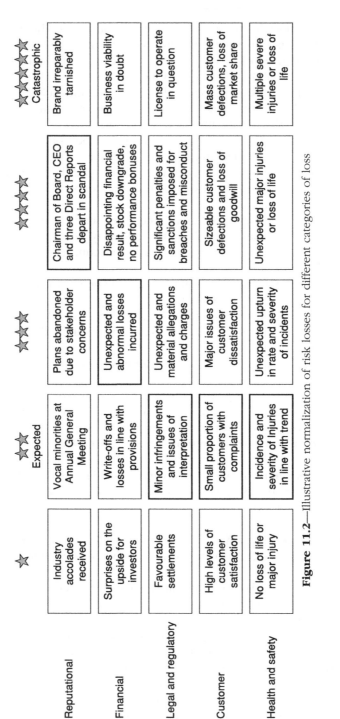

Figure 11.2—Illustrative normalization of risk losses for different categories of loss

	⭐	⭐⭐⭐ Expected	⭐⭐⭐⭐	⭐⭐⭐⭐⭐	⭐⭐⭐⭐⭐⭐⭐ Catastrophic
Reputational	Industry accolades received	Vocal minorities at Annual General Meeting	Plans abandoned due to stakeholder concerns	Chairman of Board, CEO and three Direct Reports depart in scandal	Brand irreparably tarnished
Financial	Surprises on the upside for investors	Write-offs and losses in line with provisions	Unexpected and abnormal losses incurred	Disappointing financial result, stock downgrade, no performance bonuses	Business viability in doubt
Legal and regulatory	Favourable settlements	Minor infringements and issues of interpretation	Unexpected and material allegations and charges	Significant penalties and sanctions imposed for breaches and misconduct	License to operate in question
Customer	High levels of customer satisfaction	Small proportion of customers with complaints	Major issues of customer dissatisfaction	Sizeable customer defections and loss of goodwill	Mass customer defections, loss of market share
Health and safety	No loss of life or major injury	Incidence and severity of Injuries in line with trend	Unexpected upturn in rate and severity of incidents	Unexpected major injuries or loss of life	Multiple severe injuries or loss of life

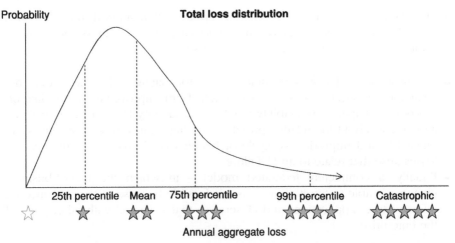

Figure 11.3—Qualitative to quantitative risk analysis mapping

Aligning roles and responsibilities for risk management

Risk management responsibilities are typically allocated widely across the business:

- Line-of-business managers held 'fully accountable' for managing risks that impact 'their patch' as part of the delegation of general managerial responsibilities. These managers are the organization's risk-takers.
- Specialists in risk management, typically associated with a central function (e.g. group risk, risk analytics) assigned to provide support to the line-of-business managers, to provide risk management tools, and to ensure the application of policies, processes and standards is consistent, including standardized methods and metrics for expressing risk.
- Specialists with a narrow focus on specific types of risk events, with attempts to minimize their occurrence and severity of impact: fraud, credit losses, industrial action, money laundering, damage to physical assets, theft, etc.
- Specialists, typically in cross-company functional roles, attempting to minimize the consequences and impact of all risks on the business (including quantifiable losses), focused individually on different areas of consequence: reputational, financial, customer, legal and regulatory, etc.
- Specialists working with non-IT risks and issues that can cause various impacts: people, process, policy, business strategy, etc.
- Auditors (internal and external) typically exert independent whole-of-business review responsibility, to monitor and confirm compliance and adequacy of controls.
- CFOs and others responsible for rationing the allocation of capital across the enterprise intent on seeking the best risk-return outcome.

With this existing complexity, it is readily apparent that support functions, such as IT, with responsibility for delivering services across the business, must take an integrated risk management approach, because:

- The head of IT, if held accountable alone for managing IT risks, would not wear the consequences of loss or benefit from improvements. The line-of-business manager accountability would be eroded by IT's perceived arbitrary judgements about the relative priorities and importance of different risks. An inevitable and unproductive cycle of blame would arise when unexpected losses arise that relate to an IT failure.
- Equally, a completely federated model – in which the line-of-business manager is able to 'go it alone' – is not feasible because of their reliance on infrastructure, applications and IT services that is shared with other parts of the enterprise.

So we have the complexity of shared responsibility, matrix organization and functional specialists working with line-of-business managers. On top of this we are dealing with the challenging topic of business risk and the complexities of IT.

This suggests a strong teaming approach is necessary, bringing together the multiple perspectives and specialists and supporting them with a common language and common risk management processes, supported by common tools and information systems.

Where to focus team efforts

To work out where the most active teaming is required, it is most useful to look at the universe of risks being managed across your business. For each of the risks, you can identify to what extent IT is:

- A potential cause or an important part of the control environment; or
- A key tool to aid risk management activities, particularly through risk information system support.

For those risks that achieve high ratings you will find a requirement for the most active teaming between business and IT specialists on joint risk management activities.

Some generic examples are illustrated in Table 11.1. Summarizing from the example table, most active teaming – between IT and others across the business – would be required on fraud, privacy and credit loss risk management in this case. In particular, advanced IT measures for risk mitigation will be required or expected. For your organization, you would need to identify, for all major risk consequences, the level of IT cause (or control) and how much help you'll need from the IT people.

Table 11.1—Effect-cause chart for typical risk consequences, showing level of IT cause or control, and the level of team support needed from IT staff

Risk consequence	IT cause or control	IT support in team
Product liability	Low	Medium
Fraud loss	High	High
Theft loss	Medium	Medium
Workplace injury	Low	Low
Property damage	Low	Medium
Failure to disclose	Medium	Low
Penalty for breach of privacy	High	Medium
Credit loss	Medium	High
Reputation impact of improper market practices	Low	Low

Banking industry operational risks

The universe of risks and how it is segmented for management purposes differs for each industry. Significant leadership in risk management, including IT, is demonstrated in airlines, military, intelligence, police and emergency services as well as some high-hazard mining and exploration industries.

Banking has been selected as an example because of the elevated position and importance of enterprise-wide risk management within banks, the recognition that banks are at the forefront of operational risk management practice and the particular importance of IT to banking operations makes lessons beneficial to others.

In banks, enterprise-wide risks are commonly defined in four broad categories:

1. Business risks – regulatory, political, competition, reputation, litigation, systemic events;
2. Credit risks – billed receivables, delivered unbilled and forward credit risks;
3. Market risks – commodity price, volatility and correlation, commodity volume, financial (interest rates and Foreign Exchange) and liquidity;
4. Operational risks – processes, technology, people and external events.

The Bank for International Settlements has focused significant recent efforts on the development of risk management frameworks and models, to be enshrined in the New Basel Capital Accord (also known as Basel II) that is to be implemented in member countries by year-end 2006 (BIS, 2003b, 2003c). A primary focus is on capital adequacy of reserves held by banks to cater for risk-related losses.

Operational risk in Basel II terminology deals with 'losses resulting from inadequate or failed internal processes, people and systems, or external events' and is structured into defined risk event-type categories (see Table 11.2).[93]

Risk events directly related to IT risk comprise a small proportion (approximately 3%) of the total value of the reported loss events. If treated as a 'siloed' risk management issue in banks, IT risk wouldn't get much oxygen – leaders of the business would be far more likely to consider the other 97% of risk event-types! In practice banks will rank risks by the capital provision that they need to make.

However, risk events indirectly related to IT risk, where IT can mitigate or control the risk, comprise a large proportion (over 50%) of the total value of the reported loss events. The extent to which IT can make a contribution varies across these risk event-type categories. Let's explore a few:

- External theft and fraud perpetrated via electronic channels may be reduced through improving IT authentication and access control methods;
- Transaction capture, execution and maintenance failures may be reduced through improving user interfaces, data validation and integrity checking at point of entry and rules-based workflow routing for managing processing exceptions; and
- Disclosure of information to clients may be made more consistent through on-line information delivery.

We have also assumed an indirect IT risk relationship between the damage to physical assets and the disasters and other events category, where IT and information assets may be amongst those threatened and damaged.

Notwithstanding the importance of IT-related risks, it is apparent that many types of risk events unrelated to IT risks do comprise a significant proportion of the total value of the reported loss events. Investments in IT won't save the businesses from these types of loss as the root cause lies elsewhere. Minimal contribution by IT specialists to risk management activities in these areas would be appropriate.

Risks of compartmentalizing IT-related risks

If we consider a recent incident at National Australia Bank, where traders were found guilty of 'hiding' mounting market losses – in part to secure individual bonuses of up to A$265 000 – inevitably the 'systems' were brought into the dock along with the traders, their supervisors, auditors, risk management functions, members of the board, etc. All were found to be guilty or inadequate and to

---

[93] Banks provided information about all individual operational risk loss events with gross loss amounts above €10 000 for 2001 within the defined categories.

Table 11.2—Basel standard risk events, categories and their extent (BIS, 2002, 2003a), IT risk relationship added by authors

Event-type category (Level 1)	Categories (Level 2)	Percentage total value of loss events	IT risk relationship
Internal fraud	Theft and fraud	3.77%	Indirect
	Unauthorized activity	1.54%	Indirect
	(No info)	1.92%	
External fraud	Theft and fraud	14.49%	Indirect
	Systems security	0.28%	Direct
	(No info)	0.77%	
Employment practices and workplace safety	Employee relations	5.49%	Unrelated
	Safe environment	0.76%	Unrelated
	Diversity and discrimination	0.39%	Unrelated
	(No info)	0.11%	
Clients, Products and Business Practices	Improper business or market practices	5.32%	Indirect
	Suitability, disclosure and fiduciary	4.63%	Indirect
	Product flaws	0.16%	Indirect
	Selection, sponsorship and exposure	0.70%	Indirect
	Advisory activities	0.27%	Unrelated
	(No info)	2.05%	
Damage to physical assets	Disasters and other events	24.21%	Indirect
	(No info)	0.07%	
Business disruption and system failures	Systems	2.70%	Direct
	(No info)	0.03%	
Execution, delivery and process management	Transaction capture, execution and maintenance	22.08%	Indirect
	Monitoring and reporting	1.80%	Indirect
	Customer intake and documentation	0.32%	Indirect
	Customer/client account management	0.58%	Indirect
	Trade counterparties (U)	0.29%	Unrelated
	Vendors and suppliers (U)	0.29%	Unrelated
	(No info)	4.05%	

varying degrees bearing responsibility for the direct financial losses and associated reputational damage.

Reports on the incident by independent reviewers and the regulator have been made public,[94] and it is a fascinating case. The IT system 'Horizon', which was custom-built, allowed traders seemingly to manipulate at will the information on trades and exposures to conceal their true position.

Of course, on its own these system features would not have caused damage – but if we add unethical and fraudulent intent on behalf of the risk-takers to incompetence in the checkers and overseers and then whisk them together, the result is: A\$360 million lost, four traders and their manager summarily dismissed. Collateral damage losses have also taken the chairman and the CEO (both resigned) and, following the appointment of a new CEO, a 'clean sweep' of executive ranks associated with the debacle: the head of corporate and institutional banking, the head of risk management and the head of global markets.

This case illustrates that IT controls are *necessary but not sufficient* in major bank trading desks, as in many other areas of business.

Let's look at another worrying area: identity theft.

A lot of identity theft is occurring now – the US Federal Trade Commission estimated losses to business, including financial institutions of US\$47.6 billion.[95] To what extent should IT shoulder the blame? Surely 'the systems' should play a part in 'stopping this' or 'picking this up'?

A friend of the authors had her identity stolen and used by the thief at Pizza Hut. She was offended the thief stole her identity and didn't order from a top restaurant! The bogus transaction was mundane and wouldn't have stuck out even if you were looking for it.

Perhaps more obvious was the counterfeit use of a new 'gold' credit card of the wife of one of the authors: three gold ingots purchased from three separate jewellers in Hong Kong in a morning.

Although fraudulent transactions are in many cases handled electronically, which system or systems are we suggesting should pick up the fraudulent transactions? For example, the merchant, the provider of authorization services, the credit bureau, the credit-card issuer, the international credit-card schemes, the banks and financial institutions processing transactions and managing customer accounts may all have a part to play in a solution.

If it isn't possible for a human to distinguish between a real and a bogus transaction, let alone prevent a new customer credit account from being created based on fraudulent records, how can IT alone plug the gap?

---

[94] In a break with the 'sins of the past' the National Australia Bank has opted for full disclosure and has made public all reports on their website.

[95] The US\$47.6 billion is comprised of an estimated US\$14 billion from misuse of existing accounts (both credit card and non-credit card) and US\$32.9 billion from new accounts and other frauds (US FTC, 2003).

It can't. The design of the entire business system – encompassing people, process and technology – must contribute to cost effectively reducing risks to acceptable levels. Where business relies most heavily or entirely on IT to do the task, then most of the opportunity for improvement in risk management controls must come through IT.

In summary, a particular business risk can be looked at in various ways. Where useful, the risk should be compartmentalized, labelled and addressed in a specific way – either on the basis of cause, risk-event type or on business impact or consequence. Certainly we have argued extensively that IT risks require their share of special attention as 'root causes' you should be seeking to control.

However, any scheme to categorize or compartmentalize business risks should not create risk management silos. Our particular concern is that distinctions between IT vs. non-IT risk do not result in a suboptimal response.

Let's now look at the key areas that IT can make a difference to the way your business manages risk.

Supporting risk-based management with IT

Whenever IT is the sinner there is also the opportunity for it to be the saint. When our IT controls fail us, we learn from our mistakes and turn again to IT for the answer: a smarter form of authentication, better encryption, smart cards, biometrics, real-time anomalous transaction reporting, etc.

Just as IT can be applied to yield results that were not previously possible in many fields so too in the field of risk management. In doing so, let's not conceive of a search for an IT 'silver bullet'. No one technology is the complete answer, even to today's problems and issues, let alone tomorrow's more challenging questions.

Next generation technology will certainly be incrementally improved from the last; however, the next generation of thieves, attackers and subversives will also be better equipped and better informed and the next generation of legislation, regulation and compliance more demanding and specific.

The wired organization (now going wireless)

If your organization is wired up – moving to Bill Gates' vision of 'Business at the Speed of Thought' – then it is most probably highly reliant on IT, or else you all sit in the same room or share an extrasensory perception gift.

Rather than traditional end-of-month reports that may have been relied on to identify a dip in demand for a particular product, today's systems might be producing daily or real-time equivalents. Perhaps management intervention has been bypassed altogether and the stock control systems automatically reschedule the plant to maintain inventory levels within the desired band. This example illustrates cost-effective risk reduction of inventory management through the application of IT – bringing risks down to acceptable levels through measured expenditure.

More generally, when a globally distributed management team can be informed of an issue within minutes – and all provided access to a forum in which to debate the right course of action – you have the basis for a better response, particularly when time is money, as is frequently the case during major and unexpected risk events.

Locked-down operating

You can use IT to build in business process controls (Hanseth *et al.*, 2001). Historically, for business processes with low levels of automation there was an option to run ad hoc: open to the whim and idiosyncrasies of the operators. Automation requires precision. As a consequence of automation, the routine aspects of business are increasingly locked-down to a repeatable and predictable pattern. Where variation and variance is the enemy, predictable translates as low risk. Automation is the preferred route towards a six-sigma (one defect per million cycles) or zero defect goal.

Applications enforce business rules: 'mandatory' fields required before a record can be saved, lookup fields used to ensure valid codes are entered, approvals above a certain value routed via workflow for management approval, ATMs won't disgorge money without a valid account and PIN combination, etc. This is an absolutely essential part of controlling normal business operations. It also allows human resources to be busy doing other things, as long as the systems reliably perform the handling as well as the checking and balancing.

In the creative realm, where predictability rapidly leads to commoditization and loss of competitiveness, IT tools are set out in front of the knowledge worker as enablers. Even here, prescribed forms are common, 'suggesting' or 'encouraging' through IT rather than explicit enforcement. How much easier is it to create a letter according to your company's template than start one from scratch? Incidentally, in using the template, you are far more likely to achieve a compliant result.

Constant surveillance

IT can keep an eye on your company and – at least in theory[96] – maintain all the records you'll need to prosecute (or mount a defence) with.

---

[96] Allinson (2001) sets out how information systems audit trails can be used in legal proceedings as evidence and suggests that most would not withstand a serious legal challenge.

While the civil libertarians may be outraged, the majority of employees are docile in their acceptance of their employer's monitoring of their electronic information exchange and website usage. You keep a log of every email I send and receive? And every website I visit? And my telephone call records? And a transcript of my telephone calls with customers? Yep.

The Big Brother scenario is with us, and the employer – while needing to navigate the laws in all jurisdictions to ensure compliance is maintained – has the tools in hand to perform this with ease.[97]

Fortunately, merely the knowledge of the level of surveillance is sufficient to stop most from infringing. For those who trip up, the evidence is at hand.

There is a catch here. Every private email between your executive team is also indelibly etched onto the corporate record and remains open to legal 'discovery' processes for years to come. Acting honourably remains the only long-term course for all.

Decision support, risk analytics and reporting

Advanced risk-return decision-making requires advanced IT support. Can you imagine manually calculating the riskiness of your credit portfolio? Data volumes are huge and the sophisticated models require precise calibration and consistent fine tuning.

Of course your quantitative analysts will turn to IT for the large-scale analysis of risks, as we always turn to IT when the going gets tough and a large number of inputs and mathematical complexity are involved.

The objective of all management information systems is to enable faster and better decision-making; in the case of risk management information, decision-making about known and potential risks. The 'holy grail' of risk management information systems: compatible and efficient IT systems for capturing, analysing and ultimately reporting risks of all types, knitted up across the entire business (Cuneo, 2003). The consumers of output from the risk management information system are both internal – across all layers of management – and external.

Automating risk information management can assist you to embed required practices into your organization by making 'business as usual' risk management activities efficient rather than onerous.[98]

---

[97] Of course, surveillance can be surreptitious, unauthorized and evolving – refer, for example, to the exposures generated through use of instant messaging (Hancock, 2001) with vulnerabilities running well ahead of potential legal sanctions.

[98] The Australian National Audit Office note that: 'An important contribution to fraud prevention is to have a suitable management information system that assists in identifying systemic issues or control weaknesses and helps to manage cases of fraud expeditiously once they have occurred . . . Of particular concern to the ANAO was that approximately 43 per cent of agencies that had reported having experienced fraud in the previous two years also advised that they did not have any form of fraud control MIS' (ANAO, 2003c, p. 15).

Ignorance wasn't bliss, but not knowing was a convenient excuse. With more knowledge comes the obligation to act. If a risk is identified and reported and the required action obvious, the executive who does not act will be later found to be guilty – certainly of incompetence and maybe worse.

As with any application, the risk information management systems may fail – refer to Chapter 8 for further exploration of defects and their impact. In such a case your risk decisioning may be flawed, and systematically so.

The dependence of IT risk management on broader enterprise competencies

Finally we consider how IT risk management relies on advanced levels of competence in other functions of your organization, in particular human resource management, strategy and planning, legal, financial management and physical security. The key question here: Despite best efforts in managing IT risk, what other management capabilities that we rely on might let us down?

Human resource management

People's performance has a strong bearing on IT risks, from the top-notch IT project manager who drives hard to meet a deadline to the diligent systems administrator who checks the integrity of the nightly back-up tapes.

Recruitment When people are brought in carry out an IT role – either as employees or contractors – they need to be 'processed' by HR. We are looking beyond simple payroll form-checking and security card dispensing. Thorough background reference checks can assist you mitigate the downstream threat of insider attacks or other malicious acts.

Performance management Once people are working for you, the system should identify and allow you to weed out underperformers and provide appropriate incentives and encouragement for high performers. We are looking for a balanced regime that rewards both risk-taking and risk-minimizing behaviours. We would have expected destructive effects at National Australia Bank to have been lower if traders' personal bonuses had been risk-adjusted.

Retention A high rate of staff turnover can result in a rapid dilution of your knowledge base and dramatically impact productivity. In particular, if significant systems expertise is lost suddenly from a specialized development team, the ability to make changes confidently and without introducing defects is impaired.

Training and development Sufficient investment is required to maintain the basic competencies, including those required for operating and administering the company's IT and conforming with standard operating procedures and policies.

Strategy and planning

Setting direction for IT starts with setting direction for the business as a whole. What objectives are important for the company? There should be only one IT strategy. This will define the criteria for selecting the right mix of projects amongst other things – both the business initiatives and the counterpart IT projects.

Is a ten-year deal with a major IT service provider desirable? Potentially not, if divestment of one or more business units is on the cards.

Should we stick with our current vendor's technology or is another viable candidate emerging that we should consider?

A business-IT dialogue should differentiate between at least three different planning horizons:

- Short-term: Over the next six to 12 months, what are the top priorities for IT? This indicates where today's limited IT resources need to be allocated and focused now and what they will be doing next. Milestones should be agreed for each month.
- Medium-term: Over the next one to two years, what are the emerging business requirements for IT? This indicates where IT capability needs to develop, perhaps where resources need to be shifted and external expertise bought in. Milestones should be agreed for each quarter.
- Longer term: Beyond two years, what is the direction for the business and IT? This indicates where investment will be allocated and which of today's services may be in the 'sunset phase' and no longer relevant. Milestones should be agreed for each year through to five years out. Beyond this timeframe is challenging.

The IT function serves many parts of the business that may not be completely aligned in their thinking. A process for dealing with ambiguity, disagreement and 'multiple business strategies' may be required – involving the CEO as arbiter if required.

Finally, in many companies, plans can be quite fluid. The cost of 'churning' IT projects (stopping one and starting another in its place) beyond 'concept and feasibility' can be enormous. It is most important, therefore, that greater precision over the short-term plan is agreed and tight 'change control' placed over the six-month committed program of work.

Legal

The main areas of potential IT risk for the legal function to support lie in third party contracts for IT services.

With a solid contractual framework in place, most vendor and outsource service provider relationships operate mainly on 'scope of work' and service level agreement schedules. However, when the going gets rough everyone turns to the contract. The provisions you will rely on must be enforceable.

When IT is required to play a key part in achieving legal compliance, the experts in the respective fields – for example, privacy – will need to articulate the requirements and confirm the adequacy of proposed solutions. This will require their close involvement in the IT project.

Financial management

If there are lackadaisical controls over project spend and 'blowouts' in IT projects go undetected, then the resultant wastage cannot be entirely blamed on those who spent it (in IT) but also on the business unit that channelled the money in and the bean-counters who should have been watching more closely.

It is necessary to place financial controls over the dollars spent in IT in line with the controls over money spent in other parts of the business, in two main particular areas:

- Budgeting – estimating and agreeing the amount to be spent on IT activities – and how this will be cross-charged to the business units; and
- Tracking – capturing and allocating actual spend against the defined budget categories, identifying and reconciling variances.

Physical security

While considerations of physical security have been touched on in Chapter 6 and Chapter 9, we view this as a related but distinct area of competence, apart from IT management.

Every employee, including the janitor, will play a part in securing your company's premises. While IT and information assets are not the only items of value, they are commonly the target of theft or misuse. It is important for all of your sites to raise awareness and promote practices that reduce this loss.

What to look out for? Social engineering and 'tailgating' are practised as art forms. The prescription is quite simple: allow and encourage your staff to be 'rude' and simply don't let people whom they don't recognize into the building.

Sites that house corporate application and data servers must be subject to even greater procedure: identity checking, sign-in, escorting and monitoring of visitors. On these sites it is a matter of not letting anyone in without absolute and explicit authorization.

And here we conclude our brief review of the five key areas of organizational competence that your IT risk management efforts will rely upon: human resource management, strategy and planning, legal, financial management and physical security.

In conclusion

We hope that as a business manager at risk from IT failure you will benefit from our ideas and we wish you well on your journey. Again, bon voyage! For your colleagues who may not get it, can we prompt you with a quote from Dr Seuss (Seuss, 2003):

> *I'm sorry to say so but, sadly, it's true*
> *that Bang-ups and Hang-ups can happen to you.*

Appendix 1: Review checklists

These review questions are to be supplemented by specific issues relating to the project, organization or technology. They complement the project risk health check at the end of Chapter 4. Merely answering 'yes' is not enough; these assertions need to be well supported.

Key review questions to answer: Completion of concept and feasibility stage

Business rationale

- Are targeted business benefits clearly articulated?
- Is the approach for realizing the benefits understood and planned?
- Is there clear alignment with organization objectives?
- Are business and user requirements defined?
- Do executive sponsors and user representatives agree the concept?

Solution and delivery options

- Has there been exploration of various solution options?
- Do solution options exist that are technically feasible?
- Do vendors and internal / external service providers have pre-existing products and service capability that will meet the requirement?
- Are delivery timeframes acceptable?
- Is the technical complexity of the solution understood?
- Are non-functional requirements defined?
- Can the solution achieve compliance with technology architectures and standards and fit within the existing technical environment?

Commercial value

- Is there a sufficiently robust quantification of business benefits being sought?
- Is the range of estimates of project cost comprehensive?

- Will the initiative deliver a positive net present value and / or achieve other 'investment hurdle' criteria?

Organizational impact

- Is the customer and stakeholder impact understood?
- Are related business process changes defined?
- Do the target organizations have capacity to undertake the required change?
- Are internal and external communications effective in raising awareness of the initiative?

Management and delivery

- Are all impacted organizations involved in this initiative?
- Has the project been set up properly?
- Are enough capable resources currently assigned to the project and can future requirements be met?
- Are suitable processes, methods and approaches being applied and are these consistent with policies and guidelines?
- Are roles, responsibilities and reporting lines clear?
- Are the plans for the requirements and architecture phase clear and actionable?

Key review questions to answer: Completion of requirements and architecture stage

Business support

- Are the business case assumptions still valid and is the initiative being actively supported?
- Have business and user requirements been defined at a detailed level and agreed with executive sponsors and representative users?
- Is the basis for acceptance of the solution agreed?
- Is the project on target to deliver planned benefits?

Solution and delivery choices

- Has the exploration of solution options crystallized an optimum technical solution and delivery approach?
- Has the selected solution option been confirmed as technically feasible and a good fit with the business requirements and service level requirements?
- Have the vendor(s) and internal / external service provider(s) with products and service capability to contribute been engaged in solution design?
- Are committed delivery timeframes acceptable and achievable?

- Is the technical complexity of the solution and its dependencies with other initiatives manageable?
- Are non-functional requirements defined at a detailed level?
- Is the approach to assuring and testing functional and non-functional requirements defined and agreed?
- Is the system design compliant with technology architectures and standards?

Commercial arrangements

- Have acceptable contracts been prepared with vendors and service providers including comprehensive statements of work?
- Does the contracting approach leverage your buying power and existing contractual terms?
- Will the solution as scoped for delivery support the achievement of the tangible business benefits initially proposed?
- In light of further detail on total project cost estimates, will the initiative still meet investment and funding criteria?
- Are actual costs incurred in line with original estimates?

Organizational impact

- Has the approach to implementation been developed and agreed with the impacted organizations?
- Have related business process changes been designed?
- Are internal and external stakeholders aware of and involved in the initiative?

Management and delivery

- Are the organizations and people involved in this initiative working effectively together?
- Are project composition and resource levels sufficient to meet current and future project requirements?
- Are suitable processes, methods and approaches bedded down and are these consistent with policies, guidelines and other relevant standards?
- Are the plans for the remainder of the project clear and actionable?
- Are approaches to managing dependencies with other initiatives working?
- Are project processes meeting probity and audit requirements?

Key review questions to answer: Build mid-point

Business support

- Are the business case assumptions still valid and is the initiative being actively supported?

- Have all changes to scope and / or approach been justified and accepted?
- Have users been involved in validating prototypes or designing usability features?

Solution fitness-for-purpose

- Is the technical solution design comprehensive and does it confirm the solution as a good fit with the business requirements?
- Is the system design compliant with defined technology architectures and standards?
- Is the technical complexity of the solution contained and being tightly managed?
- Are approaches to testing agreed and detailed?
- Do test strategies and plans set out what testing needs to be done to ensure acceptance criteria are met?
- Do all solution design elements (data and information management, hardware, networks, software, business processes) fit together coherently?

Delivery arrangements

- Are vendors and service providers delivering in line with agreed statements of work?
- Are interim milestones being achieved with progress in line with plans?
- Are internal activities being completed to the required level of quality?
- Are implementation plans, including handover activities, defined and agreed?

Commercial arrangements

- Will the solution being delivered support the achievement of the tangible business benefits initially proposed?
- Are vendors meeting their contractual obligations and receiving payments in line with the achievement of interim milestones?
- In light of further detail on total project cost estimates, will the initiative still meet investment and funding criteria?
- Are actual costs incurred in line with original estimates?

Organizational impact

- Has the implementation and benefits realization plan been developed and agreed with the impacted organizations?
- Do internal and external stakeholders remain involved in and supportive of the initiative?

Management and delivery

- Are the organizations involved in this initiative working effectively together?
- Are project composition and resource levels sufficient to meet current and future project requirements?
- Are suitable processes, methods and approaches delivering results and are these consistent with policies, guidelines and other relevant standards?
- Are the plans for the remainder of the project clear and actionable?
- Are approaches to managing dependencies with other initiatives working?
- Are project processes meeting probity and audit requirements?

Key review questions to answer: Testing, acceptance and implementation mid-point

Business support

- Are user representatives actively involved in testing and validating the solution?
- Are the business case assumptions still valid and is the initiative being actively supported?
- Have all changes to scope and / or approach been justified and accepted?

Solution fitness-for-purpose

- Have all solution elements been delivered and assembled in line with the plan?
- Are tests being executed in line with the test plan?
- Is the number and significance of defects being discovered acceptable?
- Has the system compliance with defined technology architectures and standards been assured?
- Are non-functional elements of the solution being tested and assured appropriately (security, resilience, capacity, performance, operability, scalability, maintainability)?

Delivery arrangements

- Have vendors and service providers delivered products and services in line with agreed statements of work and expectations of quality?
- Are test incidents being effectively investigated and defects resolved rapidly?
- Are delivery milestones being achieved?
- Are internal activities being completed to the required level of quality and timeliness?
- Are conversion, implementation and cut-over activities being planned and carried out effectively?

Commercial arrangements

- Will the solution being delivered support the achievement of the tangible business benefits initially proposed?
- Are vendors meeting their contractual obligations and receiving payments in line with the achievement of milestones?
- In light of further detail on total project cost estimates, will the initiative still meet investment and funding criteria?
- Are actual costs incurred in line with original estimates?

Organizational impact

- Are the target organizations ready for implementation?
- Have the change management activities been planned and agreed?

Management and delivery

- Are the organizations involved in this initiative working effectively together?
- Are project composition and resource levels sufficient to meet current and future project requirements?
- Are processes, methods and approaches delivering results and are these consistent with policies, guidelines and other relevant standards?
- Are the plans for conclusion of the project clear and actionable?
- Are approaches to managing dependencies with other initiatives working?
- Are project processes meeting probity and audit requirements?

Key review questions to answer: Post-implementation

Business results

- Is user take-up of the solution in line with expectations?
- Are the system users satisfied with the functionality?
- Are business benefits being realized from utilizing the system?

Solution fitness-for-purpose

- Has the solution met the required service levels since implementation?
- Have post-implementation support and maintenance issues been resolved quickly and effectively?

Operations and support arrangements

- Have vendors and service providers completed handover of products and services in line with agreed statements of work and expectations of quality?

- Have products and solutions been effectively transitioned under support and maintenance (and warranty) cover?

Commercial outcomes

- Is it credible to expect the delivered solution to support the achievement of the business benefits initially proposed?
- Did vendors meet their contractual obligations and receive payments in line with the achievement of milestones?
- Did actual costs align with original estimates and are any variances explained?

Organizational impact

- Have the change management activities been executed in line with the plan?

Management and delivery

- Has the project and delivery structure been disbanded with appropriate contribution to knowledge bases?
- Have project resources been redeployed?
- Were the selected processes, methods and approaches effective in supporting and enabling the delivery of results?
- Is there any feedback or learning to be incorporated into other initiatives, or into wider policies and guidelines?
- Did project processes meet probity and audit requirements?

References

Aalders, R. (2001). *The IT Outsourcing Guide*. Chichester, UK: John Wiley & Sons.

ABC (2000a). High price of communication failure. *ABC Online*, www.abc.net.au, 5 May.

ABC (2000b). Love bug reaches Pentagon, *ABC Online*, www.abc.net.au, 6 May.

ABC (2000c). Three suspected in release of love bug, *ABC Online*, www.abc.net.au, 9 May.

ABC (2003). Customs computers stolen from Sydney Airport, *ABC Online*, www.abc.net.au, 5 September.

Abe, J., Sakamura, K. and Aiso, H. (1979). An analysis of software project failure. *Proceedings of 4th International Conference on Software Engineering*, September.

Addison, T. and Vallabh, S. (2002). Controlling software project risks – an empirical study of methods used by experienced project managers. *Proceedings of SAICSIT 2002*, 128–140.

AFR (2000). Hacker in credit card extortion attempt. Chavez, P., *Australian Financial Review*, 15 December.

AFR (2004a). Cadbury's Australian profit slides again. Evans, S., *Australian Financial Review*, 2 June.

AFR (2004b). SCO rides out the Mydoom storm. Lebihan, R., *Australian Financial Review*, 4 February.

AFR (2004c). Unisys loses appeal in RACV case. Connors, E., *Australian Financial Review*, 18 May.

AFR (2004d). Customs cargo system faces further delays. Connors, E., *Australian Financial Review*, 18 May.

AFR (2004e). ANZ cancels network project. Crowe, D., *Australian Financial Review*, 7 April.

AFR (2004f). Contracts $750 million over budget. Woodhead, B., *Australian Financial Review*, 15 January.

AFR (2004g). Jetstar rush: website cracks. Harcourt, T. and Skulley, M., *Australian Financial Review*, 27 February.

Age (2004). $26m speed payout. Gray, D., Ketchell, M. and Silkstone, D., Melbourne, 15 May.

Allinson, C. (2001). Information systems audit trails in legal proceedings as evidence. *Computers and Security*, **20**(5), 409–421.

ANAO (2000). Business continuity management: keeping the wheels in motion. *Better Practice – a Guide to Effective Control.* Canberra, Australia: Australian National Audit Office, January.

ANAO (2001). Implementation of whole-of-government information technology infrastructure consolidation and outsourcing initiative. *Audit Report No. 9*, Canberra, Australia: Australian National Audit Office.

ANAO (2003a). Business continuity management and emergency management in centrelink. *Audit Report No. 9 2003–04*. Performance audit. Canberra, Australia: Australian National Audit Office.

ANAO (2003b). Business continuity management follow-on audit. *Audit Report No. 53 2002–03*. Business support process audit. Canberra, Australia: Australian National Audit Office.

ANAO (2003c). Survey of fraud control arrangements in Australian public service agencies. *Audit Report No. 14 2003–04*. Performance audit. Canberra, Australia: Australian National Audit Office.

ANAO (2004). Intellectual property policies and practices in Commonwealth agencies. *Audit Report No. 25 2003–04*. Performance audit. Canberra, Australia: Australian National Audit Office.

AS/NZS 4360 (1999). *Risk Management*. Strathfield, Standards Association of Australia.

ASX, 2003. *Principles of good corporate governance and best practice recommendations*. Sydney, Australia: Australian Stock Exchange Corporate Governance Council, March.

Aubert, B., Rivard, S. and Patry, M. (2004). A transaction cost model of IT outsourcing. *Information and Management*, **41**, 921–932.

Auditor-General of Victoria (2003). *Results of special reviews and 30 June 2002 financial statement audits: Implementation of RMIT University's Academic Management System No. 4*. Melbourne, Australia: Government Printer for the State of Victoria, February.

The Australian (2004). Why does this website cost $5.3 M?. Riley, J., 16 March.

Bandyopadhyay, K., Mykytyn, P. and Mykytyn, K. (1999). A framework for integrated risk management in information technology. *Management Decision*, **37**(5), 437–444.

Barki, H., Rivard, S. and Talbot, J. (2001). An integrative contingency model of software project risk management. *Journal of Management Information Systems*, **17**(4), 37–69, Spring.

Barros, M., Werner, C. and Travassos, G. (2004). Supporting risks in software project management. *Journal of Systems and Software*, **70**, 21–35.

Beard, J. W. and Sumner, M. (2004). Seeking strategic advantage in the post-net era: Viewing ERP systems from the resource-based perspective. *Journal of Strategic Information Systems*, in press.

Bell, C. (2000). *E-corruption: exploiting emerging technology corruptly in the NSW public sector*. Sydney, Australia: NSW Independent Commission Against Corruption. Intelligence Assessment.

Bergeron, F., Raymond, L. and Rivard, S. (2003). Ideal patterns of strategic alignment and business performance. *Information and Management*.

Besnard, D. and Arief, B. (2004). Computer security impaired by legitimate users. *Computers and Security*, **23**, 253–264.

BIS (2002). *Operational Risk Data Collection Exercise – 2002*. Basel: Basel Committee on Banking Supervision, Bank for International Settlements, 4 June.

BIS (2003a). *The 2002 Loss Data Collection Exercise for Operational Risk: Summary of the Data Collected*. Basel: Basel Committee on Banking Supervision, Bank for International Settlements, March.

BIS (2003b). *Trends in risk integration and aggregation*. Basel: Basel Committee on Banking Supervision, Bank for International Settlements, August.

BIS (2003c). *Overview of the New Basel Capital Accord*. Consultative document. issued for comment by 31 July 2003. Basel: Basel Committee on Banking Supervision, April.

Broadbent, M. and Weill, P. (1997). Management by maxim: How business and IT managers can create IT infrastructures. *Sloan Management Review*, 77–92, Spring.

Broadbent, M., Weill, P. and St Clair, D. (1999). The implications of information technology infrastructure for business process redesign. *MIS Quarterly*, **23**(2), 159–182, June.

Burden, K. (2004). The voice of reason – finding middle ground in IT contracts. *Computer Law and Security Report*, **20**(3).

Caelli, W. (2002). Trusted or trustworthy: The search for a new paradigm for computer and network security. Invited paper to the IFIP/SEC2002 Conference, Cairo, Egypt, 413–420, May.

Carr, N. G. (2003). IT doesn't matter. *Harvard Business Review*, May.

CCCA (2000). *Information Technology Infrastructure Library: Service Support*, Version 1.01 (CD version). Stationery Office for Central Computer and Communications Agency.

Chang, K.-C., Jackson, J. and Grover, V. (2003). E-commerce and corporate strategy: An executive perspective. *Information and Management*, **40**, 663–675.

Charette, R. (1996). The mechanics of managing IT risk. *Journal of Information Technology*, **11**, 373–378.

CIO (2003). Cigna's self-inflicted wounds. Bass, A., 15 March.

Clemons, E. (1991). Strategic investments in information technology. *Communications of the ACM*, **34**(1).

COSO (2003). *Enterprise Risk Management Framework*. Committee of Sponsoring Organisations of the Treadway Commission. www.coso.org

CSI/FBI (2003). *Computer Crime and Security Survey*. Computer Security Institute.

Cuneo, E. (2003). Accepting the risk. *Banking Systems and Technology*, September.

Dhillon, G. and Backhouse, J. (1996). Risks in the use of information technology within organizations. *International Journal of Information Management*, **16**(1), 65–74.

Dhillon, G. and Moores, S. (2001). Computer crimes: Theorizing about the enemy within. *Computers and Security*, **20**(8), 715–723.

Drummond, H. (1996). The politics of risk: Trials and tribulations of the Taurus project. *Journal of Information Technology*, **11**, 347–357.

EMA (2002). *Business Continuity Planning and Disaster Recovery*. Business-Government Task Force on Critical Infrastructure. Emergency Management Australia, 19 March.

Ewusi-Mensah, K. (1997). Critical issues in abandoned information systems development projects. *Communications of the ACM*, **40**(9), 74–80, September.

Farrell, D., Terwilliger, T. and Webb, A. (2003). Getting IT spending right this time. *McKinsey Quarterly*, **2**.

Financial Times (2000). Glitch halts share trading in London. Boland, V., Mackintosh, J., and Van Duyn, A. 6 April.

Fitzgibbon, M. (1998). *Burnt but Back on Track*. Sydney, Australia: Bankstown City Council.

GAO (2002). *Coast Guard's Vessel Identification System*. GAO-02-477, Washington, USA: US General Accounting Office.

GAO (2003). *High Risk Series: An Update*. GAO-03-119, Washington, USA: US General Accounting Office, January.

GAO (2004a). Testimony before the Subcommittee on Technology, Information Policy, Intergovernmental Relations and the Census, House Committee on Government Reform. GAO-04-478T, Washington, USA: US General Accounting Office, 16 March.

GAO (2004b). *Human Capital – Opportunities to Improve Federal Continuity Planning Guidance.* GAO-04-384. Washington, USA: US General Accounting Office, April.

GAO (2004c). *Electronic Government Initiatives Sponsored by the Office of Management.* GAO-04-561T. Washington, USA: US General Accounting Office, March.

Gogan, J. and Rao, A. (1999). Assessing risk in two projects: A strategic opportunity and a necessary evil. *Communications of the Association for Information Systems,* **1**, Paper 15, 1–34, May.

Gordon, L., Loeb, M. and Sohail, T. (2003). A framework for using insurance for cyber-risk management. *Communications of the ACM,* **46**(3), 81–85, March.

Guardian (2004). Planes grounded by computer crash. Clark, A. 4 June.

Hammer, M. and Champy, J. (1993). *Reengineering the Corporation: A Manifesto for Business Revolution.* New York: HarperCollins.

Hancock, B. (2001). Security views. *Computers and Security,* **20**(5), 353–363.

Hanseth, O., Ciborra, C. and Braa, K. (2001). The control devolution: ERP and the side effects of globalization. *DATA BASE for Advances in Information Systems,* **32**(4), Fall.

Heemstra, F. and Kusters, R. (1996). Dealing with risk: a practical approach. *Journal of Information Technology,* **11**, 333–346.

Hinde, S. (2003). Nimbyism, dominoes and creaking infrastructure. *Computers and Security,* **22**(7), 570–576.

Hone, K. and Eloff, J. (2002). Information security policy – What do international information security standards say?. *Computers and Security,* **21**(5), 402–409, 1 October.

Hovav, A. and D'Arcy, J. (2003). The impact of denial-of-service attack announcements on the market value of firms. *Risk Management and Insurance Review,* **6**(2), 97–121.

ICA (1999). *Internal Control: Guidance for Directors on the Combined Code.* London: Institute of Chartered Accountants.

IDG (2002). CA says it has cash, confirms SEC inquiry, Rohde, L. and Chidi, G. *IDG News Service,* 25 February.

IFAC (1999). *Enhancing Shareholder Wealth by Better Managing Business Risk.* Study 9. New York: International Federation of Accountants, June.

IFAC (2002). *E-business and the Accountant.* New York, International Federation of Accountants, March.

Iheagwara, C., Blyth, A., Timm, K. and Kinn, D. (2004). Cost effective management frameworks: The impact of IDS deployment techniques on threat mitigation. *Information and Software Technology,* **46**, 651–664.

Infosecurity (2004). Are you prepared?. Trickey, F. *Infosecurity,* January.

IntoIT (2003). Courts Libra System, *IntoIT Journal,* London: National Audit Office, August.

ISACA (2000). *COBIT ® Executive Summary* (3rd edn). Information Systems Audit and Control Foundation / IT Governance Institute.

ISACA (2001). *Board Briefing on IT Governance.* Information Systems Audit and Control Foundation / IT Governance Institute.

ISO (1998). *ISO/IEC 9126-1, Information Technology – Software Product Quality – Part 1: Quality Model.* Paris: International Organization for Standards.

Jacobsen, I., Booch, G. and Rumbaugh, J. (1999). *The Unified Software Development Process.* New York: Addison-Wesley.

Jiang, J. and Klein, G. (2000). Software development risks to project effectiveness. *Journal of Systems and Software,* **52**, 3–10.

Jiang, J., Klein, G., Hwang, H.-G., Huang, J. and Hung, S.-Y. (2004). An exploration of the relationship between software development process maturity and project performance. *Information and Management*, **41**, 279–288.

Jordan, E. (1994). A global strategy for leveraging information assets. *Working Paper 94/6*. Hong Kong: Department of Information Systems, City University of Hong Kong. www.is.cityu.edu.hk

Jordan, E. (2003). Performance measures in business continuity. *Proceedings of the Australasian Conference on Information Systems*. Perth, Australia.

Jordan, E. and Musson, D. (2001). Public and private sectors: Contrasts in IT risk governance. In S. Fischer-Hubner, D. Olejar and K. Rannenberg (eds), *Security and Control of IT in Society – II*. Proceedings of the IFIP WG 9.6/11.7 Working Conference, Bratislava, Slovakia, 15–16 June 2001.

Jordan, E. and Musson, D. (2003). The board view of electronic business risk. Proceedings of 16th Bled eCommerce Conference, Bled, Slovenia, 9–11 June 2003.

Keil, M., Cule, P., Lyytinen, K. and Schmidt, R. (1998). A framework for identifying software project risks. *Communications of the ACM*, **41**(11), 76–83, November.

Keil, M. and Robey, D. (2001). Blowing the whistle on troubled software projects. *Communications of the ACM*, **44**(4), 87–93, April.

Keil, M., Wallace, L., Turk, D., Dixon-Randall, G. and Nulden, U. (2000). An investigation of risk perception and risk propensity on the decision to continue a software development project. *Journal of Systems and Software*, **53**, 145–157.

Kern, T. and Willcocks, L. (2000). Exploring information technology outsourcing relationships: Theory and practice. *Journal of Strategic Information Systems*, **9**, 321–350.

Kontio, J., Getto, G. and Landes, D. (1998). Experiences in improving risk management processes using the concepts of the RiskIT method. *Proceedings of SIGSOFT 1998*. Florida, USA.

Lacity, M. and Hirschheim, R. (1993). *Information Systems Outsourcing*. Wiley Series in Information Systems. Chichester, UK: John Wiley & Sons.

Lacity, M. and Willcocks, L. (1998). An empirical investigation of information technology sourcing practices: lessons from experience. *MIS Quarterly*, **2**(3), 363–408, September.

Lander, M., Purvis, R., McCray, G. and Leigh, W. (2004). Trust-building mechanisms utilized in outsourced IS development projects: A case study. *Information and Management*, **14**, 509–528.

Lauer, T. (1996). Software project managers' risk preferences. *Journal of Information Technology*, **11**, 287–295.

Lawson, H.W. (1998). Infrastructure risk reduction. *Communications of the ACM*, **40**(6), 120.

Losavio, F., Chirinos, L., Matteo, A., Levy, N. and Ramdane-Cherif, A. (2004). ISO quality standards for measuring architectures. *Journal of Systems and Software*, **72**, 209–223.

Lyytinen, K. (1988). Expectation failure concept and systems analysts' view of information system failures: Results of an exploratory study. *Information and Management*, **14**, 45–56.

Lyytinen, K., Mathiassen, L. and Ropponen, J. (1996). A framework for software risk management. *Journal of Information Technology*, **11**, 275–285.

Mahaney, R. and Lederer, A. (1999). Runaway information systems projects and escalating commitment. *Proceedings of SIGCPR 99*. New Orleans, LA.

Markus, M. L. (2000). Toward an integrative theory of risk control. In R. Baskerville, J. Stage and J. I. DeGross (eds). *Organizational and Social Perspectives on Information Technology*. Boston, MA: Kluwer Academic Publishers, 167–178.

Markus, M. L. (2004). Technochange management: Using IT to drive organizational change. *Journal of Information Technology.* **19**(1), 4–20, March.

Markus, M. L. and Benjamin, R. I. (1997). The magic bullet in IT-enabled transformation. *Sloan Management Review,* 55–67, Winter.

McCartney (2000). Successful IT: Modernising government in action. review of major government IT projects. *The McCartney Report.* London: United Kingdom Cabinet Office.

McFarlan, F. W. (1981). Portfolio approach to information systems. *Harvard Business Review,* **59**(5), 142–150.

Milis, K. and Mercken, R. (2004). The use of the balanced scorecard for the evaluation of information and communication technology projects. *International Journal of Project Management,* **22**, 87–97.

Mitroff, I. and Alpaslan, M. (2003). Preparing for evil. *Harvard Business Review,* 109–115, April.

Moulton, R. and Coles, R. S. (2003a). Applying information security governance. *Computers and Security,* **22**(7), 580–584.

Moulton, R. and Coles, R. (2003b). Operationalizing IT risk management. *Computers and Security,* **22**(6), 487–493.

Musson, D. and Jordan, E. (2000). *Managing for Failure: The Macquarie University Survey of Business and Computer Contingency Planning in Australia.* Sydney, Australia: Macquarie Research Ltd.

NASA (2002). *Probabilistic Risk Assessment Procedures Guide for NASA Managers and Practitioners.* Washington, USA: Office of Safety and Mission Assurance, NASA, August.

Neumann, P. G. (1995). *Computer-Related Risks.* New York: Addison-Wesley.

Neumann, P. G. (1998). Protecting the infrastructures, *Communications of the ACM,* **41**(1), 128.

Neumann, P. G. (2000). Risks in our information infrastructures, *Ubiquity,* www.acm.org

Neumann, P. G. (2002). Risks to the public in computers and related systems, *Software Engineering Notes,* **27**(1), 7–17.

NSW Auditor-General (2003). Review of Sydney water's customer information and billing system. *New South Wales Auditor-General's Report to Parliament, Volume One.* Sydney, Australia.

NZ Commerce (1998). *Report of the Ministerial Inquiry into the Auckland Power Supply Failure.* Wellington, New Zealand: Ministry of Commerce.

OECD (1999). *OECD Principles of Corporate Governance: SG/CG(99)5,* Paris: Directorate for Financial, Fiscal and Enterprise Affairs, Organisation for Economic Cooperation and Development.

OECD (2002). Guidelines for the security of information systems and networks: Towards a culture of security. *Recommendation of the OECD Council at its 1037th Session,* 25 July 2002.

Pacini, C., Hillison, W., and Andrews, C. (2001). The international legal environment for information systems reliability assurance services: The CPA/CA SysTrust. *Commercial Law Journal,* **105**(4), 351–398.

Peppard, J. and Ward, J. (1999). Mind the gap: Diagnosing the relationship between the IT organisation and the rest of the business. *Journal of Strategic Information Systems,* **8**, 29–60.

Peppard, J. and Ward, J. (2004). Beyond strategic information systems: Towards an IS capability. *Journal of Strategic Information Systems.* In press.

Pfleeger, S. (2000). Risky business: What we have yet to learn about risk management. *Journal of Systems and Software*, **53**, 265–273.

Phelps, R. (1996). Risk management and agency theory in IS projects – an exploratory study. *Journal of Information Technology*, **11**, 297–307.

Pidgeon, N. and O'Leary, M. (2000). Man-made disasters: Why technology and organizations (sometimes) fail. *Safety Science*, **34**, 15–30.

Pounder, C. (2001). The Council of Europe Cyber-Crime Convention. *Computers and Security*, **20**, 380–383.

Powell, P. and Klein, J. (1996). Risk management for information systems development. *Journal of Information Technology*, **11**, 309–319.

Public Technology (2004). For sale: UK eUniversity. One careful owner, 10 May 2004, www.publictechnology.net, accessed 27 June 2004.

RAE (2004). *The Challenges of Complex IT Projects*. Report of a working group from the Royal Academy of Engineering and the British Computer Society, London: Royal Academy of Engineering, April.

Rainer, R., Snyder, C. and Carr, H. (1991). Risk analysis for information technology. *Journal of Management Information Systems*, **8**(1), 129–147, Summer.

Roessing, R. (2002). Auditing business continuity management. *Continuity: The Journal of the Business Continuity Institute*, **6**(3), 10–11.

Rannenberg, K. (2000). IT security certification and criteria: Progress, problems and perspectives. In S. Qing and J. Eloff (eds), *Information Security for Global Information Infrastructures*. Proceedings IFIP/TC11 15th Annual Working Conference on Information Security, 22–24 August 2000, Beijing, 1–10.

Rayner, J. (2003). *Managing Reputational Risk: Curbing Threats, Leveraging Opportunities*. Chichester, UK: John Wiley & Sons.

Sabherwal, R. (2003). The evolution of coordination in outsourced software development projects: A comparison of client and vendor perspectives. *Information and Organization*, **13**, 153–202.

Sauer, C., Southon, G. and Dampney, C. (1997). Fit, failure, and the house of horrors: Toward a configurational theory of IS project failure. *Proceedings of International Conference on Information Systems*. Atlanta, GA, 349–366.

Schmidt, R., Lyytinen, K., Keil, M. and Cule, M. (2001). Identifying software project risks: An international Delphi study. *Journal of Management Information Systems*, **17**(4), 5–36, Spring.

Schneier, B. (2000). *Secrets and Lies*. Indianapolis: Wiley Publishing, Inc.

Schwarz, A. and Hirschheim, R. (2003). An extended platform logic perspective of IT governance: Managing perceptions and activities of IT. *Journal of Strategic Information Systems*, **12**, 129–166.

Scott, J. and Vessey, I. (2000). Implementing enterprise resource planning systems: The role of learning from failure. *Information Systems Frontiers*, **2**(2), 213–232.

Segars, A. and Grover, V. (1996). Designing company-wide information systems: Risk factors and coping strategies. *Long Range Planning*, **29**(3), 381–392.

Seuss, Dr (2003). *Oh the Places You'll Go*. London: HarperCollins Children's Books.

Sherer, S. A. and Paul, J. W. (1993). Focusing audit testing on high risk software modules: A methodology and its applications. *Journal of Information Systems*, **7**(2), 65–84, Fall.

Sjoberg, L. and Fromm, J. (2001). Information technology risks as seen by the public. *Risk Analysis*, **21**(3).

SMH (2000). Airport blackout crisis, Wainwright, R. *Sydney Morning Herald*, 7 July.

SMH (2003). Customs contrite but not alarmed over break-in. Morris, L. *Sydney Morning Herald*, 6 September.

Softbank (2004). Results to date in authentication of leaked customer information and measures for the future. Press release. http://www.softbank.co.jp/english/index.html, 27 February.

Standard and Poor's (2004). Google faces challenges as it expands beyond core search engine competency, says S&P research services in Google pre-IPO report. Press release, Standard and Poor's, New York, 7 June.

Strassman, P. A. (1997). *The Squandered Computer – Evaluating the Business Alignment of Information Technologies*. Connecticut: Information Economics Press.

Straub, D. and Welke, R. (1998). Coping with systems risk: Security planning models for management decision making. *MIS Quarterly*, December.

Suh, B. and Han, I. (2003). The IS risk analysis based on a business model. *Information and Management* **41**, 149–158.

Sumner, M. (2000). Risk Factors in enterprise wide information management systems projects, *Proceedings SIGCPR 2000*, ACM Press, 180–187.

Sun (2001). UK higher education forms alliance with Sun to deliver eUniversity programmes worldwide. 19 October, www.sun.com, accessed 27 June 2004.

SWIFT, 2002. *Annual Report, 2001*. Society for Worldwide Interbank Financial Telecommunications, March.

Thorogood, A. and Yetton, P. (2004). Reducing the technical complexity and business risk of major systems projects. *Proceeding of the 37th Hawaii International Conference on System Sciences*.

The Times (2004). E-university shutdown joins list of IT failures. Information technology issue of the week, 4 May.

Trammell, S., Lorenzo, D. and Davis, B. (2004). Integrated hazards analysis. *Professional Safety*, 29–37, May.

Tricker, R. I. (2000). Corporate governance – the subject whose time has come. *Corporate Governance*, **8**(4), 289–296, October.

UK NCC (1998). *Systems Analysis Techniques*. NCC Education Services.

UK OGC (2001). *Information Technology Infrastructure Library: Service Delivery*, Version 1.0 (CD version). London: Stationery Office for Office of Government Commerce.

ukeu.com (2004). General enquiries, UK eUniversity, www.ukeu.com/enquiries.htm, accessed 27 June 2004.

US Commerce (2003). Digital Economy 2003. Washington, USA: US Dept of Commerce.

US FTC (2003). *Identity Theft Survey Report*, Washington, USA: US Federal Trade Commission. September.

US Homeland Security (2003). *Presidential Directive Critical Infrastructure Identification and Protection*, Bush, G. W., 17 December.

US NIST (1998). *Guide for Developing Security Plans for Information Technology Systems*. US National Institute of Standards and Technology, Federal Computer Security Program Managers' Forum Working Group, Special Publication 800-18, December.

US NIST (2001). Stoneburner, G., Goguen, A. and Feringa, A., *Risk Management Guide for Information Technology Systems – Recommendations for the National Institute of Standards and Technology*. National Institute of Standards and Technology Special Publication 800-30. Washington, USA, October.

Verhoef, C. (2002). Quantitative IT portfolio management. *Science of Computer Programming*, **45**, 1–96.

Von Solms, S. H. (1999). Information Security Management through Measurement. Presented at SEC99, Johannesburg, South Africa.

Wallace, L. and Keil, M. (2004). Software project risks and their effect on outcomes. *Communications of the ACM*, **47**(4), 68–73, April.

Ward, P. and Smith, C. (2002). The development of access control policies for information technology systems. *Computers and Security*, **21**(4), 356–371.

Watkins, M. and Bazerman, M. (2003). Predictable surprises: the disasters you should have seen coming. *Harvard Business Review*, March.

Weill, P., Subramani, M. and Broadbent, M. (2002). Building IT infrastructure for strategic agility. *Sloan Management Review*, 57–65, Fall.

Whitman, M. (2003). Enemy at the gate: Threats to information security. *Communications of the ACM*, **46**(8), 91–95, August.

Willcocks, L., Lacity, M. and Kern, T. (1999). Risk mitigation in IT outsourcing strategy revisited: Longitudinal case research at LISA. *Journal of Information Systems*, **8**, 285–314.

Williams, P. (2001). Information security governance. *Information Security Technical Report*, **6**(3), 60–70.

WHO (2002). *World Health Report, 2002.* Geneva: World Health Organization.

WSJ (2004). Navy contract almost sinks EDS. McWilliams, G. *Wall Street Journal*, printed in *Australian Financial Review*, 20 April.

Yusuf, Y., Gunasekaran, A. and Abthorpe, M. S. (2004). Enterprise information systems project implementation: A case study of ERP in Rolls-Royce, *International Journal of Production Economics*, **87**, 251–266.

Zviran, M., Ahituv, N. and Armoni, A. (2001). Building outsourcing relationships across the global community: The UPS-Motorola experience. *Journal of Strategic Information Systems*, **10**, 313–333.

Index

Printed and bound in the UK by
CPI Antony Rowe, Eastbourne

nted and bound by CPI Group (UK) Ltd, Croydon, CR0 4YY

23/04/2025

14660964-0001